Max Weber
the New Century &

Max Weber & the New Century

Alan Sica

Transaction Publishers
New Brunswick (U.S.A.) and London (U.K.)

Library of Congress Catalog Number: 2003063396
ISBN: 0-7658-0190-6
Printed in Canada

Library of Congress Cataloging-in-Publication Data
Sica, Alan, 1949-
    Max Weber & the new century / Alan Sica.
        p. cm.
    Includes bibliographical references and index.
    ISBN 0-7658-0190-6 (alk. paper)
    1. Weber, Max, 1864-1920—Influence. 2. Sociology—Philosophy. 3. Rationalism. 4. Historiography. 5. Philosophy, Modern—21st century. I. Title: Max Weber and the new century. II. Title.

HM479.W42S55 2004
301—dc22   2003063396

This book is for
Paolo, Enzo, and Carlo

Contents

Acknowledgements

I am happy to thank Anne Sica for splendid technical help and editorial opinions; Julie Pelton for stalwart library and computerized research assistance; Irving Louis Horowitz and Mary Curtis at Transaction Publishers for their cheerful and cheering support throughout our multi-book relationship, and for being my patient friends; Larry Mintz for his expert editorial labors; and John McCarthy and Glenn Firebaugh for providing research assistants and a congenial work setting.

For some years useful intellectual sustenance pertaining to this book and other matters has come from Robert J. Antonio, Lawrence A. Scaff, and Stephen P. Turner.

Preface: Using Weber Today

A dozen years ago the editor of a series of theory books for which this one and its companion volume, *Max Weber: A Comprehensive Bibliography*, were originally intended asked that I write a brief Weber treatment noticeably dissimilar in design and scope from the two volumes that finally broke free of their traces. Having reviewed my earlier Weber study with characteristic generosity,[1] he thought I could readily produce a succinct, moderately synthetic exposition of Max Weber's ideas and scholarly achievements, but with a particular emphasis. We shared a belief that Weber continued to be of enormous importance, but in ways that were sometimes obscured by the ritualized nature of references to his work, flatteringly ubiquitous but often vacuous as well. To help alleviate this problem, he asked me to relate Weberianism along several main axes to the way one might best theorize today about social life in our troubled world; or, put in the language of the late 1960s, he hoped I could document Weber's "relevance" to our current analytic concerns. Like many, probably most, such projects—gleefully and rather casually taken on—this one irresistibly outgrew its borders, slowly becoming a creature from the library that bore but faint resemblance to its initial genus. Because so much time has elapsed since the invitation was issued, two main reasons for this unforeseen delay must be offered, one mundanely pragmatic, the other more theoretical in nature. Despite appearances, these do not so much constitute a mea culpa (though one is surely due) as an oblique introduction to the deep, ill-lit cavern that faces the miner determined to dig out the seam of scholarly gold that has accrued around the name of Max Weber during the eighty-three years since his death.

Immediately after agreeing to write the requested book, I was chosen editor-in-chief of *Sociological Theory*, a journal of the American Sociological Association, a welcome but harried position I held from mid-1989 until early 1995. Almost simultaneously I moved my Weber library (and everything else) back and forth across the country several times within a few years at the invitation of three universities. Such wholesale removals do not aid scholarly work, especially when added to journal-editing duties. Though I had begun work on the book by 1992 in desultory fashion, most of my time went, as it should have, to editing, enlarging, and improving the ASA journal, as well as to teaching in several new settings. Not until mid-1996 did I pursue the Weber project in earnest, and at that time found myself squarely faced by a question of a quasi-theoretical sort which was naturally posed to the project after it began to acquire more discernible shape.

Expressed more simply than it probably ought to be, a puzzle began to overshadow what had begun as the fairly unmysterious task of assaying Weberianism as we entered a new century: just how broad and deep, *in fact*, is Weber's influence today across the social sciences and humanities? It is easy enough to speculate or to assume without hesitation, if based only on textbook treatments or the rate of what are properly called "ceremonial citations,"[2] that Weber becomes a larger force in the social sciences with every passing year (abetted, no doubt, by the temporary eclipse of Marx). But "empirically," as it were, there ought to be a clearer answer, so I thought. But how to go about finding it?

"Content analysis," once the favored methodology for answering questions of this sort, hardly seemed feasible in terms of Weberiana, since already by 1988 when the last Weber bibliography appeared, 900 English-language works, small and large, had been found which depended in one way or another on Weberian thinking. Proficient hermeneutics, a demanding art when done properly,[3] could never be carried out amidst such a mass of material, even if handled in a highly selective manner. Instead, I decided to attempt "an answer" to the question by systematically putting to use what were then the newly available electronic means of access to sources here and abroad. What I had been doing the "old-fashioned" way, searching from one printed source to another, was substantially augmented when computer-based search engines began to appear around 1995, giving me access to books and journals that do not come readily to hand even in large academic libraries.

In short, I began what might be called a "global search" for Weber materials in English which had eluded previous bibliographers or had appeared since theirs were published. The unrelieved tedium that accompanies this sort of project, the mule-like insistence upon locating whatever is pertinent and recording details accurately, is not an activity, especially when spread over some years, that I would recommend to friends. Yet how else but to search in this way, by shaping a "definitive" inventory, can one know what Weber has meant and continues to mean within the larger world of intellectual labor? In fact, his name has now reached well beyond the academy and into the less airy realm of journalism, recently having figured prominently in the *New York Times,* the *Economist, U.S. News and World Report,* the *Atlantic Monthly,* and similar middlebrow publications—as explained in detail in chapter 3. Thus, what ought to have been a single, slim volume discussing Weber's ideas in today's context became two intimately related volumes, one which served as the "empirical basis" of the other. In order to write about Weber, *Werk und Person*, first I had to find out "which Weber" was still vibrantly influencing so much published work.

Naturally, such a strategy might be accused of confusing quantitative for qualitative meaning. It is probably true, for example, that one part of a book by Leo Strauss, Eric Voegelin, Herbert Marcuse, or Jürgen Habermas that treats Weber's ideas seriously is "worth" scores of routine articles in specialty journals, aimed more than anything else at persuading peers to accept this or that small alteration in received Weberian wisdom. How else could one explain the thousands of articles in a dozen major languages which have been created solely to "test empirically" the Protestant ethic thesis? Further, if it is true, for example, that Arnaldo Momigliano's small article on Weber's concept of the Jews as a "pariah people" carries more intellectual payload than a shelf of journeyman works (which I think it does), why bother listing the latter? Aside from the obvious fact that a single compiler of a large bibliography is incapable of assessing the "ultimate" quality of every identified item, there are other good reasons for using an all-inclusive principal of "selection" in an undertaking of this kind. Fashions change in intellectual matters nearly as quickly as in the clothing business, so what seems at one moment of capital import for Weber students loses its primacy in the next—for instance, Mannheim's invocation of substantive versus formal rationality and irrationality, or the relationship, real or imagined, between Carl Schmitt's right-wing theory of the state and Weber's notions of nationalism and power. Only by risking "over-inclusion" can one be sure that the next generation's interests will be preserved in a bibliography such as the one I compiled. The only decisive characteristic of a given item is that it has to do with Weber in some non-trivial way, and that can be ascertained, as has been done here, only by examining the piece in question.

My intention in this book was to examine Weber and his legacy from a number of angles, some of which have very seldom been treated, at least in English-language scholarship. My rhetorical study of *Economy and Society* (the pivotal opening passages) attempts to show what a full-scale hermeneutic analysis might entail were one given time and space enough to do it properly. The conversation that could arise between the reader and Weber by means of this kind of work would help overcome the chronic decontextualization that has affected so many of Weber's "choice morsels" as they pop up repeatedly in social science writing. The following chapter, which treats Weber as an increasingly standard ingredient of mass media writing, is also not something done before so far as I can tell. By means of computerized searches and the old-fashioned kind as well, I isolated a large number of references (to Max Weber the sociologist versus Max Weber the painter!) in the sub-scholarly print media, trying to divine whatever patterns arose from them. It is truly fascinating to see how much Weber has penetrated popular consciousness at the higher reaches, but how very limiting this distorted portrait of his work can be, even when invoked by the more learned journalists and popular writers. As with Freud, Marx, and Adam Smith, the name has become a popular totem for various causes, and bears strikingly little relation to the "works themselves." My chapter on Weber's concept of rationalization reworks an old chestnut (going back to Karl Löwith's work in the 1920s) from a slightly different point of view, bringing in film and fiction that speaks to the concept in a way that denizens of contemporary society can easily understand. Whereas Benjamin Franklin's *Autobiography* lit up Weber's imagination when he read it for the first time when young, subsequent wholesale rationalizing of personal behavior along economic or general lines is now more persuasively conveyed through modern fiction and film—or so I argue in the chapter. Another venture into more or less fresh terrain occurs in the following section wherein I ask the question of how much Weber's ideas have influenced American historians as they have portrayed the formation of this country's culture beginning in the colonial period. This chapter could have been much longer, but I think that enough connections were made between Weber's ideas and those of some leading U.S. historians to demonstrate how vital he became to our self-understanding as a civilization distinct from Europe's, particularly in histories written since the 1950s. I end the book with three shorter forays: Weber's role as a philosopher (one he would have vigorously repudiated in favor of his colleague, Heinrich Rickert, and his younger friend, Karl Jaspers, among others), an historically specified connection between Vilfredo Pareto and Weber that I discovered some years ago and was the first to do so, so far as I could tell, and a short commentary on the utility of viewing Weber's work in tandem with Thomas Mann's great fictional legacy, prompted by the excellent monographs of Harvey Goldman.

Writing still another book on Weber, in addition to compiling the bibliography, after already having contributed two monographs to "Mount Max," might well seem a waste of time to those social scientists who work outside the ever-expanding international Weber-*Kreis*. What automatically springs to mind is Robert K. Merton's unintended immortalization of Whitehead's stern warning (from the 1916 essay, "The Organisation of Thought"): "A science which hesitates to forget its founders is lost." (Never mind, for the moment, that neither Whitehead nor Merton meant we ought to be excused forever from the burden, so-called, of studying the history of theorizing; they objected only to "ancestor worship" of a pathological, debilitating type, as Whitehead's next sentence indicates: "To this hesitation I ascribe the barrenness of logic.") The fact that this form of scholarly labor has not seemed so to me, nor to the thousands of other authors who over the years have been inspired by the person and writings of Weber, perhaps requires more explanation than, say, wishing to add yet another book on feminist or postmodernist theory might, given recent academic tastes. Yet rather than arguing abstractly that "we still need Weber," it might be wiser to allow these two books in toto to make the case. Could the authors—including myself—of the 4,900 entries which make up *Max Weber: A Comprehensive Bibliography* be deluded about the vitality of the Weberian worldview? We shall see.

Notes

1. Charles Lemert, review of Alan Sica, *Weber, Irrationality, and Social Order* (Berkeley: University of California Press, 1988), *American Journal of Sociology*, 95:2 (September, 1989), 453-455.
2. In a letter to me of September 16, 1998, Robert K. Merton alluded to Richard Lewontin's phrase, "ceremonial citations" which the latter used in a letter to Merton (12/18/79), but which, unknown to Lewontin, was previously offered in print by Jonathan and Stephen Cole (*Social Stratification in Science*, Chicago: University of Chicago Press, 1973, p. 209): "...ceremonial citations to the early work of colleagues of new prominence[;]...ceremonial citations might be better made to the more recent work of these men, the work which has elevated their reputation." I do not have anything this in technical mind. For me, ceremonial citations are simply those essentially cosmetic references to a "classic" author meant to self-award immediate legitimacy to a contemporary argument or study, even though the classic material is unnecessary on purely intellectual grounds, or may, indeed, prove to be contrary to the present-day argument—if, that is, the classic work were actually read rather than merely cited.
3. See, for example, Gary Shapiro and Alan Sica (eds.), *Hermeneutics: Questions and Prospects* (Amherst, MA: University of Massachusetts Press, 1990); Alan Sica, "Hermeneutics and Social Theory: The Contemporary Conversation," *Current Perspectives in Social Theory* (Greenwich, CT: JAI Press, 1981), vol. 2, 39-54; Alan Sica, "Hermeneutics and American Historiography," pp. 669-681 in Mary Kupiec Cayton and Peter W. Williams, eds., *Encyclopedia of American Cultural and Intellectual History* (New York: Charles Scribner's Sons, 2001).

1

Weber and the Future of Social Thought

Why Must We Still Read Weber?

As the twentieth century ended, there were signs that the best-educated segments of Western society seemed more eager each day to dispense wholesale with the received past, to hold a monumental garage sale of cultural items in order to make room for those enlightening shifts of viewpoint and values that were widely anticipated to appear soon after the new millennium began. Most of this apparent, almost titillating, newness was a product of computerization and its willing handmaiden, globalization. Implied in this urge to toss out the past's achievements is the belief, typical of millennial sentiments, that such new ways of seeing the world and of analyzing social life would sharply outdo all those efforts which had captured the imagination of the discarded century. In contrast to this general approach to the change of calendars, this book—by means of its exposition as well as the "data" provided by the large mass of information in its companion volume, *Max Weber: A Comprehensive Bibliography*—holds to a view which, in such an atmosphere, risks seeming quaint.

I have several arguments to make on behalf of both books, and, at the same time, in support of the claim that during the last dozen years or so, Weber has become the theorist whom informed parties need most urgently to reread and reclaim. In brief, my argument is this: Max Weber's social theory, inspired by cultural currents and sensibilities available only within the preceding fin de siècle, continues to speak directly to our extant and emerging conditions of social life in a way that overshadows every other available large-scale theory. That is, analyzing contemporary life in industrialized societies by means of ideas conceived or elaborated by Max Weber will bring one closer to a reliable understanding of the immediate future than will using the key ideas of any other social theorist or philosopher still being read with care. Now that Marx has

1

been set aside via an historical transformation of the sort he would have enjoyed observing, and with Freud being denigrated on every side by platoons of detractors, both learned and ignorant, only Weber survives as the principal social theorist of the twentieth century whose ideas can lead us with cognitive confidence into the upcoming era. Durkheim surely remains useful for certain analytic tasks, but his core values as a scholar and person are much more a creature of the nineteenth than the twentieth century and noticeably less applicable as we begin to deal with the twenty-first. And of all the nineteenth and twentieth century theories which most persistently animate discussion and social research, none will survive so much intact as Weber's—not those of Freud, Marx, Jung, Piaget, nor anyone else. Though there are plenty of social scientists and informed laypersons who might not find this a revolutionary notion, others will surely regard it as blind hero-worship of an almost willfully stupid kind. But before allowing this contrary view to carry the day, allow me to explain why I take a standpoint which might initially seem quixotic or worse to knowing participants in today's global culture.

Born on April 21, 1864 and dying prematurely on June 14, 1920, a victim of the global influenza pandemic, Weber has proven beyond any real doubt to be the single most creative, influential, diagnostically accurate, and inspiring social theorist and social analyst of the twentieth century. There were many others who at one point or another might have been so designated, but their grand moments are gone. If one equates influence with books in circulation, then it must be said that Oswald Spengler's *Decline of the West* sold extremely well for twenty years after its publication in 1920—90,000 copies in English alone between 1922 and 1930—especially in view of its extreme length, conjectural quality, and expense. By contrast Weber's masterpiece, *Wirtschaft und Gesellschaft*, sold fewer than 2,000 copies between 1925 and 1945 (according to Hans Gerth, who learned this directly from Paul Siebeck, Weber's publisher [Gerth, 1994: 555]). Yet who but antiquarians mentions Spengler today except with an ironic smile, admitting that his sweeping theory of culture, borrowed in spirit from Goethe and Nietzsche, is no longer tenable or even interesting considering what has since become known about history, and, along with this, the prevailing tastes for the specific and non-metaphysical. Likewise, one could mention Vilfredo Pareto's *Mind and Society*, its four fat volumes for a time in the thirties the very embodiment of "advanced" social thought (so it was claimed at length in May, 1935 *Saturday Review of Literature* cover story), yet now entirely neglected by social theorists and long out of print. Similarly Pitirim Sorokin, originator and powerhouse of the Harvard sociology department, gave the world his four-volume *Social and Cultural Dynamics* in the late 1930s, along with dozens of other works, and today has devolved into little more than a historical footnote to the early work of Talcott Parsons, with whom he fought between 1930 and Sorokin's death in 1970.

It does not require much imagination to see why Weber should be today's social theorist of choice for those wary denizens of the postmodern condition who hope to comprehend, as best they can, the new century. The only worthy competitors for the title of Master Social Analyst, Marx and Freud, have not proved as durable as Weber in the face of the political and intellectual forces of the last several decades. While it's quite true that much of Marx's critique of capitalist social practices remains as telling now as when he wrote it, "Marx" qua political or cultural symbol has so besmirched Karl Marx, the scholar, that it will take some time (in league with a global economic depression) for the latter to reassert himself and regain his rightful place in the pantheon of the indispensable. As for Freud, his ideas—or the universal popularization of them that overtook the postwar West—has become the victim of his own wild success. "Everything is sexual" or "the unconscious rules" might well be summarizing slogans of consumerist societies and the advertising industry that propels it. And this impetus came largely from Freud's hypotheses about humanity's fundamental nature, first brought to common awareness in 1900 with his *Interpretation of Dreams* (and read immediately by Weber). Yet his famously supple German prose, and the subtle persuasiveness that this gave his ideas, have long since been lost from most of what is now considered, however imprecisely, the "Freudian."

Freud was almost eight years old when Weber appeared on April 24, 1864, and Marx died at sixty-five, just before Weber turned nineteen. If Marx had been granted the same seventy-five years of life as his confederate, Engels, he might well have begun to hear about the young Dr. Weber, a precocious expert on Roman economic history, medieval trading companies, and the political-economy of contemporary agribusiness in Prussia. These were topics close to Marx's heart, and given his gargantuan appetite for reading technical materials, he would probably have come across Weber's name. As it was, Weber spent his early career in dialogue "with Marx's ghost" (as Albert Salomon put it in 1945), as well as those of his followers, teaching his earliest students by means of a careful reading of *Das Kapital*, and always thinking about the relationship between ideas and economic activity along lines similar to Marx's. In the case of Freud, Weber's connection was much closer. He not only read Freud's work as it appeared, but also in 1914 defended before an Italian court some of Freud's more literal followers, those who practiced "free love" and other liberated social activities under the banner of a kind of crypto-Freudianism that cropped up again in the 1960s. Weber, then, enjoyed an accident of birth which positioned him between Marx's revolution in social analysis and Freud's recalibration of humankind's internal life. And he was gifted enough to take advantage of these (and many other) intellectual sources in forging his own version of socio-economic and cultural analysis, the type of thinking that now goes by his own name: Weberian.

In 1935, Ezra Pound, the founder of American literary modernism, began his famous manifesto, *Make it New*, by announcing that "criticism has at least the following categories" or forms: by means of discussion, by translation, by "exercise in the style of a given period," "via music," and "criticism in new composition." The final form is the most intense and risky, and might affiliate with Thomas Kuhn's famous notion of "paradigm shifts." Pound goes on to explain that criticism has "two functions," first, to "forerun composition," to serve as a "gunsight," and second, "excernment - the general ordering and weeding out of what has actually been performed - elimination of repetition." With this in mind, let us consider where we are in relation to Weber's gigantic oeuvre, and along the way, to recall another European who during his time defined his national cultural character even more than did Weber.

In 1906, seventy-five years after Hegel's death, the greatest Italian philosopher of the modern period, Benedetto Croce, asked a rhetorically charged question. It has been repeated ever since, applied not only to Hegel, but to nearly every other thinker of note who lived before our own time: "*Ciò che è vivo e ciò che è morto nella filosofia di Hegel*" (What is Living and What is Dead in the Philosophy of Hegel?). We must ask the same question as it pertains to Max Weber, yet with much less defensiveness than was the case with Croce's spirited reclamation of Hegel's repu-tation, which, by the turn of the last century, was tarnished very nearly beyond saving. Yet the history of thought is a strange animal, for now Croce is forgotten while Hegel's troops continue to stream out of the academy. And whereas Pound's most famous clarion call, to "make it new," is burdened by a heavily ironic load of meaning that it surely did not have in the mid-thirties, Weber's work seems almost *en-tirely* alive in ways that Pound's seems almost entirely bypassed—for good or ill.

Forty-three years ago the Harvard social theorist, Talcott Parsons, who at that time was as widely esteemed by his peers as today he is sidestepped, began a review-essay in the *American Sociological Review* with this judgment: "Just forty years after his death the figure of Max Weber stands as a kind of great hovering Presence [*sic*] over the disci-pline of sociology, to say nothing of the broader intellectual situation of our time" (Talcott Parsons, "Max Weber" [review of Reinhard Bendix, *Max Weber*], *ASR*, 25:5 [October 1960], 750-752.) He ended the review by suggesting that Weber's "theoretical contribution as such" should be further examined—something Bendix had not done in his admirable primer—and that "a broader treatment of the place of Weber in intellectual history" ought to be undertaken as well. Dozens of similar published statements between 1920 and today could be trotted out to demonstrate that Weber continues to influence how the social, economic, and political worlds are perceived globally, not only by social scientists, but increasingly by the informed laity as well. We are now as far removed in time and historical memory from Parsons' observations as he had been from Weber's death when he published the essay quoted above. Yet nothing seems to have changed in terms of the veneration in which Weber's achievements continue to be held. Acknowledging his indispensability to a wide range of intellectual projects in multiple disciplines has become a ritual act.

It has turned out to be rhetorically convenient that Talcott Parsons quoted Crane Brinton in 1937 when he asked, a bit waspishly, "Who now reads Spencer?" since it gave ample license for theorists in succeeding generations to retort: "Who now reads Parsons?" This was both ironically amusing and humanly understandable given the ideological distance that had grown up between Parsons and his younger detractors. But the humor eventually faltered when newer theorists of "The Postmodern" leeringly upped the ante. They fired an even more potent piece of rhetorical artillery by converting Parsons's attack on his immediate intellectual past to their own, more damaging devices: "Who now reads *anything*?" they want to know, in a mixture of chipper obedience to the onrushing wave of electronic communications, combined with token shock at what has been lost—to the extent it can be remembered. "Read" in this context means, of course, examining print in the "traditional" sense of studying words on paper that make up a coherent narrative, rather than staring at printed advertisements, or rapid-fire images projected from electronic screens.

With this bad news for readers in mind—a general phenomenon lately christened "the Gutenberg elegies"[1]—it might reasonably be argued that the exhaustive bibliography of Weberiana mated with this Weber treatment renders the expository material that precedes it superfluous. Even moderately good libraries already own worthy primers about Weber's ideas—those by Bendix (1962), Freund (1968), and Käsler (1988) have weathered particularly well. And given that the definitive edition of Weber's work in German is still a very much a work in progress,[2] where, one might fairly ask, on the steep slopes of Mount Weber might this book secure a foothold?

A reflex animus against non-living, non-colored, non-Asian, non-homosexual, non-females who thrived during the epoch of high imperialism has sprung up over the last two decades. With it one perceives a widespread assumption, most noticeable among those whose knowledge of social theory begins, for example, with Foucault's later works or Judith Butler's writing of the 1990s, that little is left to learn from theorizing that was created prior to our immediate cultural period. Whereas this view lightens considerably the load that would-be theorists must bear in terms of "start-up costs," it can easily turn out to be a crippling error of judgment. It correlates with the fantasy sometimes voiced regarding modern music which holds that because we have Stravinsky, Haydn becomes dispensable; or, with the Beatles on tap, Irving Berlin's tunes can safely be deleted from cultural memory. For many of the same reasons, while thrown into a different register, disregarding what has oddly become known as "classical" theory runs the gravest risks for those who wish to understand our plight today, and our chances for societal improvement. And casually minimizing Weber's importance to the ongoing project of self-clarification and social critique, prior even to a study of his work, is the most worrisome part of the wholesale rejection of the immediate past that has so taken over much of the avant-garde and its imitators. These may seem to be strong and heterodox claims, but they are not made lightly or without reasons.

First of all, Weber personifies and exemplifies, perhaps as no one else of his large circle, a quintessential practitioner of that "high literacy" peculiar to the Victorian age, so much written about.[3] Whereas most of the famous Victorian polymaths and polyhistors were students or creators of literature, comparative religion, philosophy, or history, Weber is unique in bringing together all these areas, in addition to law and legal history, musicology, economics, social policy, comparative politics, survey research, and the first glimmerings of German sociology. If there is still much to be learned from the great "Victorian sages"—Carlyle, Ruskin, Arnold, George Eliot, Darwin, Huxley, Max Müller, and others—the same could be said about their direct descendants, those Edwardian creators of social science, like Weber, Simmel, Troeltsch, and Durkheim.

Moreover, behind even the most abstract presentations and analyses of his work, one senses profound admiration for Max Weber the man. It is this obvious attachment to his character that motivates the best Weber scholarship, and not disembodied theoretical interest alone. The key to his personal narrative was a Kantian acceptance of "tension"— *Spannung* or *Streckung*—and its theoretical and practical unavoidability in his century. He was not the first German social theorist or moralist to fasten on to the term, but he pursued it, as it pursued him, more exhaustively than any predecessor. Marx, by comparison, always claimed to know where science and politics met, and he tried to position himself at their nexus without much handwringing. Perhaps this is why, though it is still easy to admire Marx's boisterous political adventures, American and German ("bourgeois") theorists today feel almost "natural" standing in the queue headed by Weber, with fact on one side, value to the other. Precisely what angered those like Georg Lukács (*The Destruction of Reason*, 1980: 601ff), this willingness to put on and take off the scientist's uniform, rationally and apolitically, is the central characteristic of Weber, man and scholar, that has guaranteed his symbolic sponsorship of Western sociology for a half-century. Voices against him are small in compass or intensity of attack, and his importance accordingly grows with time. Twenty years ago, *Against Weber* by Greg Philo was announced for publication, then did not appear, almost as if the presses refused to commit this sort of sacrilege; meanwhile, Bryan Turner's *For Weber*, a substantial and lavish book in two editions, does not cause surprise, unless one expects from it more coals to Newcastle. In this happy spirit the Weber Industry—now with its own journal, *Max Weber Studies*—steams along, not pure hagiography to be sure, yet hardly tearing at its object's imperial robes. One wonders what the old man would think of this.

Secondly, Weber's vitality for today's readers can easily and without casuistry be linked to our complex concerns that surround the idea of "diversity," particularly regarding those various cultures which have vied for hegemony over the last several centuries of global history. Weber's methodological basis for social analysis lies principally within the practice of comparison. His ceaseless pursuit of fine-grained information about a dozen major cultures, historically and in his own period, propels his theorizing to generalized heights neither his contemporaries nor successors could reach. His ambition for cross-cultural knowledge knew no real limits, and given his exquisite education and the social setting provided him by his class position within Bismarck's Germany, he was able to synthesize and appropriate to his unique purposes a stock of knowledge that no other individual could claim up to that point, or probably since. In short, his work has not been superseded or equaled by any single scholar, and the worldview that it expresses can be found only in his work. He was and remains in this regard "an original."

There are ways to demonstrate—even to the recalcitrant or harried postmodern citizen who lives in a post-literate condition—that Weber's ideas speak in a language that is our own, but with more rigor and with a degree of historical and cultural sensitivity which elude most writers today. Take, for instance, two popular claims made today by cultural critics. One argues that computer programming has not exhibited much originality in China because Chinese students, taught to think by means of ideograms, find it difficult to conceptualize in computer "language," which takes alphabetical form. Another, not unrelated notion holds that with pictures, still and in motion, playing an ever larger role in children's education and in adult amusement, the power of *logos*, the word, literacy, will diminish steadily until genuine literacy, especially multilingual, will become as rare as the knowledge of Latin became after the beginnings of modernity. There are many ways Weber might respond to each of these "postmodern" observations, one of them in his *Religion of China*. In explaining the rise of the mandarin class of "literati," he notes that "In spite of the logical qualities of the language, Chinese thought has remained rather stuck in the pictorial and descriptive. The power of *logos*, of defining and reasoning, has not been accessible to the Chinese." By forcing prospective mandarins to paint 2,000 ideographs over and over until perfected, "The lack of all training in calculation, even in grade schools, is a very striking characteristic of Chinese education" (p. 125).

Nearby in the same section, Weber offers some observations about music which seem, almost eerily, to address today's debates about the ultimate fate and apparent demise of "classical" music in Western culture, and the rise of a global rock or pop music culture that has entirely displaced it. In reference, again, to the Chinese, Weber writes, "Music improves man, and rites and music form the basis of self-control. The magical significance of music was a primary aspect of all this. 'Correct music'—that is, music used according to the old rules and strictly following the old measures—'keeps the spirits in their fetters" [quoting the *Siao-Hio*, official schoolbook] (p. 123). With these observations in mind, it is much easier to understand the stern, sometimes violent, resistance offered by the Chinese government when students begin indulging in Western musical experiment or when they try to embrace postmodernist culture via computers and the Web (witness the governmental monitoring of e-mail which resulted in recent arrests). This is not simply the perpetual struggle between generations; it is a world-historical shift in which an entire worldview, essentially Confucian and mandarin in nature, is fighting for its political legitimacy against a range of cultural behaviors and traditions about which Weber was perfectly cognizant ninety years ago.

Another reason to read Weber today, if one reads anything in this general realm of endeavor, is to learn about ethical tolerance for the Other. Beginning life as an unapologetic nationalist, in obvious imitation of his father's potent example, Weber shifted over time to a position more universal or world-historical in intention—perhaps unconsciously following the lead of his boyhood hero, Goethe. Weber's young friend, Karl Jaspers, the existentialist philosopher, political moralist, and psychiatrist, sensed this in Weber long before anyone else, when he wrote, shortly after his death, that with Weber's premature passing, Germany and the world had lost one of its finest political ethicists and philosophers of human life. Weber had examined the data of human cultural and political-economic history with extraordinary care, had isolated patterns that achieved or failed to achieve certain ends, and only following this exhausting effort, offered opinions about how the contemporary world might be organized to promote his *summum bonum*—individuals' freedom within a context of ethical responsibility. Yet his work did not slide into that dangerous egocentrism that today goes by the name "libertarianism" of the less thoughtful variety. Never did he lose sight of the Greek's realization that individual freedom meant nothing unless it matured within the context of social organization that, within practical limits, assured general liberty rather than freedom by caste or class membership. Just as many other scholars have written histories of freedom, Weber's entire project, multi-layered as it was, could bear a similar title.

Today's scholarly world is confused in its mission and its methods. The dual attack upon conventional knowledge mounted by the cult of political correctness on the one hand, the electronic diminishing, even erasure, of the printed word on the other, has left the well-intentioned academic or policy-oriented writer without the trusted signposts common to Weber's era. It is true that he did constant battle with scholars and journalists whose main ambition was to persuade rather than inform, but at least he knew which sources he could draw upon to defeat his enemies in polemical battle, and his audience seemed to know a knockout when they read one. This scholarly environment encouraged, even demanded, from its participants a level of factual precision and detail that is no longer amenable to our time. Things now are entirely different. As Lester Thurow put it not long ago, "Logical appeals can be made on the electronic media, but it is a far better medium for stirring emotions than for transmitting logical information." The generalized learning and sensitivity to language that made the political speeches of Greece and Rome, of Lincoln and Bryan, such powerful public performances, are "simply impossible today."[4]

In order to evaluate precisely Weber's treatments of law, music, Hinduism, ancient Judaism, the origins of capitalism in Europe, the 1905 revolution in Russia, or the logic and methods suitable for social science, the reader must immediately come to grips with an argument that was fashioned by means of thorough immersion in pertinent "facts"—a word that is itself today suspect in many circles. And all of them were connected within a logical tissue that absolutely rejected simplification or trivialization. Theodor Adorno, working in Weber's shadow as a young man during the 1920s, perhaps had the preceding generation in mind when he insisted that any argument too easily comprehensible was not one worth making, for it could not possibly be "true" in any serious sense. Analyses of this caliber and density do not lend themselves to sound-bites and similar barbarisms that cramp and distort knowledge-workers in today's transformed environment, which by their very nature hamper original or complex thinking about social and cultural life. In an atmosphere in which earnest, well-intentioned, and relatively attentive college students can write that "Ferdinand Tennessee" (i.e., Tönnies) or "Immune [*sic*] Kant" were important to nineteenth-century social theory[5], the great distance between Weber's intellectual environment and ours becomes too clear.

Finally, by way of justifying my claim for Weber's continuing "relevance," "resonance," or general applicability to our own perturbed epoch, consider what is, in fact, a postmodern observation, despite my hesitation to name it as such. For aside from his monumental "Presence" among social scientists that Parsons identified in 1960 and continues today, there is also a component to Weber's appeal what nowadays might be termed the "personal dimension." Following Mitzman's psychoanalytical biography in 1969 and the appearance of Green's collective portrait (1974), compounded by the English translation of Marianne Weber's biography the following year, Weber qua disturbed soul became almost as important to his iconic status as Weber the titanic social scientist. Just over one hundred years ago in the fall of 1898, without warning, the most promising mind in social science began a rapid descent into a peculiar kind of madness which would last in earnest for five years. The crippling symptoms of this collapse—hysterical paralysis, insomnia, lassitude, anxiety, probably impotence, and others, including the need for narcotics for sleep—would wax and wane until the victim's death twenty-two years later. At thirty-three years of age, Max Weber—already a famous economist, legal scholar, survey researcher, and historian—verbally fought with his father, Max Weber, Sr.—a nationally known politician and powerbroker in Bismarck's Germany—over his mother's right to visit her eldest son's home by herself for several weeks each summer, and over her control of an inheritance. As commentators have observed over the years since, a more perfectly Oedipal conflict has rarely been recorded in the life of a modern intellectual. Within weeks of this strident and unprecedented argument, which culminated in Max, Jr. ordering his father to leave his home in Heidelberg, Max, Sr. died in Riga while on a trip on August 10, 1897. The possibility for reconciliation forever lost, the grieving son slipped into a process of psychological decomposition which would eventually rob him of sleep, the ability to write, to lecture, to read serious material, and to control his body. His father, as it were, had walked into the hereafter carrying with him his son's soul.

At almost the same time this event was transforming Max Weber's life forever—and, as it turned out, most definitely for the best in terms of his contributions to social science—not far away in Vienna, Freud was developing psychoanalytic theory and practice which spoke directly to his condition. Weber was not won over by most psychoanalytic explanations of human action, nor for those people he knew who claimed to follow Freudianism by practicing "free love" and related repudiations of Victorian mores:

> Freud's theories, which I now know of also from his major works, have admittedly changed considerably over the years, and I have the impression, speaking as a layman, that they have not yet by any means reached their final form: important concepts, such as that of "abreaction," have unfortunately very recently been garbled and watered down until they have lost all precise meaning. . . for all that, there is no doubt that Freud's line of thought *could* become very important in suggesting interpretations for whole series of cultural phenomena, especially in the area of the history of *religion* and morality. . . . An essential precondition would be the creation of an *exact casuistics* of a scope and a certainty which, despite all assertions to the contrary, does not exist today, but will perhaps exist in two or three decades: one has only to follow through all the changes which Freud has made in one decade, and to see how alarmingly thin, in spite of everything, his material still is (all of which is understandable and is certainly *no reproach*). (From a letter of September 13, 1907; in Runciman [ed.], *Weber: Selections*, 1978: 383-384; original emphases)

Yet despite his serious intellectual misgivings about Freud's ultimate success as a social analyst, he was much too insightful about himself and others not to realize that his own crisis, beginning after a vacation to Spain in the summer of 1898, revealed sets of unresolved, perhaps irresoluble, conflicts within his psyche that had been sown by the relationship of his parents, and the *Spannung* (tension) that conditioned their conventional, bourgeois marriage.

Later studies of Weber, heavily influenced by and participants in the explosive feminist revaluation of social theory's past—for example, Bologh (1990) and Gane (1993)—though adding nothing archivally original to our knowledge of Weber's mental collapse in 1898 and his life-long episodic disturbances thereafter, gave pride of narrative place to a dire assessment of Weber's psycho-sexual difficulties, even if the data for such examinations is "alarmingly thin," as Weber wrote about Freud. While nothing definitive is likely at this point to be discovered regarding Weber's transformative crises, linked with his parents, wife, and alleged lovers (Mina Tobler and Else von Richthofen), without at minimum the publication of letters now withheld from public scrutiny, this lack of "hard" data has not prevented various scholars from writing *as if* we knew much more than we do. (His "Letters from Ascona" do not shed much light on these matters, as interesting as they otherwise are; see Whimster [ed.], *Max Weber and the Culture of Anarchy*, 1999: 41-71; also Martin Green, *Moutain of Truth*, 1986). Put another way, the temptation to play at anachronism by casting into Weber's social world certain predilections and mores peculiar to our own, pulls vigorously at the storylines composed by a number of recent writers.

That said, and without going into all the available details here, a case could be made that Weber's tidal wave of productivity and creativity, beginning in 1904 with *The Protestant Ethic* and continuing throughout his remaining sixteen years, is not only an expression of neurotically inspired work habits, but, and more importantly, the necessary result of psychopathology that was in a strange and somewhat pathetic sense "ideal" for the Wilhelminian scholar. As he explained to his wife on many occasions, he believed that unless he could work with absolute concentration "until one in the morning," if he could not bear to brutalize himself with intellectual labor, then he did not deserve to be a professor, an intellectual, a social researcher. He felt the need to be burdened with *Pflicht* (duty) on a daily basis, as if to embody the German proverb in literal form: "*Ich schlief und träumte das Leben ist Freude; Ich erwachte und sah das Leben ist Pflicht; Ich handelte und siehe die Pflicht ward Freude*" (I sleep and dream that life is joy; I awoke and saw that life is duty; I behaved and saw that duty became joy). Perhaps he lived this way to prove to himself or his parents that he was worthy of their approbation, or because he understood that his life of privilege rode on the bowed backs of the proletariat, or, more in keeping with today's vocabulary of motives, in order to keep libidinal energy harnessed to the traces of nonsexual labor. Whatever his motivation, self-understood or not, the result was a level of sustained workmanship and theorizing which very few theorists or social analysts have ever attained. It is instructive, then, to see his life as a work of scholarly art, a self-creation borne of misery and perpetual discontent, which a less determined or neurotically energized scholar might well have found overwhelming and paralyzing. There is something here for us postmoderns to consider as we look over our own regimens of work, leisure, and anxiety. It may also be worth admitting this: like most innovators, Max Weber did not venerate his intellectual forbearers, and would therefore probably object heartily to the 4,900 items which comprise the bibliography that makes up this book's sister volume.

Notes

1. Sven Birkerts, *The Gutenberg Elegies: The Fate of Reading in an Electronic Age* (Boston: Faber and Faber, 1994).
2. See Guenther Roth, "The Complete Edition of Max Weber's Work: An Update," *Contemporary Sociology*, 25:4 (July 1996), 464-467; also Lawrence Scaff, "Review of Max Weber Briefe 1909-1910," *Contemporary Sociology*, 25:4 (July 1996), 469-471.
3. There are many studies which document Victorian scholarly virtuosity and the astonishing complexity of the intellectual setting, for example, Peter Allan Dale, *In Pursuit of a Scientific Culture: Science, Art, and Society in the Victorian Age* (Madison: University of Wisconsin Press, 1989); Regenia Gagnier, *Subjectivities: A History of Self-Representation in Britain, 1832-192* (New York: Oxford University Press, 1991); John Holloway, *The Victorian Sage: Studies in Argument* (London: Macmillan, 1953); William Irvine, Apes, Angels, and Victorians (New York: McGraw-Hill, 1955); Thas E. Morgan (ed.), *Victorian Sages and Cultural Discourse* (New Brunswick, NJ:
4. Lester Thurow, *The Future of Capitalism: How Today's Economic Forces Shape Tomorrow's World* (New York: William Morrow and Co., 1996),
5. Papers of otherwise able students in my undergraduate social theory course were marred by these infelicities in the 1995-96 academic year—though I must admit that they provide a type of comic relief one cannot buy at any price.

2

Weber as a Writer:
Rhetoric and Reason in
Economy and Society

"A sound, natural, and harmonious relationship between the rational and the irrational forces of life is all important for men of modern culture and civilization. For it is precisely modern culture and civilization which by its peculiar character threatens this equilibrium"—Friedrich Meinecke, *The German Catastrophe,* Harvard University Press, [1946] 1950: 34).

"The German professoriate as a whole was sucked into the vortex of nazism partly for ideological reasons but mostly because its members were too unworldly, naive, timid, lazy, and selfish to resist the Nazis. Even Meinecke, who could have obtained a chair in any country in the world, did not budge from Berlin. Late in 1945 he published a book on naziism called *The German Catastrophe.* That wasn't hard to do when the British and American armies already occupied West Germany. He had said nothing in public during the twelve-year Hitlerian Reich, not even against the Holocaust." (Norman Cantor, *Inventing the Middle Ages,* New York: Morrow, 1991, p. 89) [It is interesting that Meinecke referred to Weber as "the German Machiavelli"; see Jameson, 1974: 54.]

"The only really interesting thing is to climb inside a great writer's mind and watch how it worked—to the extent one is able to do so. Everything else is floral arranging." Bertrand Russell's brother-in-law, Logan Pearsall Smith, might have said this had he lived long enough.

Every theoretical text is like a military cemetery: the quiet obscures a terrible battle that went before. "Anonymous," more or less.

Defining the Target Text

Aside from the laudable and seldom mentioned exception of Bryan Green (Green, 1988), plus some shorter inquiries by David Chalcraft (Chalcraft, 1994; 2002), few informed Weber scholars have evaluated his prose as a defining ingredient in the makeup of his theorizing. Even the unforgettable preface to *From Max Weber,* in which Gerth and Mills (surely

15

more the latter than the former) visualize Weber's sentences as "gothic castles" meant for the eye and not the ear, full of Platonizing word usage and other troubling, untranslatable tendencies, did not inaugurate a tradition of research into Weber's stylistic mannerisms. Given the tone of the 1950s and 1960s when Big Science inspired sociological research, even among theorists, this is not too surprising. Gerth and Mills did refer to Weber's "tributes to German philosophy and jurisprudence, to the style of the pulpit and the bureaucratic office" (Gerth and Mills, 1946: xi), which in part was ably explicated many years later by Turner and Factor: "If Weber had a consciously chosen model for the structure and discursive character of *Wirtschaft und Gesellschaft*, it may well have been this book," that is, Rudolf von Ihering's *Der Zweck im Recht*, published in 1877 and 1883 in two volumes (Turner and Factor, 1984: 24). Yet these rare ventures into Weber's peculiar linguistic tics have not yet inspired emulation in English vis-á-vis what is now thought of, rightly or not, as Weber's magnum opus.

The thorny textual problems associated with *Economy and Society* at the most basic level regarding its composition and posthumous construction have been well-documented by Weber specialists, often in exasperated tones. The dean of such studies, Wolfgang Mommsen, has recently summarized in English the existing knowledge of the work's haphazard construction and publication (Mommsen, 2000), and in German, Hiroshi Orihara has added his discoveries (see Mommsen, 2000: 365, note 4 for details). Yet more than twenty years ago, Dirk Käsler had already remarked at the opening of his partial exegesis of the work, "The undoubtedly difficult editorial situation of this ultimately unfinished text makes any presentation and interpretation of it is a tricky exercise" (Käsler, 1988 [1979]: 143). More recently, Eliaesen has seconded and elaborated this opinion:

> The key passage in Weber is the classic opening from the introduction to "Basic Concepts of Sociology" [those parts of *WuG* which are also included in *GAW*]: "Sociology . . . is a science which attempts the interpretative understanding of social action in order thereby to arrive at a causal explanation of its course and effects" (*GAW*: 542). This might be understood in two ways, either (1) that through an act of understanding one has achieved explanation; or, the opposite, (2) that explanation has to pass through the stage of understanding, as an inalienable but not sufficient element in the process of explanation. *Here, in the very cornerstone of his sociology, Weber manages to confuse posterity with a formulation resistant to unambiguous interpretation.* It is clear, however, that we cannot ignore either understanding or explanation. (Eliaeson, 2002: 43; emphasis added).

Eliaeson's frustration at not being readily able to discern Weber's precise intentions vis-à-vis the crucial distinction between "understanding" and "explanation"—more crucial, perhaps, for philosophers of social science than for regular practitioners of social research—echoes dozens of previous commentators. What exactly Weber meant to convey in this terse, dry introduction to sociological reasoning has never been entirely clarified by any single interpreter.

We know that Weber oversaw the correction of galleys for the first part of the work, and that his wife, Marianne (along with her assistant, Melchior Palyi), inserted titles and subtitles at will while working through a mountain of incomplete manuscripts after his death. We also now know that Weber began to think about these general problems of sociological method and scope almost immediately upon beginning his truncated teaching career in 1892. By 1905 he was drafting materials that eventually found their way into the compendium or "handbook," even though he did not contractually agree to write it (or something like it) until 1909. Yet if we leave aside all of these complexities, some of them irresolvable, there exists still another layer of hermeneutic inquiry which is less commonly addressed regarding the rhetorical structure of the work. It is this other zone of interpretation that I will begin to tackle in this chapter.

Was Weber a Rational Writer?

Weber can be viewed not exclusively as a social scientist, but as an author ("modernist" or otherwise) who wrote under tremendous pressures, internal as well as external (e.g., relating to publishers, his small but sophisticated public, and his private demons), as is the case with many creative genii. The results of this perspective can be evaluated from at least two points of view: what he thought he said, even in draft form, and what the text reveals about the more obscure logic of his creative process, over which he probably would not have exercised complete control, nor understanding. Given his speed of composition, obsessive attention to detail, and ingrained resistance to imposed deadlines, it makes some sense to consider the distance between his intentions and what the texts actually realized, particularly given their canonical status within the social sciences. (Cf. Hennis's casual remark about a minor piece: "Max Weber's 'Parliament and Government in a Reconstructed Germany' of May, 1918 has for me always been the model for situational political analysis"; Hennis: 2000a: 226.) Textual analysis— even when applied to the English translations that have become the lingua franca of international Weberianism—might be able to divulge not only what he capably understood and described, but may also illuminate those elements of social life and their pertinent theorizing that remained fundamentally opaque to him, even as they became progressively more transparent to later readers.

Put another way, if Weber's achievement is evaluated as a "prose performance" rather than principally or exclusively as a set of analytic ideas that we now selectively choose to apply to contemporary concerns—if he is read as a modernist writer, even as a philosopher of culture, rather than merely as a late-nineteenth-century political-economist—then it becomes necessary to take seriously the way he chose to express himself rather than to think exclusively about "the ideas per se." As the practiced Weber translator, Keith Tribe, recently put it in the opening line of a "Translator's Appendix" to a vital piece of Weberian analysis: "Max Weber was a writer who chose his words carefully" (in Hennis, 2000b: 205). It is not that the ideas become less interesting or important than the rhetoric which gave them life, but rather that they came to Weber's mind and to public attention via an apparatus of expression which cultivated certain kinds of knowledge and inhibited others, the combination of which, I will argue, affected their "substantive" content more than has usually been noted.

The most revealing commentary regarding Weber's outlandish rhetoric appeared thirty years ago in an idiosyncratic English-language study published in Denmark, yet with most of the many Weber excerpts reprinted in their original German. The author (the Danish ambassador to France as of 2001) seldom again wrote about Weber in English, which is our loss, since the book was quite sophisticated for its time, and nowhere more so than in the opening paragraphs:

> On one point at least, this book will surprise and probably dismay the reader: in many places, passages quoted in it are left in the original, mostly in German, unaccompanied by a translation into English. This may seem paradoxical and even perverse in a work the purpose of which is avowedly to help the reader to understand the complexities of Max Weber's thought, since this help is of course above all required when the reader is not prepared to read Weber in the original German.
>
> However, the practice indicated has been adopted precisely because of the peculiar, and peculiarly difficult, character of Weber's German text. In fact, Weber's thought, at least in the field of methodology, is far from clear. His arguments do not progress in straight lines and logical chains, but on the contrary derive much of their effect from being rich in ramifications, modifications, digressions, and exemplifications. This tortuous, even tortured, density of Weber's intellectual texture is reflected in his language, which is full of long, involved, carefully balanced sentences (sometimes running to half a page or more). These intricate linguistic constructions pose an almost insuperable problem to the would-be translator. If they are rendered accurately, they grow very obscure; and if the translator opts for clarity, he runs the risk of destroying the intricate balance of Weber's thought. To this must be added a second difficulty: the meaning of many of Weber's concepts "shimmers" and is difficult to grasp accurately; thus, any *translation* of his text automatically implies an *interpretation* which, like all

interpretations (particularly of Weber's thought), is debatable. (Bruun, 1972: vii; emphases in original).

The notion of Weber's prose "shimmering" is surely the most adventurous such comment in the small literature about Weber's style, and even though it is impossible to know precisely what Bruun had in mind when using the word (in quotation marks, no less), it hints at the built-in ambiguities, most of them quite intentional I suspect, which marked much of Weber's professional writing. Bruun is precisely right about the nature of Weber's prose, even if his decision to lard his book with untranslated fragments of Weber's work probably detracted from its usefulness. Commentators on Weber, it would seem, are damned if they do, damned if they don't.

In so circumspect a writer and thinker as Weber, his particular attention to matters of expression and style if properly examined—even the fact that he chose to camouflage his writerly abilities under tangles of formalist expression, while putting them fully on display only in private letters— might yield a fuller understanding about what constitutes "Weberian social theory" today, both negatively and positively. By way of comparison, one might recall Herbert Spencer's "Literary Style and Music," an odd entry in his oeuvre—perhaps inspired by his close friend, George Eliot (see Paxton, 1991)—but no less interesting for being so (Spencer, 1973; for a literary critic's comments on this unusual document, see Kennedy, 1973). A scamp might note that if one so constitutionally deaf to the aesthetic subtleties of life and art as Spencer nevertheless found time to evaluate the puzzle of literary style, we might well follow his example. Or more recently, and exhibiting an elaborate analytic apparatus, one might also imitate Conal Condren's uniquely rigorous study of classics in political theory, *The Status and Appraisal of Classic Texts*, wherein each examined text is evaluated in terms of its "originality," "contribution and influence," "coherence," and "ambiguity"—the last of which, interestingly, getting the lion's share of attention (Condren, 1985).

Works in social theory have too seldom received this kind of scrutiny. That social theorists were writers and rhetoricians as well as sober analysts should by now be too obvious to cause much surprise, yet the rarity of studies along these lines continues to limit contemporary understanding of what these nineteenth-century thinkers were doing "in full." Works like William Johnston's analysis of Marx's early versifying are much fewer in number than they ought to be (Johnston, 1967). And Kölwel's analysis of *Das Kapital* along strictly stylistic lines—highlighting Marx's almost chronic use of chiasmus, puns, allusions to classical work and so on—is simply unknown within the vast Weber literature

(Kölwel, 1962). Except for a few recent studies of Weber and Nietzsche, capable Weberians have contributed virtually nothing analogous, even though Marianne names in her biography a large number of writers who were close to Weber's heart, both when he was forming himself and as a mature reader later on. His unrealized ambition to write at length about Tolstoy (not unlike Marx's parallel desire to write a monograph about Balzac) only hints at what might be uncovered were one to examine this angle carefully enough. From a slightly different vantage point, the nude etchings of Max Klinger so highly prized by the young Weber couple, and which embarrassed Weber's mother when she visited his home, surely indicate something about the Webers' jointly constructed *Weltanchauung*, as we now know through the creative spadework of David Chalcraft (in Whimster, 1999: 196-213).

It is along these general lines that this chapter has been conceived, though not without the usual misgivings that must be associated with any investigation of Weber's creative acts. Thus, it is wise to recall the polysemous difficulty that blocks an easy journey for readers seeking a clear understanding of Weber's ideas and practices by considering a celebrated denunciation issued nearly twenty years ago, and aimed particularly at Anglophone Weberians: "Friedrich Tenbruck has recently observed that this critique, the seventy-five-year [now ninety-year] enterprise of coming to terms with Weber's methodology, has failed. Indeed, Tenbruck goes so far as to claim that the "core" of Weber's writings as a whole has not been discovered. As a result, his work remains *so utterly alien and unintelligible* to us that we are unable to reach any consensus about what it means" (Oakes, 1988: 5; emphasis added). Is it not possible that such a consensus may never be established, nor even be necessary or desirable?

The Tale Itself

Imagine two kinds of soup simmering on the stove of culture. One is the notorious nineteenth century version, made in a twenty-gallon kettle of lukewarm water, into which a few mealy potatoes are thrown, and through which a small piece of dehydrated meat is dragged, but briefly, so that the concoction sports what we might call "essence of beef." This is the insubstantial mixture that Dickens's sorry waif, David Copperfield, would have known, as would all the inmates during that time who were incarcerated within the walls of our own imaginations. The other brew is made nowadays, say, in Wisconsin, by a self-abnegating Protestant housewife and mother—I will assume, for the sake of hungry nostalgia, that there still remain one or two such women in that state, and that they are wheeled out for special occasions to remind people of what the glorious 1950s were like. Into a thick and healthily prepared base, she carefully insinuates large chunks of precooked meat, freshly cut vegetables, and aromatic seasonings of the kind which, when the family smells it as they climb off their tractors or out of their SUVs, causes everyone to grin from ear to ear. They enter the spacious kitchen, and the English major of the sib-group says, "Golly, Mom, life surely takes on enhanced meaning when you prepare this soul-sustaining food for us. Hallowed be thy name!"

Now that one's imagination is swimming in soup, I will, of course, propose an analogy. The heartiness and palatal satisfaction that would surely come from eating today's Wisconsin soup on a wintry day, and which puts to such shame the gruelish liquid of the nineteenth century, well represents the textual density of Weber's writing as against a great deal of what has been written since, and particularly in the last third of the twentieth century, even by academics whose job it is to compose "thick texts." Put another way, the more electronically dependent and gratified Western culture has become since the widespread use of electric lighting, the more dimly has the literate past been perceived or understood as thoroughly or precisely as it might be. Such a notion has become an article of faith among historians of political thought, such as Quentin Skinner and the aforementioned Condren. It has less thoroughly penetrated the interpretative mindsets of those scholars in charge of bringing to life sociological theory for the younger generations. Though arguments which began in the 1960s about "presentism" versus "historicism," and the related anguish caused by anachronistic readings, are commonly known to intellectual historians, specialists in social theory seem not yet enough acquainted with them to have changed their way of doing business. More often the question is "what can Weber teach us today," rather than "what was Weber doing when he did it, and why did he do it that way?" My position, *in nuce*, is that the former cannot be properly answered until the latter has been grasped, even if only approximately.

These issues become particularly sharp if one more or less accepts Dilthey's definition of *Verstehen*, and tries to comprehend a given writer's consciousness at the moment when his or her works were being composed. As Dilthey put it in 1910, "Understanding and interpretation is the method used throughout the *Geisteswissenschaften* and all functions unite in it. It contains all the truth of the human studies. Everywhere understanding opens up a world" (Dilthey, 1961: 116). Recalling that Dilthey visited Weber's home when the latter was young and clearly influenced not only his methodology, as ritually noted in the literature, but more importantly, his definition of what the human sciences ought to comprise, revisiting Dilthey's arguments becomes suggestive in trying to identify those elements which seem to have made up Weber's scholarly persona. Here I second Hennis's contention that Heinrich Rickert was not the principal inspiration for Weber's scholarly method along these lines, as some scholars have argued; moreover, Dilthey—and Burckhardt, as an examplar of historical practice—are more important for Weber's methodology than the formalist, logical studies of his friend and colleague in Freiburg. In this I am pointedly disregarding Rickert's own deep hostility (and envy?) toward Dilthey: "See Rickert's critique of Dilthey as a *Lebensphilosoph*, which condemns him to the lowest circle of philosophical hell along with Nietzsche, Bergson, Simmel and Scheler" (Oakes, 1988: 169, n. 8).

By way of a beginning, I want to reiterate and question the last phrase from the Dilthey quotation: what does it mean to "open up a world" and how does one go about it? From an encyclopedia of advice on the process and practice of *Verstehen* that Dilthey left behind, these comments are characteristic:

> The interpretation of what is transitory is also determined by the moment. It is terrible that in the struggle of practical interests every expression can be deceptive and its interpretation changed with a change in our situation. But, in great works, because some content of the mind separates itself from the creator, the poet, the artist, or the writer, we enter a sphere in which deception ends. No truly great work of art can. . . wish to give the illusion of a mental content foreign to its author; indeed it does not want to say anything about its author. Truthful in itself it stands—fixed, visible, permanent; and because of this a skilled and certain understanding of it is possible. Thus there arises in the confines between science and action a circle in which life discloses itself at a depth inaccessible to observation, reflection, and theory. (ibid., 118-119).

Similarly, from a chapter which bears the interesting title "Neither Philosophy of History Nor Sociology is Really a Science," these related remarks occur:

> There are various persons within each of us: family member, citizen, colleague; we find ourselves bound by moral obligations, belonging to a legal system, and part of a purposive system of life directed toward satisfaction. Only in self-reflection do we discover within ourselves the unity and continuity of life which maintains and supports all these relationships. In this way the life of human society too consists of the production and formation, differentiation and integration of these enduring systems of interaction, without thereby possessing—and without any of the individuals who support them possessing—an awareness of the over-all connection of those systems. (Dilthey, 1989: 136)

These could well have been Talcott Parsons's words in the 1960s had he been more sensitive to phenomenological issues, or even George

Herbert Mead's—but instead they are Dilthey's from 1883. It was during this period that he developed what Guy Oakes has termed "psychological hermeneutics," and only later did he begin to create the more formalistic "cultural hermeneutics," somewhat closer in spirit to Rickert's philosophy of the *Geisteswissenschaften* (in Simmel, 1980: 57-61).

Today it is perhaps difficult to comprehend the full meaning of Dilthey's intentions, and these snippets hardly substitute for the sort of detailed knowledge, personal and intellectual, that Weber was privileged to have of this titan in the German academic firmament. As H.P. Rickman, Rudolf Makkreel, and other Dilthey specialists have repeatedly argued, a fair estimate of Dilthey's profound influence cannot be gained from bite-sized quotations. Nevertheless, just within these few words lies a prolegomenon to what I would call a "full-bodied hermeneutic" that remains as compelling today as it must have been during Weber's early career. In fact, parts of the last quotation read almost like a scholarly catechism for the young Weber as he was preparing, unbeknownst even to himself, for an unrelievedly scholarly existence. It is here, in assaying the contextual and sociological bases of intellectual and literary composition, that we must struggle to comprehend the major works of the nineteenth and early twentieth centuries—before radio and "the talkies" forever altered the way humanity perceives and then analyzes itself and its cultural artifacts.

I am fully aware, as is surely every attentive Weberian, that one of Weber's explicit epistemological goals was to shy away from Dilthey's and Windelband's enormous presences within the so-called "human sciences" —*perhaps*, indeed, in favor of Rickert's philosophy of science— during that period when he was beginning his career (recalling that Dilthey lectured at Berlin until six years before he died in 1911, and only nine years before Weber's own demise). Simmel similarly sought to escape their weight, simply by refusing to mention Dilthey in his work, even while explaining identical matters (Simmel, 1980: 58). Even though Weber appreciated the firm distinction they had made between the social and natural sciences, he refused to give up the virtues of one for the other, and like all innovators (cf. Randall Collins's sociology of philosophical schools) was very keen to carve out for himself an alternative methodology for the genuinely new science he thought sociology could become; nevertheless, he retained one of Dilthey's favored terms, *Verstehen*. Even though the word itself has become quite familiar to students of social thought, most readers, particularly during the last twenty years or so, do not seem nearly so aware of its origins as were earlier scholars who covered this terrain, among them Carlo Antoni, H. Stuart Hughes, or H. P. Rickman. If we remind ourselves of this persuasive way of looking at the social world—one which helped shape the worldviews of

Husserl, Heidegger, Croce, and other notables of lesser magnitude—it might make sense to reconsider Weber's own magnum opus from the point of view of a truncated hermeneutic inquiry that is suitable for a brief foray such as this.

Weber's Reading

One way of beginning such a task is to consider which textual references might have sent Weber down one analytic road rather than another. And though we do not have, to my knowledge, studies equivalent to Michael Reynolds's *Hemingway's Reading, 1910-1940* or Gillian Beer's "Darwin's Reading and the Fictions of Development," there are plenty of signposts in Marianne Weber's biography and his own untranslated *Jugendbriefe*, pointing out which authors and ways of thinking influenced him during what we like to think of as one's most "impressionable" years. Let's listen in on what Marianne had to say in her indispensable volume regarding the precocious boy whom one day she would marry: "At the beginning of 1877, before his fourteenth birthday, Max wrote— evidently as a belated Christmas present—two historical essays, 'after numerous sources,' one 'About the Course of German History, with Special Regard to the Positions of the Emperor and the Pope,' the other 'About the Roman Imperial Period from Constantine to the Migration of Nations'. . . Two years later, again around Christmas, he wrote, "Observations on the Ethnic Character, Development, and History of the Indo-European Nations." These essays already incorporate the results of original thought—in the "philosophy of history," so to speak" (Marianne Weber, 1975: 45-46).

The obvious, discomforting comparison between the sort of mental work the young Weber was producing at thirteen or fourteen when set beside even the brightest children of our own time is not really my point here, though it's surely an interesting one. My question instead revolves more around the Diltheyan question of how one "gets inside" another's mind in sufficient detail to understand the author's intentions, a singular goal that, according to those classic hermeneutic principles set forth in the early nineteenth century by Friedrich Schleiermacher and others, leads to reliable understanding of texts. That this point of view is less popular than it was before the onslaught of postmodernist theorizing is not presently at issue. That is, no matter what one's position about "identity," "presence," "agency," and so on, the fact is that Derrida's readings of Plato or Freud, for example, are either illuminating and useful, or they are perverse. The classical hermeneutic discipline aimed for the former condition, of course, as I am doing here.

Returning, momentarily, to Marianne's report in an early chapter of her biography, one can picture how young Max Weber became the titan whose work today is scrupulously reconsidered and also, if truth be told, venerated: "But books were the most important thing in his rich boyhood. At an early age Max studied on his own whatever he could get his hands on, history and the classics above all. But he also read philosophy. . . Spinoza and Schopenhauer. . . he especially read Kant. At the age of twelve he told his mother that someone had lent him Machiavelli's *The Prince* and that he was going to read *Antimachiavell* [by Frederick the Great in 1739], and also look into Luther's work." At fifteen he had this to say about himself: "I don't daydream. I don't write poetry, so what else shall I do but read? So I am doing a thorough job of that." His wife reported that "Around that time he was already taking notes on his reading....'My progress is slow because I make many notes as I read.'"

Marianne then begins several important pages on which she records Max's reading during this period of early adolescence, including Homer and Ossian (James Macpherson), and all forty volumes of Goethe's works in the Cotta edition, which he consumed during class hours while he was a sophomore in high school, presumably because he was bored otherwise. Then she reproduces his self-reports, which seem, in context, nearly incomprehensible: "The adolescent did almost no work for school, and only occasionally paid attention in class. . . . He was always the youngest and weakest of his class. He remembered being 'lazy as sin' devoid of any sense of duty or ambition" (p. 48). His other readings include works of Theodor Mommsen on Roman history, Treitschke on political philosophy, U.S. history, Walter Scott's *Heart of Midlothian* ("one of the most stirring novels I know"), Herodotus, Virgil, Cicero, and Sallust. In September, 1878, at fourteen, he wrote in a letter to his older cousin, Fritz: "I do not like Virgil nearly so well as Homer. In Virgil's *Aeneid* he seeks to arouse a certain suspense, but one hardly feels it, or, if one does, it is not a pleasant sensation. This clearly comes out in Book Four, where the catastrophe of Dido is described. He succeeds in part, but the feeling it gave me was not a pleasant one—because the tension does not arise naturally from the material itself but is artificially created by means of various devices. To be sure, little bourgeois epics like Goethe's *Hermann und Dorothea* would be pointless, they would be idylls rather than epics if there were no suspense, but they simply are middle-class epics" (p. 51).

Finally, from the untranslated *Jugendbriefe*, we read some post-Christmas reflections of a young man who appears to be possessed of an adult-like mind. This letter is dated December 29, 1878, which Marianne summarized but did not quote in her book:

Dear Fritz,

We have proceeded through the celebration days really happily and I do not doubt you have, too. In the last days before Christmas and especially at Christmas Eve, one is in a festive mood, although sometimes also impatient when one has to wait too long. Then we always sit together in the next room, which was only dimly lit with a somber red gaslight and we sing Christmas songs in anticipation of the things to come. . . I want to enumerate my gifts. There was first an English Shakespeare, which at the present time I cannot use, due to my insufficient knowledge of the English language. This is because I have had only a quarter-year of English lessons. I think, though, that I will gain enough knowledge by Easter to understand it to some extent by then. Also got three volumes of Curtius's *History of the Greeks* which I mainly wished for and which I find especially interesting. I have already read a lot in it, and can only admire the beautiful, well-written language and the attractive style with which all events are told. Then I got a book about *Cicero and His Friends* [cf. the American juvenile favorite, *Duck and His Friends*, a Golden Book, Western Pub. Co. 1949], a German edition of a French work by Boissier. I have not yet read in this book much, but believe I will be greatly interested in it. In addition I also received so-called art history, illustrated broadsheets, which appeared in different collections, and a history of architecture, sculpture, and paintings with illustrations. I already own parts of it, this is the second, and I have every piece beautifully bound individually. In addition I was sent two novels from Bielefeld by Walter Scott, which are *The Talisman* and *Quentin Durward*. I have immediately gotten stuck in it and read them through. [The former novel is 358 pages long in a standard edition, and the latter was first published as a three-decker of 273, 331, and 360 pages each.] I find Walter Scott's novels generally very interesting, even though occasionally a little bit thick and long-winded. Anyhow, they are the kind of art that allows one to go deeply into them, as I have done. Otherwise, I have read. . . a really interesting but difficult book by Victor Hehn about the movement of cultivated plants and pets from Asia to Europe. The book deals with every useful animal and plant, one after another, and tries to demonstrate how the individual plants and animals from Asia came to us and how and when they established themselves. Otherwise, I'm busy also with Latin Authors, reading Livy's *History of Rome* and related works. [The Penguin edition of Livy in 4 volumes comes to 2,100 pages, so perhaps Max, at fourteen, read an abridged edition, but almost surely in Latin.]. (Weber, 1936: 15-16)

It is trite to observe that Weber's critical sense was already leagues ahead of his age-mates, and his acumen obviously befuddled one close relative, who discretely hinted that young Weber had lifted opinions from famous books, then tried to pass them off as his own. On October 25, 1878, at fourteen, Weber responded with indignant politeness, as he would throughout his life:

What you have said about the influence of bookreading on a person is very true. . . I admit that everything may indirectly stem from books. What are books for but to enlighten people about things that are not clear to them, and to instruct them? It is possible that I am very sensitive to books, that is, their comments and deductions; this you can judge better than I, for in certain respects it really is easier to know a person other than oneself. Yet the content of my—perhaps completely untrue—statements does not come directly from any book. For the rest, I cannot resent any of your criticism, for I have now found out that quite similar things are contained in Mommsen. At any rate, I believe that what I said about Cicero may be derived from a mere knowledge of Roman history of the period. If one reads the first three Catilinarian orations [55 pp. in the Penguin edition] and at each sentence asks himself why Cicero spoke it, one comes to the identical conclusion. (Ibid.: 54-55)

Note two very important phrases: "in certain respects it really is easier to know a person other than oneself," which sounds remarkably like something Dilthey or even William James might have written. And when one recalls the titanic struggle for his own sanity that overtook Weber at the age of thirty-three, virtually crippling him intellectually until he was almost forty, this sentence takes on special meaning. More to the immediate point, consider his advice to his older cousin, then in college: "If one reads...and *at each sentence* asks himself why Cicero spoke it..." [emphasis added]. This is the mark of a hermeneutic virtuoso in the making who, at fourteen years of age, is already preparing himself for a lifework of critical reading, commentary, polemic, and interpretation, even if quite unselfconsciously at the time, given his father's robust political career and his extended family's vast commercial connections (as detailed in Guenther Roth's recent book, *Max Webers deutsch-englische Familiengeschichte, 1800-1950*). If Dilthey was a founder of *Lebensphilosophie* and hermeneutic philosophy, culminating most recently in Hans-Georg Gadamer, then Weber, it could be argued, helped found a hermeneutically based form of theorizing and analysis that has more to do with rhetorical intention and punch than any so-called "logic of scientific discovery" as understood in its common form. In short, early on he became a great reader of great material, and he learned exactly what to do with these "data" after making them his own, via elaborate, earnest annotation.

How are we to deal with this level of intellectualism—one might even say, this "Olympic level"? How can we avoid the "inventive misinterpretation" (to quote from the first page of Roth's introduction to *Economy and Society*) that has so often been associated with the reception of Weber's work? There is, of course, what one might call the "piecemeal option." An English-language bibliography pertaining to Weber that I have been assembling for some years currently numbers over 4,100 published items, plus 400 dissertations and hundreds of reviews. Within it one can find dozens of experts in a given area of scholarship—say, medieval trading companies in the Italian port cities—who can pick at some of Weber's earliest work based on newer methods or better archival materials. But it's almost invariably the case that by the time the article in question reaches its end, a phrase turns up that seems to be generated by the same computer—probably hidden in the Weber Archives in Munich—which duly reports: "Even though Weber was incorrect on some details, overall his conclusions about this particular phenomenon were right." And when the rare critic does take radical exception to one of Weber's main ideas, he or she often find themselves on very thin ice—a recent example being Jacques Barzun's comically inadequate dismissal of the Protestant Ethic thesis within two paragraphs of his latest and grandest work, *From Dawn to Decadence* (pp. 36-38). There is an expression, I believe, from the world of spectator sports—"Too good"—indicating that an opponent is so overwhelmingly superior to all competitors, that authentic competition is proscribed. (Perhaps for the time being one could introduce novices to Weber by means of the phrase "the Tiger Woods of sociological analysis"; in the thirties it would have been "the Bill Tilden of social thought"; my own favorite is "the Jascha Heifetz of analytic brilliance.")

Rhetorical Sources

Having done my best within this short space to hint at the difficulties peculiar to understanding and then elaborating Weber's ideas and his unique method of creating social theory, I will use the remaining pages to sketch in barest form some of the rhetorical ploys that characterize the opening sections of *Wirtschaft und Gesellschaft*. My goal is not to humble or "update" Weber as much as to hunt for that elusive "fusion of horizons" which Gadamer in *Truth and Method* commends to those whose scholarly goals include hermeneutic appropriation of classic works. First, it must be admitted that the opening chapters of Weber's masterwork seem almost universally disdained or dismissed, with the notable and energetic exception of Richard Swedberg's recent revaluation, though even he refers to it as "very tough reading" (Swedberg, 1998: 8, 208-209). Swedberg quotes three critics of the opening chapters. Herbert Marcuse, in his notorious comments at the 1964 centenary celebration, writes of "veritable orgies of formal definitions, classification, and typologies." Guenther Roth notes that chapter 2 has "proved a waste of effort" and "economists and sociologists [with minor exceptions] have ignored it." Only Marianne Weber, as one would expect, wrote about these dense passages with Olympian appreciation: "Whereas the first, abstract part employs historical material everywhere essentially as a means to illustrate concepts, thereafter ideal-typical concepts are, conversely, put in the service of the interpretive illumination of world-historical circumstances, events, and developments" (German Preface to

Wirtschaft und Gesellschaft; quoted in Baier et al. 2000: 108). Some years ago I myself referred to "the almost unreadable accretion of definition piled upon definition" that makes up Weber's introductory remarks (Sica, 1988: 146). How charmingly ironic that I now find myself analyzing, even defending, what is surely among the least inviting parts of the entire Weberian oeuvre.

That said, however, these pages indeed deserve special scrutiny since we know (from Marianne Weber's biography, as well as Wolfgang Mommsen's recent work) that Weber went over them in galley form before suddenly dying, so they at least had the benefit of his final ruminations and annotations, unlike the rest of the huge work assembled by his wife and collaborators. Mommsen points out that if strict chronology were the goal of editing *Economy and Society*, these chapters ought to have come at the end, since they were written last, in 1919/20. Nevertheless, through a long history of usage, at least since Parsons's first translation in 1947, they have been read as Weber's opening salvo in his battle to set sociology on a course that suited his own scholarly interests and values—and, not incidentally, would finally give long-suffering Paul Siebeck something to publish after waiting a dozen years.

There are, of course, a number of hermeneutic postures one might assume in dealing with this famously "dry" material. While trying to come to terms with this problem, I recalled a unique article I had first read while in graduate school, but had not revisited in many years. In the inaugural issue of *New German Critique* (1974), Fredric Jameson published an uncanny piece in what has since become the celebrated body of his own critical writings, which he called "The Vanishing Mediator: Narrative Structure in Max Weber." Though seldom mentioned since in the secondary literature, it seemed even then to me a tour de force. Jameson craftily applied a quasi-mathematical structuralist formula invented by A. J. Greimas (inspired by Lévi-Strauss's analysis of myths) for use in taking apart various forms of literature to see how their subtexts operate. Jameson put A.J. Greimas's "semantic rectangle" to use, first in considering Weber's four types of social action, and then, more elaborately, by examining some of his main claims within the "storyline" of *The Protestant Ethic*. (He does not pretend to be a Weber specialist and is therefore preserved from certain hesitations: "Such an approach [myth analysis] will require a distance from Weber's work and an attitude towards it quite different from that of official sociology" (Jameson, 1974: 52). Although the article is too complex to deal with thoroughly here, a taste of Jameson's project can be gleaned by examining several of his graphics in the order he presented them, first, with regard to the four types of action, and then concerning magicians' power versus the bureaucratized condition of priests within an established church.

In the order in which they appear below, the first represents Greimas's original schema for myth analysis, where binary oppositions are highlighted, so that S is contradicted by -S (anti-S), and then by complex and neutral terms created by their opposites. Jameson explains:

> The premise of this schema, which distinguishes between the contrary of a given term S (-S or what we may term anti-S), and its simple negative or contradictory (S or not-S), holds that all concepts are implicitly or explicitly defined in terms of conceptual oppositions. Its advantage lies in the possibility which it suggests of generating other supplementary and related elements out of that initial pair of contrary terms. Thus for example, we observe that the contrary of S or -S (anti-S) logically possesses a contradictory of its own in not-anti-S. Moreover, it should be noted that each side of the rectangle constitutes the possibility of a synthetic term (S united with -S) is termed a "complex" term, while the union of not-anti-S and not-S is a "neutral" one which marks out as it were the closure or outer limits of the thought system in question. (Ibid., 64).

The second diagram is Jameson's way of arranging Weber's four types of social action in Greimas's terms, which will immediately strike practiced Weberians as far too simple, in that the action types cannot really be conceived as simple opposites. Still, the formulation has its appeal. The third arrangement is meant to convey Weber's insight within his *Sociology of Religion* (a subsection of *Economy and Society*) that magicians and priests draw on different sorts of power in order to persuade their auditors to follow their dictates, one from personal, charismatic appeal, the other from received dogma. Moving to Weber's *General Economic History* (p. 265), Jameson offers his most complex graphical portrait, where he compliments Weber for being able to convert static categories into a fluid portrait of social change—in short, for producing a credible and interesting "narrative account." The prophet nullifies the magician's idiosyncratic power by helping to bureaucratize religious action, and thus unknowingly setting a table at which eventually the bourgeoisie will dine through its control of bureaucratic administration.

I am not persuaded that Jameson succeeded quite so much in freshly illuminating Weber's argument as he did in ingeniously extending the reach of structuralist methodology, at that time so much in vogue among Francophile literary critics. In fact, his final display reminds me more of Parsons's last forays into tabular representations than of the "richness" of Weber's own narrative.

The essential point, however, is that Jameson tried to treat Weber *as a writer*, and that the tools of the trade common to critics served him well as he struggled to make sense of a text which he described as follows: "Such a vision of history is doubtless what lends these dry pages, interlarded with dead theology and the most unbearable scholarly appara-

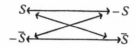

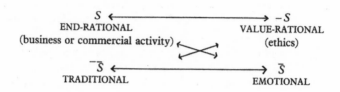

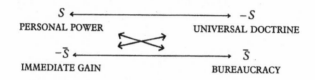

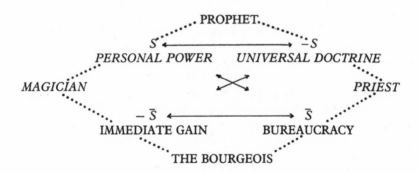

tus, their emotional impact: *de te fabula narratur!*" If Jameson thought *The Protestant Ethic* was "dry" and "unbearable," he clearly never looked at the opening pages of *Wirtschaft und Gesellschaft*. More astutely, Jameson continues: "Weber's monograph has about it some of the dizzying pessimism of Freud's *Civilization and Its Discontents*, or of the early novels of H. G. Wells, which, contemporaneous with it, offer the same remorseless gaze into a dwindling future" (ibid., p. 71). And moving in directions very sympathetic to my own, he evaluates Weber as a narrativist and as a polemicist with notions of historical truth that operated, as Burckhardt and others knew full well, on the level of refined artistry: "we may characterize Weber's objection to the vulgar Marxist position as an aesthetic one, one that detects the weakness of the earlier explanation through flaws in the latter's narrative construction (and it may be suggested in

passing that all historical 'revision,' all the 'great debates' about historical interpretation, whether of the class basis of the English civil war, or
of origins of the Cold War, or whatever, may be understood in narrative
terms in precisely this way)" (ibid., p. 70). In my view, this is precisely
correct, and opens an avenue toward understanding Weber's theorizing which has heretofore been rarely explored, or even mentioned. As
we know from Harold Bloom and others, all writers must position themselves in relation to competitors and opponents in order to win the
public's ear, especially if, as in Weber's case, the "public" was extremely
small and just as extremely well educated in the materials to be debated.
In simplest terms, Weber simply did not like "the Marxist story" of how
religious beliefs affected capitalist accumulation, so he proposed a new
story which suited him, aesthetically and historically. His new melody
fit the materials at hand in ways that, for example, Kautsky's or Sombart's
did not.

Whatever the limitations of Jameson's approach, in combining the
structuralist formulae of Lévi-Strauss with the "semantic rectangle" of
A.J. Greimas, his unique purchase on Weber's work is the result of this
general argument: "we find ourselves confronting a theoretical problem
which may alternately be characterized as that of history or that of narrative, depending on whether we raise it in connection with the object of
our study or our own method of analyzing that object respectively. . .
narrative analysis, in other words, requires us to explain the imaginative illusion of change, or time, or of history itself, by reference to basic
components of the narrative line which are bound to be static ones"
(ibid.: 69). Jameson's immediate concern is with how theory portrays
diachronic movement, which to my mind is too narrow a problem when
thinking of Weber's historical works. The larger and more important
the topic he undertook, the more narrative artistry he applied to it, so
that by the time he composed his *Zwischenbetrachtung* near the end of his
life, he had left far behind the prose aesthetics revealed in the two essays
that made up *The Protestant Ethic* in 1904/05.

Whether or not Jameson's general approach was successfully applied to the broad outlines of *The Protestant Ethic*, my preliminary attempt to do similar labors on the opening chapters of *Economy and Society*
were met with frustration, probably because the "narrative line" is much
weaker than in the better known "tale" and because Jameson is slicker
than I am. Yet Jameson's larger point remains suggestive: to consider
Weber as a modernist writer, to examine his use of rhetorical forms, to
chart his linguistic maneuvers, is in some ways at this advanced stage
of Weber scholarship a more satisfying endeavor than simply once again
to puzzle out whether his analyses of the *oikos*, or of Chinese
patrimonialism, or of the Jews as a pariah people still hold water.

Weber perennially appeals to attentive readers because—and I realize this viewpoint is heretical given contemporary norms of readerly tastes—his mode of expression is exciting, though *not* because he controlled language in the way that Nietzsche or Stefan George or even his houseguest, Oswald Spengler, did, but precisely because he did not. He told certain stories well because he knew enough to make them "particularistically" fascinating, in a way that is somehow more akin to Chekhov than it is to, for instance, the more inflammatory, almost hallucinatory Dostoyevsky. Very few Weber scholars have remarked on his attentiveness to the telling phrase or image, obsessed as they have been with the "meaning" of this or that concept. Quite recently Guy Oakes broke the mold by commenting, even if only in an endnote, about these matters (although his subtextual goal is to demean Jaspers in favor of Rickert, a longtime strategy of his):

> Karl Jaspers, perhaps the most eminent and unrestrained of Weber's hagiographers, maintained that Weber, "always dedicated to substance and oblivious to language," was indifferent to the literary quality of his work (1931: 71). Perhaps Jaspers had no ear for Weber's many resonant metaphors. The Weberian penchant for figurative expression is not confined to his disposition to express the pathos of human affairs in a language with richer resources than the austere discourse of science. Weber often betrays a preference for allusion over analysis when problems become conceptually difficult, a habit that is especially evident when he moves from historical and sociological issues to philosophical problems. His discussions of the theory of value rest overwhelmingly on metaphors such as the polytheism of values and the struggle between the gods of value spheres. . . .This is a surprising practice on the part of a thinker who consistently represented himself as a hardened apostle of objectivity. Instead of following a puritanical rule of plain-speaking and rigor, Weber seems to have embraced an anti-puritanical principle classically formulated by Mae West: "I generally avoid temptation unless I can't resist it" (Oakes, 2003: 42n.5).

Along similar lines, reconsider the *Zwischenbetrachtung*, now so much admired (and to which Oakes, among many, pays special attention): if one removes the details of comparative religion, what would be left except the frailest skeleton of pure imagining? Weber was always in search, it seems to me, of that which in German might be called *"richtig"* (correct, right, proper), as in his specification of the perplexing *Richtigkeitsrationalität*, translated by Käsler as "means-ends-rationality" (Käsler, 1988: 179, 183), or by Graber as "objectively correct rationality" (Weber, 1981: 154), but literally meaning "the rationality of correctness or accuracy"; could one even risk rendering it as "the correctness of rationality"? There existed within Weber's unannounced philosophy of prose style the remnants of a strong categorical imperative, and in this unforgiving Kantian morality he found his ultimate grounding for scholarly work. He wrote as if his life depended on it; which, of course, it did, aside from material concerns.

Yet these are all claims for which I have not yet offered proof, so-called, and in the pages left to me here, I would like to explore some of the rhetorical terrain that Weber inhabited as he laid out his unique plan for the social sciences, built around the activity of interpreting "meaningful action." Roth refers to "Science as a Vocation" and "Politics as a Vocation" as "these two rhetorical masterpieces," yet he goes on to explain that despite the chilly formality that opens *Economy and Society*, it is "full of irony, sarcasm, and the love of paradox" (Roth, 1968: xxvii). We know from contemporary documents that Weber was famous among friends and students for using just these rhetorical tropes in conversation and public debate. (Paul Honigsheim's memoirs are an especially good source for this, reissued not long ago; Honigsheim, 2000.) We also have his wife's testimony that despite years of complaints, false starts, reformulations, and altercations with his harried publisher, "At last he concentrated on a uniformly great task," so his tendency to pursue all possible topics simultaneously was temporarily, and fruitfully, contained (Marianne Weber, 1975: 419).

Yet late in his foreshortened life, Weber dressed himself in an expressively ascetic mode, bringing his stylistic tendencies to heel in much of his writing in order to walk the strict line of value-neutrality that he thought he owed his audience when speaking as a professor. In contrast, it is perhaps worth reminding ourselves that Weber's "love of paradox" was shared by Marx, of course, who indulged in it almost to a fault, over-using what rhetoricians call "chiasmus," the inverting of parallel phrases, for example, Samuel Johnson's famous version, "Your manuscript is both good and original; but the part that is good is not original, and the part that is original is not good." Or, from Marx's *Early Philosophical Manuscripts*, this memorable passage: "Being the external, common *medium* and *faculty* for turning an *image* into *reality* and *reality* into a mere *image...money* transforms the *real essential powers of man and nature* into what are merely abstract conceits and therefore *imperfections*— into tormenting chimeras—just as it transforms *real imperfections and chimeras*—essential powers which are really impotent, which exist only in the imagination of the individual—into *real powers and faculties* (Tucker, 1978: 105; emphasis in original). More simply, "He [the worker] is at home when he is not working, and when he is working he is not at home" (ibid: 74). Whereas Weber avoided mannered rhetoric of such stridency, he did, after all, teach *Das Kapital* very early in his career, and the stylistic panache of the great polemicist must have left some mark on his own writing.

And Nietzsche's influence is perhaps too obvious even to mention, though less in *Economy and Society* than in his speeches and similarly expressive writings when he was more eager to connect emotionally with his audience. Of a hundred possible examples, consider only Nietzsche's often quoted analysis of German anti-Semitism from section 475 of *Human, All Too Human,* and compare it with Weber's extremely sober *Ancient Judaism*:

> Incidentally, the whole problem of the *Jews* exists only within national states, inasmuch as their energy and higher intelligence, their capital of spirit and will, which accumulated from generation to generation, in the long school of their suffering, must predominate to a degree that awakens envy and hatred; and so, in the literature of nearly all present-day nations (and, in fact, in proportion to their renewed nationalistic behavior), there is an increase in the literary misconduct that leads the Jews to the slaughterhouse as scapegoats for every possible public and private misfortune. (Nietzsche, 1984: 228-229)

It was to this steaming level of scholarly rhetoric that Weber would at times aspire (the final pages of *The Protestant Ethic* are the best-known examples), and when one considers not only Nietzsche, but also Schopenhauer, Goethe, Ibsen, and like writers whom Weber read with care and appreciation, it becomes much easier to think about his prose works as artful rather than exclusively analytic.

The Opening Paragraphs

In the opening pages of the work, within "The Definitions of Sociology and of Social Action," Weber uses twenty-six pages divided into fourteen sections trying to explain what an interpretative sociology might entail (Weber, 1968: 3-28). These are among the most important pages he ever wrote, at least methodologically. Here he concisely expressed his unique conceptual amalgam, a heterodox brew that came from all the philosophies of social science and their epistemologies that had been swirling around him since he was a young student thirty years before. As already noted, these pages were also among the last he wrote and proofed before his unexpected death (Marianne Weber, 1975: 675-76). Though it is impossible within the constraints of a few pages to explore these texts thoroughly without putting most readers to sleep, with the possible exception of myself, perhaps we can quickly review a few key passages with the idea of reading them primarily as writerly productions rather than in the way they are normally taken, as pragmatic guides for social science practitioners. In this way, I believe, one can come closer to Weber's intentions, misattentions, creative breakthroughs, and uncertain stumblings than would otherwise be likely.

As always, his wife's commentary is indispensable to understanding what he meant to accomplish in these last feverish months of his scholarly labors. She explains that the book has two parts, one purely conceptual, the other arranged by ideal-type, which more or less illustrate the preceding concepts' raison d'être. She also advances a wise estimate of Weber's compositional practices that is available virtually nowhere else in the literature, and given her witnessing of the events, her version of the book's long-term coming together carries special weight. She wrote:

> The mastery of facts he had acquired early in life placed an inexhaustible wealth of illustrative material at his disposal for clarifying scientific and theoretical connections or practical and political matters.. . . the conceptual constructs used in the descriptive parts for the penetration of historical processes are in the first part arranged systematically and presented as unambiguously as possible. The theory of concepts, then, presupposes a comprehensive mastery of history, because it is not deduced from major terms or principles, as speculative intellectual systems are, but is directly evolved from the concrete factual material and *composed* inductively [in contrast to Spengler]. This is why Weber wrote his historically analytical and descriptive treatises before the war and "from memory"—without notes. He did not need any material or *apparatus criticus*, for he had universal knowledge at his disposal. (Marianne Weber, 1975: 306, 676)

Notice that Weber's approach to the problem of writing "theory" is first of all to have become a professional-level historian, a self-imposed task begun in early adolescence. Of all the many differences between his generation of what we now term "social theorists" and those scholars today who practice an analogous craft, this single feature is probably the most significant. Even if his knowledge was not quite "universal," it was probably close enough when compared with even the best-read theorists in today's academy, so that his wife's point still stands. Her unexpressed argument, then, is this: without the vast historical data at this fingertips, he could not and would not have "composed *inductively*" the categories which occupy the opening chapters of *Economy and Society*. Many of today's model-builders in theory circles seem to have in mind, first of all, their own immediate social and intellectual environment when they propose "likely behavior" among the social actors whose actions they hope to anticipate, understand, even control by means of their abstractions. Despite Weber's commitment to science and rigor, this was most definitely not his way of working, which is perhaps why his work continues to be read while any number of formal models—going back to J. L. Moreno's "sociograms" in the 1930s (Moreno, 1934; 1943)—have predictably grown stale over a relatively short time.

Marianne continues in her analysis of her husband's magnum opus:

> Only later did he set down his theory of categories. He had to do this for the lectures he gave in Vienna in 1918 and in Munich a year later. Now, a few months before his death, it was given its final form. He kept remolding the difficult concepts and made many changes in the proof sheets.
> Weber finally achieved a concision of expression that satisfied him. To be sure, "People are going to shake their heads." He realized that his method, which was filling well-known historical, economic, juridical, and theological systems with a completely new substance, would at first not only be hard to understand but would also strike people as strange. . . The language of the entire work, particularly of the theory of concepts, is very different from that of his other writings. (Ibid)

People have indeed shaken their heads for decades, yet they seem nevertheless drawn to parts of the conceptual exposition that opens the work, particularly as they prepare to present their own schemes for interpretative analysis.

Gottl

For my purposes it is noteworthy that Marianne refers to "the language of the entire work," especially since Weber himself (as pointed out by Marianne) invoked a 1901 book that has made no impact at all in the anglophone sphere, Friedrich Gottl's *Die Herrschaft des Wortes* (The Domination of the Word). Gottl was a political economist ten years Weber's junior whose goal in this book was to clarify the lexicon of concepts that had swept into his field during the last part of the nineteenth century, and to enunciate an "ontologically" valid philosophy of social science. He wanted to participate in the *Methodenstreit* as it was winding down in Germany. Clearly, Weber's intentions were similar regarding the field he finally in 1919 permitted in his own work to be called *"soziologie"* (Mommsen, 2000).

Though very seldom noted in the secondary literature, Weber's intellectual relation with his "colleague Gottl" (Marianne Weber, 1975: 312) illuminates fundamental properties within Weber's own philosophy of social inquiry, along with some sense of his ideas about how language should be used within sociological and economic analysis. The only text within Weber's oeuvre in which he wages close hermeneutic combat with a long list of such contemporaries was translated nearly thirty years ago as *Roscher and Knies*, surely the least-often cited of his many larger works. In these linked essays, Weber bequeathed many pages of blunt, though polite, polemic to Gottl, and while a thorough consideration of his sentiments is impossible here for lack of space, a few of his remarks ought to be recalled as we evaluate Weber as a rhetor and writer.

In the fifteen pages or so dedicated to probing Gottl's ideas, Weber is principally interested in the hoary question first introduced into hermeneutic theory a century before by Friedrich Schleiermacher, then elaborated by Dilthey. In short, the puzzle that fascinated historical economists during the last quarter of the nineteenth century was this: is there an epistemological (Weber repeats Gottl's "ontological") distinction between interpreting the "leaden diffuseness" of everyday human life as opposed to "the dead nature" of the natural world which stand outside human control or cognition (Weber, 1975: 216; 162)? In today's jargon, can social scientists and natural scientists use the same mental operations in their work, or are they separated by distinctions in their conceptual tools which are insuperable? Gottl, Dilthey, Münsterberg, and many other scholars of Weber's day strongly held for the latter position, whereas a growing band of economists, following Menger and opposing Schmoller, thought otherwise, mostly because they were so intrigued by the nascent mathematization of their field and its imagined "maturing" into an "exact science." Quite characteristically, Weber objected to the strongest arguments of both camps. He neither believed that "interpretation" (which he insisted on trapping within quotation marks) of human actions was utterly different from interpreting the data of natural science, nor would he accept the idea that studying meaning-seeking humanity could be neatly subsumed under a general model of science most perfectly rationalized in physics. He fully understood both positions, and he took strong exception to both. And yet there is clear evidence, particularly in his altercation with Gottl, that Weber found especially irritating and unsupportable those writers who insisted that the *Geisteswissenschaften* were at an ontological remove from the *Naturwissenschaften*. As he put it, "The role which our 'historical'—or more generally, interpretive—imagination plays in the 'inference' of historical processes is no different from its role in the domain of physical knowledge" (ibid.: 156). On the other hand, he is perfectly willing to admit that understanding meaning-seeking behavior is not simply or apodictically carried out, that discovering the root causes of human action can be more difficult than dissecting natural phenomena. Advancing one of Simmel's related points (from *The Problems of the Philosophy of History*), Weber adds that "it is 'uniqueness' which establishes a relation to *value*. The specific *interest* in 'understanding' that which is significant because of its 'uniqueness' is based on this axiological relation" (ibid.: 259, n. 57). While minutely interrogating each theorist who chimed in on this complex of issues, he goes to great lengths—making the book hard to digest for readers not consumed with passionate interest in these matters—trying to prove the superiority of his points. Yet again, as usual, he is much better at destroying others' arguments than in proposing a tidy solution to these methodological puzzles, most likely because he did not believe a simple solution existed.

Some of his rhetorical moves are very sharp indeed. He wrote these long essays—along with *The Protestant Ethic*—just as he began to emerge from five years of mental instability and physical collapse. They may have taken their tortuous rhetorical form partly because he wanted to prove as much to himself as to his colleagues that the protean Max Weber of the early 1890s was back in full force. For whatever reason, his saber flashed throughout these highly argumentative position papers. Typical is this passage:

> The modest degree to which strictness can be attained and the limitations upon quantifiability are not a consequence of properties peculiar to the "mental" or "intellectual" objects of the concepts of the laws in question. On the contrary, the real question is *whether* the generally valid laws which may eventually be discovered make any contribution to the *understanding* of those aspects of cultural reality which we regard as *worth knowing*. The following point should also be noted as regards the "primal universal nexus" as perceived in our inner experience, a perception which (according to Gottl) excludes the use of naturalistic causal reasoning and abstraction. (Actually this is only the case to the extent that naturalistic causal reasoning is often useless in attaining knowledge of what we regard as essential.) It *would* reappear in the domain of dead nature (not only in the domain of biology, which Gottl concedes as an exception to his view) if we attempted to grasp a natural phenomenon in its full, concrete actuality. (Ibid., 216-217, n. 22, emphasis in original).

Note the phrase "of what we regard as *worth knowing*." If this credo were inscribed more regularly today among social scientists who have whole-heartedly adopted the Baconian model of inquiry, perhaps many of their "findings" would be received more enthusiastically than they are, winning for them more than polite applause from those few cronies who drink from the same funding trough. For Weber, it was never enough to be "statistically significant." The fruits of research, no matter how arrived at, must also meet the test of *human* significance to which he always held himself.

The material just quoted comprises one section of a footnote, the sort for which Weber became famous when the two parts of *The Protestant Ethic* appeared in 1904/05. Embellishing a German academic prose tradition, he would relegate to notes entire mini-treatises on pivotal conceptual or historical points, so that the notes often became, in truth, more valuable than the text proper. In one such four-page footnote (pp. 254-258, n. 54), Weber embroiders on the themes of Gottl's various failures to achieve clarity or plausibility when defining social science method and conceptual specification. Perhaps in a bit of self-mockery (yet who can know), he notes that Gottl's "extremely ingenious work. . . *The Domination of the Word*, reached a very limited audience because of the form in which Gottl chose to write it" (p. 254). As is so often true, he is as much referring here to himself as to the beleaguered Gottl.

One of the most charming features of Weber's writing—and I use the adjective without irony—is his technique of switching from the epistemologically highflown to what he himself mocked as "the 'gaucherie' of 'everyday life'" (ibid.: 256, n.54). He could write mandarin German with the best of them, but seems at pivotal moments in his arguments to prefer a more relaxed and earthbound mode of expression. To wit:

> Suppose Gottl made the (hopeless) attempt to provide an exact account of *all* the everyday experiences in *all* of their aspects from just a single day of his own life. He would be very easily convinced that it is impossible to include absolutely *every* action of whatever sort in a scientific account, no matter how comprehensive that account might be. An account of the "cultural" contents of an era, even if it is very comprehensive, is invariably an inquiry into the "experience" of this era conceived in terms of a plurality of qualitatively different "*points of view.*" These points of view are oriented to values. The same holds for those "*everyday* experiences" which become objects of investigation in the "cultural sciences." (Ibid.: 256-57)

What could be clearer? And coming after many pages of inventively relentless textual dissection, it reminds the reader of Weber's basic humanity and his desire to help create a social science that is capable of explaining *and* understanding "ordinary" human action, both of the synchronic as well as diachronic types. His goal, in part, is to show how values guide interpretative labors, and how such rigorous interpretation can help elevate researchers out of "the inchoate stupor" (ibid.: 162) which normally precedes intellectualized cognition.

Weber's Other Inspirations

I have taken this short detour into Weber's sustained critique of Gottl from *Roscher and Knies*—which, done properly, would require many more pages—because of the "Prefatory Note that opens *Economy and Society*. The bibliographical doffing of his cap which makes up this note was originally drafted for the famous *Logos* article in 1913, "Some Categories of Interpretive Understanding" (Weber, 1981: 179). His friends and colleagues, including Rickert, complained that the piece was unnecessarily dense, so when he adapted the article for renewed use in *E&S*, he simplified it somewhat and made a few small changes in the note itself (e.g., omitting mention of Vierkandt and Radbruch). The second version is as follows:

On the concept of "understanding" compare the *Allgemeine Psychologie* of Karl Jaspers, also a few observations by Heinrich Rickert in the second edition of the *Grenzen der naturwissenschaftlichen Begriffsbildung* and particularly some of Simmel's discussions in his *Probleme der Geschichtsphilosophie*. For certain methodological considerations the reader may here be referred, as often before in the author's writings, to the procedure of Friedrich Gottl in his work *Die Herrschaft des Wortes*; this book, to be sure, is written in a somewhat difficult style and its argument does not appear everywhere to have been thoroughly thought through. As regards content, reference may be made especially to the fine work ["euduringly significant" in the original] of Ferdinand Tönnies, *Gemeinschaft und Gesellschaft*, and also to the gravely misleading book of Rudolf Stammler, *Wirtschaft und Recht nach der materialistischen Geschichtsauffassung*, which may be compared with my criticism in the *Archiv für Sozialwissenschaft* [see Weber, 1977]. . . . This criticial essay contains many of the fundamental ideas of the following exposition. The present work departs from Simmel's method (in his *Soziologie* and his *Philosophie des Geldes*) in drawing a sharp distinction between subjectively intended and objectively valid "meanings"; two different things which Simmel not only fails to distinguish but often deliberately treats as belonging together. (Weber, 1968: 3-4)

As has often been noted, Weber was reserved in his praise of others' theories—if not downright niggardly, then surely cautious. I do not think this reflected a refusal to share the limelight (what little there was of it for this kind of work in those days), but instead was his unvarnished response to thinkers whose breadth of knowledge and theoretical ambitions did not quite equal his own, even when they were close friends and colleagues.

Such a posture makes the quoted paragraph all the more remarkable and particularly valuable from a hermeneutic viewpoint. Here he frankly lays out his debts to Jaspers (Jaspers, 1963), Simmel (Simmel, 1977; also Simmel, 1978 and Wolff, 1950), Rickert (Rickert, 1986; cf. Oakes, 1988), Tönnies (Tönnies, 2001), Stammler (1896; cf. Weber, 1977), and, as we have seen, Gottl. Much could be made of this "honor roll" of influences. To begin with all of these very different kinds of scholars were known personally to Weber, and several were close friends. In a way, then, this becomes an "in-house" production of a very small, very bright circle of stars, as the brightest star of the lot vigorously comes to terms with ideas that he regarded as central to the development of social theory and political economics. Given Weber's notorious honesty, to the point of causing himself and his friends frequent interpersonal problems, one might well assume that this list is exhaustive of his principal inspirations, and that no one was named for mere show. Once again, then, in keeping with preferred hermeneutic procedure, an examination of each of these fruitful works should precede a close reading of Weber's own formulations since he claims them as foundational works.

Tönnies

Except for Guy Oakes's markedly partisan inquiry into the Weber-Rickert connection—which contradicts, among others, Jaspers's eyewitness account— the result of which has not been universally accepted—no-one has yet carried out careful studies of Weber's borrowing and upgrading (his *Aufhebung*) as they pertain to these half-dozen key sources. Each of these books, with the possible exception of Gottl's, has turned out to be a minor landmark in the progress of the *Geisteswissenschaften*, particularly as absorbed by English-language scholars. Consider, for example, Tönnies's pathbreaking work, *Gemeinschaft und Gesellschaft* (1887), perhaps the most immediately recognizable *title* of any book published by a sociologist in the nineteenth century, whether or not its "content" (to use Weber's term) has been assimilated by recent generations. The first retranslation in sixty-one years (bearing the fourth version of the title and as such less easily interjected into introductory sociology textbooks than was the handy *Community and Society* [1940]) may help bring readers back to Tönnies's ideas, since his reputation by now is almost wholly related to his two key terms, and not to the book in toto (Tönnies, 2001). Weber, of course, knew Tönnies personally and worked with him, Simmel, and Sombart when setting up the German Sociological Society in 1909. But the richness of Tönnies's major work (though only one of many he wrote during a long career, often in dialogue with Marx) probably appealed to Weber because of its distinctly anti-Durkheimian slant vis-à-vis the fate of modern society, and also because of its careful attention to the question of legal and ethical relations. As explained by Turner and Factor (1994), Weber's legal training strongly influenced the way he saw and theorized his world, and Tönnies's viewpoint synchronized nicely with that of his more famous colleague, even though Tönnies came to his study of "natural law" via philosophy and economics, not "legal reasoning."

Needless to say, this is not the place to investigate the book thoroughly—a task seriously entertained by no one for several decades—other than to note that if Weber found it to be a "fine work" (or "beautiful" work depending on the translation) and worth noting as such, *some* appreciation for Tönnies's ideas needs to be worked into a sound hermeneutic of *Economy and Society*. With rare exception (notably in the work of Tönnies's kinsman, Rudolf Heberle and his colleague, Werner Cahnman), this connection has not been studied, nor even mentioned in the Weber literature (e.g., Cahnman, 1995). Not since Mitzman's study thirty years ago has Tönnies been evaluated in juxtaposition with Weber and his circle (Mitzman, 1973). Even in the bulky standard work regarding Weber's relations with his peers, Tönnies is oddly slighted

(Mommsen and Osterhammel, 1987). Cahnman suggests that this may be the result of Guenther Roth's dismissal of Tönnies's influence on Weber in the 1968 introduction to *Economy and Society* (pp. xcvi-xcvii), even arguing that Weber's masterwork was written consciously in opposition to Tönnies. Given Roth's stature as a Weber expert, Cahnman's hunch seems entirely plausible. Nevertheless, if Weber himself claimed to have found sustenance in this "beautiful" book, his own testimony cannot be reasonably ignored.

Before moving on, consider for a moment Tönnies' epigrammatic observations about his fabled distinction between *Gemeinschaft* and *Gesellschaft*:

> The theory of *Gesellschaft* takes as its starting point a group of people who, as in *Gemeinschaft*, live peacefully alongside one another, but in this case without being essentially united—indeed, on the contrary, they are here essentially detached. In *Gemeinschaft* they stay together in spite of everything that separates them; in *Gesellschaft* they remain separate in spite of everything that unites them. As a result, there are no activities taking place which are derived from an *a priori* and predetermined unity and which therefore express the will and spirit of this unity through any individual who performs them. Nothing happens in *Gesellschaft* that is more important for the individual's wider group than it is for himself. On the countrary, everyone is out for himself alone and living in a state of tension against everyone else. The various spheres of power and activity are sharply demarcated, so that everyone resists contact with others and excludes them from his own spheres, regarding any such overtures as *hostile*. (Tönnies, 2001: 52)

Mitzman points out, in quoting Tönnies's private letters, that he held "a favorable view of the Middle Ages," which, along with his life in the small towns of northern Germany, gave him the lineaments of what constituted *Gemeinschaft* (Mitzman, 1973: 67). For many decades professors of social theory, most of whom live in the heart of one *Gesellschaft* or another and who therefore feel a natural existential urge to make a virtue of necessity, have chastised Tönnies's alleged "romanticism" and "nostalgia mongering," pointing out that for Marx (and Simmel), pre-urban life amounted to little more than tedium and bucolic provincialism. History has not yet had the last word on these distinctions, but the more one rereads Tönnies, the less "romantic" his sentiments might seem.

He continues in defining his pivotal distinction:

> Such a *negative* attitude is the normal and basic way in which these power-conscious people relate to one another, and it is characteristic of *Gesellschaft* at any given moment in time. Nobody wants to do anything for anyone else, nobody wants to yield or give anything unless he gets something in

return that he regards as at least an *equal* trade-off. Indeed it is essential that it should be more desirable to him than whatever he has already, for only by getting something that seems better can he be persuaded to give up something good.

It takes little imagination to see this as an 1887 critique *avant le lettre* of the "rational choice theory" that has so entranced economists and political scientists over the last two decades, and, against all "reason," makes ever-larger inroads into sociology proper. The difference, of course, between Tönnies's withering commentary and today's celebration of "cost-benefit analysis" is that he wrote before this hobbling of the imagination had become the predominant (or "normative") mode of interaction between members of "advanced" society. He was still capable of critique, whereas today's theorists and social researchers, many of them, have embraced this used-car salesman ethic as if it were a religious catechism, uniquely suited to contemporary urban life. I bring Tönnies back to life in this context because his sentiments, though much more public and fierce, resonate warmly with those of Weber, particularly in the last few pages of *The Protestant Ethic*. One could even argue that Tönnies's influence on Weber's general view of rationalized culture, contrary to Roth's opinion of it, is in fact quite profound. Given their close professional relationship, this would hardly seem surprising.

More from Tönnies:

> If everyone shares such desires, it is obvious that occasions may arise when object "a" may be better for person "B" than object "b," and likewise object "b" may be better for person "A" than object "a"; it is however *only* in the context of such relations that "a" can be better than "b" at the same time that "b" is better than "a." This provokes the question: can we in any sense at all speak of the "quality" or "value" of things independently of such relationships? (Ibid.: 532-53).

It is a cardinal principle, perhaps *the* principle, of marginal utility theory that there is no such thing as "intrinsic quality," that every object and every person is reducible and understandable in terms of market value. A verified lock of Adolf Hitler's hair would currently have gigantic market value, one would suppose, no matter what other "meanings" one might attach to such an object. Weber was as much an expert in these matters as his good friend Tönnies, but whereas the latter never hesitated to lambast contemporary urban culture for its churning rationalization and commodification of everyday life, Weber simply accepted it as a necessary and irreversible condition, theorizing about it as a given. Thus, his famous four types of social action. In a letter to his friend Friedrich Paulsen (the Kant biographer) in 1879, Tönnies weighs in with the sort of comment that Weber would have considered ill-advised and impractically "romantic": "If that is so, if men *remain selfish* in socialism, *inclined* more to luxury and idleness than to moral companionship and labor—then what use is it?" (in Mitzman, 1973: 67). Weber's critique of socialism was more along practical lines, of its likely failure as a mechanism for producing sufficient goods in proper distribution, but for Tönnies the ethical dimension was more pressing. For the latter the question was this: will socialism make for "better people" than has capitalism? At the age of twenty-four, in a moment of complete openness and what now seems unsophisticated confession, Tönnies wrote in another letter to Paulsen: "It [the Middle Ages] is a world which to us—to us as a people—is irretrievably lost. The men in whom these feeling were still living were more decent and generous than we" (Mitzman, 1973: 68). Weber would never have taken this position, even if while enjoying Wagner's heroic operas he might have sympathized with it.

As Tönnies aged he became somewhat less married to the fundamental goodness of *Gemeinschaft*. He wrote in 1907 the following remarks ("The Nature of Sociology"), which are close in spirit to a paper he delivered at the Congress of Arts and Sciences in St. Louis in 1904, in the company of Weber and Troeltsch:

> We know that the social and benevolent motives and thoughts are continually in contradiction and conflict with those of an opposite nature; that love and hate, trust and distrust, gratitude and vindictiveness cross one another; but also that fear and hope and, based on these emotions, human interest and intentions encounter each other, either in harmony or in disharmony, so that feelings as well as designs partly connect, partly divide human beings, singly as well as in groups of all kinds. (Tönnies, 1971: 89)

If Roth is right in saying that Weber wrote *WuG* in opposition to Tönnies, and that the latter's ideas did not play much of a role in the construction of his master theory of socio-economic life, then it is hard to understand the pathos that Weber artfully included in the concluding sections of *The Protestant Ethic*, or the "Prefatory Remarks" to his *Religionssoziologie* from 1920, or to the memorable sections of "Science as a Vocation" and "Politics as a Vocation" in which he rails against the "one-dimensionality" (to use Marcuse's term) that had afflicted European culture. As I suggested above, in all these essential passages, and many others, he seems very close in intention and ultimate values to Tönnies's "beautiful" book from 1887, already a classic in the field.

Jaspers

It is also instructive to glance, however briefly, at the other books written by Weber's intimates, to which he refers generously (even if at points querulously) in his "Prefatory Note" to *Economy and Society*. Perhaps the least known to social theorists is Jaspers's stupendous *General Psychopathology*, a unique compendium of 950 pages in fine print. Weber wrote: "On the concept of 'understanding,' compare the *Allgemeine Psychopathologie* of Karl Jaspers." The version of this book that Weber read (the first edition of 1913, but probably not the second of 1919) was very different from the seventh edition from which the first English translation was made in 1963, since Jaspers entirely rewrote it in 1942 for the fourth German edition. The ballooning pagination tells the tale: first German edition, 338 pp.; 2nd, 416 pp.; 3rd, 458; 4th from 1946, 748; 5th-7th, unchanged (Schilpp, 1981: 873). While most of the book brings together everything clinically known during Jasper's lifetime about mental disturbances, that part which must have most intrigued Weber—not only due to his own psychopathology, but in order to create his *verstehende Soziologie*—comes in Part II, "Meaningful Psychic Connections: Psychology of Meaning—*verstehende Psychologie.*"

But first a few words about Jaspers and Weber (see Baumgarten, 1957; Manasse, 1957/81; Henrich, 1987; Adair-Toteff, 2002). Though not much read today, Jaspers for many decades was the "good German philosopher" and leading non-Sartrean existentialist, the anti-Heidegger (a close friend of his before 1933) who, partly because of his adored Jewish wife, Gertrud Mayer, resisted the Nazis at every turn and nearly lost life and career in standing by his principles. Whereas Heidegger has of late been reviled at his easy accommodation to the Nazi regime, Jaspers's behavior in the 30s set the postwar gold standard for defiant resistance to the murderous ideological practices of the Third Reich. As Jaspers himself said and wrote on many occasions, the guiding light for his behavior at that troubled time and otherwise, as well as for his professional thinking, was always Max Weber. Jaspers met Weber in 1909 in Heidelberg when he was twenty-six and the older man forty-five, and he almost immediately became Platonically infatuated not only with Weber's ideas, but with the man himself—his "personality" or "character" were the words he often used. Jaspers delivered a commemorative oration for Weber in Heidelberg on July 17, 1920 in the University's Great Hall, and by all accounts it was an unforgettable performance. He published his remarks soon thereafter and wrote directly or indirectly about his idol for the rest of his life (Jaspers, 1921, 1928, 1964, 1989; Arendt and Jaspers, 1992). Only very late in life, according to Dieter Henrich, after seeing a dossier of love letters allegedly exchanged between Weber and Else Jaffé fifty years before (given by her when she was very old to Weber's kinsman, Eduard Baumgarten, who in turn showed them to Jaspers in order to win an argument), did Jaspers have some small misgivings about the icon he had created in Weber's memory (Henrich, 1987: 539-541; Henrich also saw the dossier).

For Jaspers, Weber represented above all else uncompromising truth, so to learn that his hero had feet of clay, even for a psychotherapist of Jasper's skill and experience, was a disturbing experience, particularly after having gone on record for decades claiming that Weber was the finest German of his era, and also a true philosopher. In this context, "philosopher" carried a heavy ethical connotation, far removed from the logical exercises that have consumed much of philosophy during the last century. Nevertheless, Jaspers's testimony about Weber is uniquely indispensable in understanding the deepest meaning of their work, the both of them, for two reasons: (1) Jaspers was the only person aside from Marianne Weber, so far as one can ascertain, who ever read Weber's autopathography, a key document that Jaspers successfully encouraged Marianne to destroy before the Nazis could use it to defame Weber's antifascist memory, and (2) Jaspers was the only one of Weber's few close friends who was trained both in psychiatric theory and technique, and who then, in a second career beginning around 1922, became a major philosopher of consciousness whose major inspiration was Weber himself. These two characteristics give Jasper's analysis of Weber, thinker and social actor, remarkable weight, along with everything else we know about Jaspers's dedication to truth, no matter how unpleasant. Jaspers felt so strongly about his veneration of Weber that five days after his death in June, 1920, when he saw Heinrich Rickert for the first time following Weber's funeral, he immediately severed all ties with Rickert because the latter claimed that Weber had been his acolyte, and that as a philosopher, so Rickert argued, Weber had no standing nor claim. For Jaspers this was blasphemy of a high order, and at great professional risk, he broke with Rickert on the spot, which probably caused the latter to do everything he could to block Jaspers's appointment to the chair of philosophy at Heidelberg when it fell vacant in 1922 (see Jaspers's autobiographical account in Schilpp, 1981: 30-34).

In his major work, *Philosophie* (3 vols., 1932), which vindicated his belief that he could transform himself from a practicing psychiatrist with M.D. degree into a philosopher proper, he begins by invoking Weber: "A decisive, clarifying step was found in 1909 when I read Max Weber and began to grasp the scientific nature of the historical sciences, in which we work by means of 'understanding.'. . . It was only after 1920, after the death of Max Weber, that the alternative appeared compelling: I could either abandom my previous reserve, start philosophizing on my own, and thus represent philosophy as a professor and teacher, or I could continue to limit myself to psychology (Jaspers, 1969: 12, 8). What Jaspers did, of course, in his *General Psychopathology* was lay out in stunning, quasi-phenomenological detail what he called *verstehende Psychologie*, thus imitating Weber's use of the term "*Verstehen*" (itself borrowed from Dilthey). It has been argued, not only by Jaspers but by his interpreters, that virtually everything he wrote of a speculative or political nature in the ensuing sixty years after meeting Weber was inspired by the Lion of Heidelberg. Jaspers even restructured his Husserlian impetus from straight phenomenology into something that much more closely resembled the approach Weber took in his sociology of religion studies. In fact, the keystone of Weber's comparative analysis of religion, the so-called *Zwischenbetrachtung* (*From Max Weber*, 323-359), was studied by the young Jaspers—Weber sent him offprints, which he had bound and preserved—and thereafter used as a measuring rod for his own success at understanding human affairs and interpreting whatever pertinent data came to hand in a way that could stand comparison with Weber's virtuoso efforts.

When the first edition of *General Psychopathology* appeared in 1913, it was hailed as an astonishing work, not least because its author was thirty years old, and had composed this sovereign volume with only four years of clinical experience behind him. Invited in 1911 by a publisher to write a textbook, Jaspers did for his field what William James had done for psychology in 1890 when he also wrote a text for introductory students, the difference being that James agonized over his book for more than ten years, whereas Jaspers created his with almost blinding speed. This verges on the unbelievable when Jaspers's frail physical condition is brought into account, a combined lung and heart disease that permitted him to work steadily for only a few hours at a time. (This is quite unlike the young Max Weber from the late 1880s who believed that any intellectual worth their salt ought to be able to work hard until 1 A.M., and then rise early the next day to start again.) But a strong difference between James's textbook and Jaspers's was that the former, so gracefully and compellingly written, was immediately embraced by everyone who read it, whereas Jaspers's, despite its great success with the informed critics who reviewed it, never succeeded in endearing itself to its intended audience. This is mostly owing to its density, unorthodox combining of research and theory streams, and ambition in viewing the "whole man," as Jaspers put it, rather than only his or her organs: brain here, eye there, and so on, which had been the case before in the world of medically oriented psychiatry. Jaspers felt that he was liberating his chosen field from the artificial, scientistic constraints that had been suffocating psychology and psychiatry, most of which he thought amounted to so much chatter and concept-mongering, and did very little to expand the reach of theory, or to help clinicians in treating actual patients.

In his desire to change all that, he committed a substantial part of the book to explaining the difference between his kind of psychiatric analysis versus more standard versions, while being careful to offer what amounted to an encyclopedic survey of everything then known to concerned parties. That portion of the book which would almost surely have most interested Weber comes in Part II, "Meaningful Psychic Connections: Psychology of Meaning—*verstehende Psychologie*" (pp. 301-450). Like Weber in the opening paragraphs to *E&S*, Jaspers commits his first footnote to bibliographical thanks regarding his key term, "understanding." He quotes the venerable Joachim Wach—known in the U.S. exclusively as a sociologist of religion, but whose major work is in hermeneutics, very broadly understood—from his compendious *Das Verstehen* (3 vols., 1926-33): "Understanding is a fundamental human activity that from time immemorial has proceeded on its own methodical, conscious and scholarly way." Jaspers then adds Droysen (*History*, 1867) and also Weber: "The work of Max Weber was mostly responsible for my deliberate use of understanding as a method which would be in keeping with our great cultural traditions. I was also influenced by *Roscher und Knies*, etc., in Schmoller's *Jahrbüchern*, Vols. 27, 29, 30 (1903-06)" (Jaspers, 1963: 301, n.1; translation corrected.) Jaspers continues in almost perfect synchrony with Weber (recalling that Weber's *Logos* article and Jaspers's book both appeared in 1913, so they may well have been sharing manuscripts with each other) as he creates his own honor role of *verstehende* inspirations: "My ideas were then carried further by Dilthey (*Ideen über eine beschribende u. zergliedernde Psychologie...*) and by Simmel (*Probleme der Geschichtsphilosophie*)." The note continues at some length, bringing in unflattering reference to Freud ("a misunderstanding of itself"), plus mention of a dozen other now forgotten writers mostly trained in psychiatry, psychology, and psychotherapy. For Jaspers the point of this opening excursus is to show that "understanding," though diminished in stature among that majority of clinicians who favored the physiological model of mental illness, was part of a "great cultural tradition" with which Jaspers, as a brilliant newcomer, wanted to reconnect his field of study. And judging from this note and his other writings, it would seem that Weber is *primus inter pares* among those who motivated him to take what was then a distinctly unpopular position.

This 150-page part of the book cannot be economically summarized, yet Jaspers makes it clear in the very beginning that he believes understanding must be put to use in a phenomenological way, but mixed with "objective" measures of illness in order to give a complete picture of the ailment in question: "1. We sink ourselves into the psychic situation and *understand genetically by empathy* how one psychic event emerges from another. 2) We find by repeated experience that a number of phenomena are regularly linked together, and on this basis *we explain causally. ...* Meaningful psychic connections have also been called '*internal causal-*

ity,' indicating the unbridgeable gulf between genuine connections of external causality and psychic connections which can only be called causal by analogy" (Jasper, 1963: 301). Fichte's *hiatus irrationalis*, which Weber occasionally recalled in his methodological essays, correlates with the "unbridgeable gulf" that worries Jaspers as a clinician, as a user of psychological data from which to draw causal conclusions. Jaspers is doing here for psychology and psychotherapy precisely what Weber was doing at the same moment in his *Logos* essay for sociology and the social sciences broadly defined. Neither of them was the least inclined toward the semi-mysticism that occasionally sidetracked Dilthey in his hermeneutic theorizing, a somewhat unfortunate legacy of Schleiermacher's "divinatory experience" that was supposed to inform and guide all interpretative work. Unfortunate, at least, for those surrounded by colleagues who were, on the one hand, obsessed with the rational model of marginal utility theory, and on the other, more concerned with brain function and other physiological parameters of mental health than with "understanding" what mental illness was about "at the level of meaning." This phrase, which crops up repeatedly in Weber's writings, is a virtual lift from Jaspers's *General Psychopathology*, or, if not literally so, then inspired by the same worldview and taken from the same original sources. It is interesting that Weber's prescription for a *verstehende Soziologie* met with success, especially after World War II, whereas Jaspers's identical call fell on deaf ears among his peers in the world of psychiatry.

The problem facing both men lies with the nature of empathy and how to reconcile such a "soft" concept with the strict demands for proof in the *Geisteswissenschaften* (Dilthey's Germanization of Mill's term) that had been in the air ever since Mill had published his *System of Logic* in 1843, then augmented by the spectacular explanatory (and publishing) success of Darwin's *Origin of Species* after 1859. Jaspers works very hard at walking the tightrope between quasi-philosophical understanding on the one hand, that he knew to be vital to psychological analysis, and the rules of inductive science on the other, which he had learned to respect as a medical student. In the next several pages of *General Psychopathology* (302-09), he lays out various forms of interpretation and understanding that range from the strongly intuitive and empathic to the sternly "objective," all of which fit snugly within Weber's sense of the terms. A few quotations will illustrate the strong connection between the two thinkers, obviously working in symbiotic harmony. Jaspers distinguishes the merely repetitive (we might say "experimental") examination of phenomena from interpretative understanding: "The psychology of meaningful phenomena is built up entirely on this sort of convincing experience of impersonal, independent and understandable connections. Such conviction is gained *on the occasion* of confronting human personality; it is not acquired inductively *through repetition of experience*" (303; original emphases). He is speaking here of clinical experience, during which the psychiatrist "confronts" the "human personality" of the patient in all its uniqueness, comes to an understanding of the pathology experienced by same, and then—carefully, and without losing sight of the idiosyncratic configuration of the patient's mind—tries to generalize from this "convincing experience" to some broader set of analytic categories for the benefit of his colleagues or for publishing purposes. Jaspers also mentions the "ideal typical" a number of times in precisely the way that Weber used the concept:

> The self-evidence of a meaningful connection does not prove that in a particular case that connection is *really there* nor even that it occurs in reality at all. Nietzsche convincingly and comprehensibly connected weakness and morality and applied this to the particular event of the origin of Christianity, but the particular application could be wrong in spite of the correctness of the general (ideally typical) understanding of that connection. (303)

Jaspers was far in advance of other Weberians by highlighting in this way the powerful meaning that Nietzsche held for Weber, something only now receiving the full study it deserves (a task for which he was well prepared, having published the masterful study, *Nietzsche*, in 1936).

After allowing that science proceeds through objectively based generalization, Jaspers insists that the purely inductive does not serve psychology (and by implication, any of the social sciences) as well as some rigorous form of "interpretative understanding": "All such objective data, however, are always incomplete and our understanding of *any particular, real event* has to remain more or less an *interpretation* which only in a few cases reaches any relatively high degree of complete and convincing objectivity. . . . The fewer these [cases] are, the less forcefully do they compel our understanding; we interpret more and understand less" (303). This should not be read as a methodological defeat, but rather a realistic assessment of how humans deal with meaningful action and words conveyed by their peers, particularly those in dire psychological circumstances, often separated by a cognitive barrier from their interlocutors. He counterpoises "genetically understandable connections" with those that are established "inductively," pointing out that the former are more likely to promote humanly meaningful knowledge than the latter, which are more keenly attuned to "causality" than to understanding per se. As he puts it, "Frequency in no way enlarges the evidence for the connection. Induction only establishes the frequency, not the reality of the connection" (304). This is an interesting way of rephrasing the warring relationship between those researchers who believe that establishing causality is the *summum bonum* of science versus their opposite numbers, who see the exhausting hunt for the causes always undermining the more important issue of "what it all means."

Becoming almost indistinguishable from Weber's own formulations, Jaspers summarizes his argument thus: "Rational understanding always leads to a statement that the psychic content was simply a rational connection, understandable without the help of any psychology. Empathic understanding, on the other hand, always leads directly into the psychic connection itself. Rational understanding is merely an aid to psychology, empathic understanding brings us to psychology itself" (304). Yet he does not draw from this the conclusion that causal linkages cannot, by the nature of the material explored, be established in the *Geisteswissenschaften*: "There is no limit to the discovery of causes and with every psychic event we are always looking for cause and effect. *But with understanding there are limits everywhere.* The existence of special psychic dispositions [etc.]. . . all constitute limits to our understanding" (305; original emphasis).

Finally, in his most sweeping, summary set of directives for proper psychological analysis, Jaspers identifies five "modes of comprehensive understanding (cultural, existential, and metaphysical)," all of which he believes are essential for proper technique, to carry out what Freud called his "archaeological" labor, building "his interpretations from fragments of human works" (307). For Jaspers the favored modal pairs are (1) phenomenological understanding and understanding of expression; (2) static and genetic understanding; (3) genetic understanding and explanation; (4) rational and empathic understanding; and (5) understanding and interpretation. The third type is closest to what Weber had in mind. Jaspers wisely concludes by admitting that "in practice, however, understanding is constantly in touch with *something more comprehensive in which all such acts of understanding lie embedded* (307; emphasis in original).

The overarching point to this trot through Jaspers's reasoning is that Weber had access not only to this stunning printed compendium of clinical and theoretical analysis, but, more importantly, to its author—in a close personal relationship (which may even have carried over into psychotherapy). Weber's relationship with Jaspers today is often denigrated as merely one of demigod to iconographer, the younger man so entirely in thrall to his senior that he could not write "objectively" about him. I regard this as a wasteful, temperocentric blunder. As one can intuit even from the few pages given here to his work, Jaspers was an extraordinary, precocious, and adventurous thinker with strong credentials as a practicing psychotherapist and analyst. Contact with such a person, particularly during his prolonged recovery period, must have been enormously helpful to Weber on several levels, not least of which in discovering what a fully rounded comprehension of "interpretative" or "empathic" understanding might mean when used skillfully.

Simmel

The relationship, personal and intellectual, between Weber and Georg Simmel is not easy to disentangle because even though they worked together professionally (and their wives were collaborating feminists of the time, thus strengthening the bond), their personalities and styles of work did not mesh well, and they often seemed to be "talking past one another" in their published work. And given the entirely different economies of each man's household—with Weber after 1898 a psychological invalid and mainly living off his wife's inheritance thereafter, while Simmel was forced to make ends meet by offering popular lectures to large crowds of paying students—plus their differing paths to social theory (Simmel via two Kant dissertations, Weber through history, law, and political-economy), it is unsurprising that their works ring differently. (Frisby's "The Ambiguity of Modernity: Georg Simmel and Max Weber" is a useful attempt to bring the two giants onto the same stage, a relatively rare entry in the literature; cf. Atoji, 1984: 45-95; Faught, 1985; Lichtblau, 1991; Vandenberghe, 1999). Nevertheless, they maintained obvious mutual admiration, and Weber went out of his way to befriend Simmel professionally, partly in a long, yet unsuccessful effort to combat the institutionalized anti-Semitism endemic to German higher education at the time which prevented Simmel from acquiring a professorship until very late in life.

When Weber in his "Prefatory Note" to *Economy and Society* refers admiringly to Simmel's *Probleme der Geschichtsphilosophie*, this can be taken as more than a polite doffing of his hat: "On the concept of 'understanding,' compare . . . particularly some of Simmel's" *The Problems of the Philosophy of History* (tr. 1977). But much earlier, in *Roscher and Knies* (1905/06; tr. 1975), Weber at his most querulous surveys a series of thinkers, and just before launching into the lengthier Gottl section mentioned above, he gives several paragraphs to "'Understanding' and 'Interpretation' in the Work of Simmel." He writes:

> First of all, we owe to Simmel the elucidation of the most extensive range of cases which fall under the concept of 'understanding'—'understanding,' that is, in contrast to 'discursive knowledge' of reality which is not given in 'inner' experience. He has clearly distinguished the objective 'understanding' of the *meaning* of an expression from the subjective 'interpretation' of the *motive* of a (speaking or acting) person" (Weber, 1975: 152).

When Weber paid Simmel this mighty compliment, he had of course not yet read Jaspers's book, as it was still several years in the future. Jaspers acknowleged Simmel's book in a footnote (p. 302), yet it is clear that his clinical work allowed him to expand upon the concept of "understanding" much further than Simmel could, who mostly came to the problem from a traditional background in neo-Kantian and aesthetic studies. And unlike so many others who were targets of Weber's barbs in *Roscher and Knies*, Simmel's theorizing is gently handled, with no more chastisement than "This is not quite right" (ibid.). By summoning up Hugo Münsterburg's idea of "commitments of real life" to supplement Simmel's "psychologistic" analysis, Weber believes that "the decisive point" is how one interprets the motives of a speaker or an author, and for this feat, "interpretation" of a special kind is needed (ibid.: 153-154). As usual in these contexts, Weber speaks of "objective meaning" and the *"logical* character of *this* sort of 'understanding'" in an automatic way that signals his desire to be precise and scientific while Simmel is more descriptive and aesthetically attuned. In the end it irritated Weber that "Simmel's ultimate *interests* are directed to metaphysical problems, to the *'meaning'* of life" (Weber, 1972: 161), which he naturally thought were quite beyond the proper realm of social science.

As I have pointed out above (as have others, e.g., Oakes, 1980: 57-59), the hidden voice behind all these lucubrations is Dilthey's (recalling that Simmel never referred to him in print, strangely enough). Even he, master of the hermeneutic motion, was tormented later in his career by the term "logical," which seems to have become throughout the German academy a fetish or totem for "right thinking scientists." A strong aversion to the intuitive, the empathic, the "sensitive," has continued among philosophers of social science into our own period, mainly due to the Vienna Circle, Wittgenstein, and the entire apparatus of linguistic analysis that has fought tooth and nail against the Hegel-Schelling-Schleiermacher trajectory always in earnest search and definition of "meaning." This general tradition, despite its wide internal divergences, holds that "re-experiencing" another's emotions or motives is an essentially aesthetic achievement, an artful mixture of historical, psychological, and biographical insight. If one does not need to be Caesar to understand him, one surely must understand a great deal about rulers and the ruled of Caesar's time in order to analyze his political acts sympathetically. It is very clear from both Weber's and Simmel's epistemological writings that they were as torn about these essential differences of perspective as the logical positivists were sure that "meaning" is "by definition" a linguistic confusion. "Re-creating" another person's mental state, reconstructing their vocabulary of motives, "re-experiencing" their sense of meaning as they voice words or commit acts all seem, even from a strict Millsian position, extremely shady and insubstantial ways of going about social "science."

In a way this is an idiotic posture for a philosopher of the *Geisteswissenschaften* to take. It is much like the first moment that a young person realizes what was entailed in their biological origins, and then struggles to come to terms with the notion that parents create children through a fairly uniform procedure, one which often shocks the tender mind. How else can one comprehend history, humankind's in general or one's own in particular, unless by putting to use this definingly human capacity? When another biography appears of, say, Henry James or Napoleon or Darwin, adding to long rows of such volumes already in libraries, the question the savvy reviewer must ask is the same one Simmel and Weber were asking about the interpretation of social action: "Does this portrait ring true? Is it a convincing replication of a life?" No-one truly believes that Leon Edel's five-volume *Henry James* or Dumas Malone's six-volume *Thomas Jefferson* are indeed perfect representations of their subjects' lives and works (any more than family oral traditions of great-grandparents' exploits are accepted as literally true in all aspects). And yet they must come as close to this idealization as one is likely to get, which is why they receive the imprimatur of "definitive biography"—at least until the next publishing generation retakes the terrain. What the hard-edged twentieth-century philosophy of social science did when it imitated linguistic philosophy and logical positivism was to turn its back on some of the central features of human cognition and evaluation which seemed terribly obvious to Dilthey, Windelband, Croce, then Simmel, Weber, and their peers. What was gained in precision was lost to forgetfulness of the necessary human capacity for understanding and interpretation, that very set of "tools" that have allowed the species to persevere against all odds. It could even be argued that this area of thought took a detour that lasted seventy-five years or so, and has only in the recent past, with the rise of Paul Ricoeur, Hans-Georg Gadamer, and their many followers, begun to rediscover the path laid out by Simmel and Weber around 1905.

The future difficulties for *Verstehen* were clearly laid out in Simmel's *Problems of the Philosophy of History*. His text worries itself about what is "objectively true" versus what the historian or social scientist simply imposes on "facticity" due to idiosyncratic intentions or needs. Like others writing in this tradition, under the cynical impact of scientism, he is suspicious of motive-imputation. And yet he writes unblushingly, "We must be able to recreate the mental act of the historical person. As this is sometimes expressed, we must be able to 'occupy or inhabit the mind of the other person.'"... It is only essential that the objective import of the ideas has the same logical form for both speaker and listener" (ibid., 64). The term "logical form" here is not easy to interpret unless one remembers Simmel's Kantian roots. He tries to clear the air:

> Although I understand the expression, I don't completely understand what is expressed. (Actually, the object of understanding is not the act of speaking, but rather what is spoken.) The situation changes immediately if the speaker's utterance is a consequence of some subjective intention: for example, prejudice, anger, anxiety, or sarcasm. Suppose we identify this *motive* for the expression or utterance. In this case, the sense in which we "understand" the utterance is very different from the sense in which we grasp its import. In this case, understanding is not only concerned with comprehension of what is spoken; it is also concerned with the comprehension of the act of speaking. (Ibid., 64-65)

Simmel was not alone, of course, in puzzling over these sorts of questions at the fin de siècle, of how one understands and then transmits to an audience the substance of a third party's sentiments. Proust thought about this, too:

> . . . none of the feelings which the joys or misfortunes of a real person arouse in us can be awakened except through a mental picture of those joys or misfortunes; and the ingenuity of the first novelist lay in his understanding that, as the image was the one essential element in the complicated structure of our emotions, so that simplification of it which consisted in the suppression, pure and simple, of real people would be a decided improvement. A real person, profoundly as we may sympathize with him, is in a great measure perceptible only through our senses, that is to say, remains opaque, presents a dead weight which our sensibilities have not the strength to lift. . . the novelist's happy discovery was to think of substituting for those opaque sections, impenetrable to the human soul, their equivalent in immaterial sections; things, that is, which one's soul can assimilate. (Proust, 1992: 116-117)

Weber never sought this level of subtlety, not because he did not understand the issue or appreciate its significance, but because he believed in ways that Simmel did not that the set of problems to which Simmel (and Proust) alluded becomes quickly insoluble through any simple or elegant means of discursive argument. Weber thought it wiser to walk around the foggy bog than to try to run through it with deft alacrity, dancing among the quicksand. In this realm of analysis the two friends disagreed, even though Weber never took Simmel to task in the way he did Knies, Roscher, Gottl, and many others. He seems instead to have accepted Simmel's elevated labors as given, and then to have proceeded along parallel but distinct paths of thought and analysis.

Back to the Text

The first two paragraphs of *Economy and Society* offer a mea culpa for the "unavoidably abstract" nature of the opening definitions and conceptual elaborations that fill the first sixty pages of the work, giving it "the impression of remoteness from reality." As explained above, this textual situation troubled him, as he related to Marianne Weber at length. These materials constituted his *Kategorienlehre* ("categorical teaching," which Roth translates as "casuistry" [*Kasuistik*], and Käsler calls "conceptual exposition" [Käsler, 1988: 149]), which might intimate a sardonic bit of self-mockery, since similar schemes, equally dry, filled eighteenth-century German epistemologies, particularly those of Christian Wolff and his successor, Kant. When Weber lectured on these materials to hundreds of students (Vienna, 1918, and Munich, 1919/20), "the course on the categories drove them away *en masse*" (Roth, 1968: XVIV). Weber's first attempt to state these ideas came in 1912-13 (not 1908-09 as often claimed) when he wrote the famous *Logos* article ("Some Categories of Interpretative Sociology"), but learning from Rickert and others that it was too dense, he tried to write it more lucidly for the version that opens his magnum opus.

Ironically enough—and Weber was nothing if not ironic, in this a soulmate of Thomas Mann, whose *Buddenbrooks* (1901) could as easily have been called *The Webers* (see Goldman, 1988; 1992)—if there is a single characteristic of social or philosophical analysis that Weber loathed, it was the perception that such work floated high above empirically knowable reality in a zone of precious irrelevance to earthly concerns. This in part may explain why he regarded such ruminations of Simmel and his other distinguished colleagues with less than absolute acceptance or good cheer. Weber did not begrudge metaphysicians per se their conceptual constructs, but he did seek to erect a strategic barrier between that sort of hypothesizing and the work of social analysis proper. Put another way, if he did not find empirical plausibility within an argument, no matter how ingenious on other grounds, Weber would leave it behind when voicing his own most important directives regarding the way social science should operate.

But there is more going on in these opening pages than the fruit of Weber's battle with competing or complementary theorists. As Wolfgang Mommsen has explained in more detail than has been available before (Mommsen, 2000), *Economy and Society*—or *Wirtschaft und Gesellschaft. Soziologie*, as it was originally titled—is also the expression of a man in dire psychological straits. He was driven almost to despair by the insistent, desperate demands of a publisher on the verge of bankruptcy, the pressing "real-world" calamities of the First World War, all magnified by Weber's own internal locomotive of frustrated ambition. Not only had he promised Paul Siebeck, his publisher, to oversee a gigantic, collectively authored social science encyclopedia, but he was trying simultaneously to create an interpretative social science single-handedly. Since about 1903 he had written some of the densest essays ever devised in the modern philosophy of methodology (*Roscher and Knies, Critique of Stammler*, the *Logos* article, the objectivity essays), invented the sociology of religion (1912-13), the sociology of comparative civilizations, the sociology of music (1910-11), and the sociology of law (1912-13). Yet given what must have seemed to him a welcome interruption by the First World War (during which Weber set his belated writing aside to help with the war effort), only two of these projects were truly "finished" by 1920, and the more Siebeck pled to have the work concluded, the more Weber fell into "irritation and despair" (Mommsen, 2000: 379, 381).

This, then, is the compositional context of what is now "Part One: Conceptual Exposition" of *Economy and Society*. It is as much a work of frustrating genius as Kant's first *Critique*, or Marx's first volume of *Capital*, or Jaspers's *Philosophy*, each of which required a decade or more to produce and which, during the gestation periods, threw their authors into fits of uncertainty regarding the ultimate results. And yet in each case the prose of the finished product has about it the air of supreme self-confidence, almost cockiness, which, in light of their subsequent influence, seem now entirely justified.

Other readers have observed that Weber's "Part One: Conceptual Exposition" is not meant to be read so much as consulted, for otherwise it is too dull, too much like a guidebook to a foreign land rather than the compelling narrative one might prefer. This seems particularly true when compared with his works on religion, which, although compactly composed, remain fascinating for their historical retailing of information Weber picked up from specialists. And yet if one does indeed read "Basic Sociological Terms" as a unified prose performance—recalling Fredric Jameson's structuralist treatment of *The Protestant Ethic*—more than a few characteristic elements that make up the Weberian modus operandi come clearly into view. And along with this overview of the larger enterprise, his wish to write a "definitive work" about the new science of sociology, the reader can also locate fissures in the smooth facade that Weber presents with undeniable cunning and circumspection. After all, he mentioned the helpful works of Jaspers, Tönnies, Simmel, and Gottl not only out of sincere appreciation for their collegial inspiration, but also because he believed his exacting prescription for how the *Geisteswissenschaften* should develop was superior to theirs. He had stood on their shoulders and seen further.

"Weberian sociology" for a half-century after Parsons's *Structure of Social Action* (1937) meant some version of "interpretative" or *verstehende* sociology (sometimes awkwardly rendered as "understanding sociology"), which was used as a polemical weapon against the advances of behaviorism or simple statistical correlations. But during the last couple of decades the notion that one can or should engage in an elaborate, Diltheyan process called "interpretation," or virtuosic understanding, when analyzing the data of social life, broadly or narrowly defined, has seemed increasingly suspicious or improbable. Partly this is due to the more modest goals for sociological research that were set by various schools in the philosophy of social science, which had become far more "reflexive" about the defensible limits to understanding than were those of Weber's own time. Or so it has been strongly implied during the last half-century. And partly, too, this newfound modesty about the likely achievements of social research turned around questions of a political nature, an environment which, for instance, accused Weber of a virulent form of imperialist nationalism that sought to undercut the authority of his work. Among many Dead White European Males whom, it was argued, deserved to be cast from the temple, he was often named *numero uno*, partly because he was obviously the smartest and also because his self-assigned project was by far the largest in scope and depth. What were once regarded as his virtues turned to defects and his very ambitions made him the mightiest available target. (Marx was mostly immune to this treatment, again for political rather than intellectual reasons, which is odd because in many ways Weber's work is a gigantic corrective footnote to Marx's study of capitalist processes.)

Without any interest in refighting the "culture wars" that now seem more or less left behind (in the wake of September 11, 2001), mostly for lack of space, what I wish to do in my remaining pages is look at Weber's "Basic Sociological Terms" with as few preconceptions as possible. This may seem preposterous, but no more than is Weber's goal itself: to reshape the raw materials of history, political economy, comparative religion, philosophy of method, rudimentary psychology, legal reasoning, and the occasional literary morsel into a new way of seeing the world which we have since named "Weberian." It is sometimes worthwhile to return to foundations, and now that everyone claims to know what Weber meant—and what he should have meant had he shared current prejudices—this might be a good time to reconsider the facts of the case as they appear on the page.

As noted hundreds of times, Weber defines sociology as "a science concerning itself with the interpretive understanding of social action and thereby with a causal explanation of its course and consequences." He complicates things substantially by adding "We shall speak of 'action' insofar as the acting individual attaches a subjective meaning to his behavior—be it overt or covert, omission or acquiescence. Action is 'social' insofar as its subjective meaning takes account of the behavior of others and is thereby oriented in its course" (Weber, 1968: 4). As famous and often quoted as theses line are, they somehow remain impenetrable if one seeks to know exactly what Weber meant, or, more importantly, how his directions ought to be used in formulating an interpretative sociological method.

First of all, what does he mean by a "science"? *Wissenschaft* in German, as is ritually pointed out, is broader than our "science," because it also connotes knowledge or disciplined inquiry, as opposed to the arts that take their fire from intuition and inspiration. Weber was trained both in the "science" of law and in political-economy, and his apprentice works in ancient and medieval history, plus his huge empirical study for the *Verein*, were each committed to the use of quantitative measures and rigorous analytic technique. His profound commitment to scientific procedure is put on display in these well-received writings, yet he was not a part of that camp (mostly economists) who envisioned a future social science entirely free of the non-mathematical. His personal relations with Dilthey, Windelband, and Schmoller, among others, plus wide reading in literature and history, protected him from holding this simpleton's view of how the social sciences ought to operate. So "science" in this context would seem to mean little else besides disciplined inquiry of a kind that might be replicated by any competent scholar who wished to do so. Whereas Stefan George, Ernst Bloch, and Oswald Spengler (visitors to the Weber salon in Heidelberg) insisted on the primacy of what one might call "private insight" as the source of their ideas and creativity, Weber dismissed their pronouncements for lack of empirically verifiable bases. And yet he did interact with them, read their work, considered their notions about the direction of Western societies, and therefore could not have been entirely untouched by their arguments in favor of a non-scientific or quasi-scientific apprehension of cultural change. Put another way, if Weber embraced "science," he did so to protect it from both political pressure and the vagaries of intuition, but he did not do it out of ignorance of how politics affected knowledge seeking, or of the essential role that aesthetic perception plays in the creative act.

The major difficulty in evaluating Weber's use of "science" lies, of course, with the phrase "causal explanation." The issue of establishing exact causality in the social sciences has been laid to rest, not because it was conquered but rather simply abandoned as too difficult. Correlations seem to be enough to please most audiences, even when they are very small and bear far more "statistical" than human "significance."

But during most of the twentieth century, interested parties expended enormous energy debating the merits of causal analysis, and Weber's name was often invoked during these endless arguments in ways he probably would not have appreciated. This is because for him, causality had to be linked with explanations that embodied *sinnhafte Adäquanz*, "adequacy on the level of meaning" (ibid.: 11). Weber used this idea many times and seems to have meant by it the need for researchers to comprehend the meaning of a social act just as it was experienced by the actor. Put another way, if the actor (say, the Dutch merchant of the seventeenth century) would read Weber's *Protestant Ethic* in good faith, he would approve of the portrait because the motives Weber attributed to him "ring true" in terms of his self-estimate. Anything short of this heroic labor of imagination (or *Nacherleben*, to use Dilthey's indispensable term) made "causal analysis" impossible so far as Weber's notion of "interpretative sociology" was concerned. As Parsons[2] pointed out long ago, however, true causality that is "adequate on the level of meaning" also requires that an "objective" evaluation of action be undertaken which need not be bound by the subjective limitations peculiar to any given actor's behavior or its self-estimate (Parsons, 1937: esp. 624-635).

Thus, the analyst is called upon to comprehend the meaning attached by the social actor to the action as it was carried out, and then to assign causal sequencing in terms of the actor's own calculus of meaningfulness. To put it mildly, this is a tall order, particularly by today's standards when so many voices clamor for attention, demanding equal time before the court of causal reasoning. The astonishing fact is, though, that Weber qua virtuoso analyst, seems to have "hit the nail on the head" many more times than he missed when it came to performances of this forbidding type. He was aesthetically and factually accurate enough, so it has seemed to subsequent generations of readers, when characterizing the Protestant merchant, the charismatic leader, the Confucian mandarin, the Jewish prophet, the soulless cog in the bureaucratic machine, etc., that these organizing metaphors for Weberian analysis are as much with us now, and as vital, as they were when he concocted them nearly a century ago. In fact, they seem to have become reified into thoroughly accepted imagery in ways that even he would have found bothersome, shorn as they now are of all the qualifications he habitually attached to his cynosures.

Weber concludes his pregnant opening paragraph by pointing out that action is "social" only when other people are involved or when their significance is somehow taken into account, even in their absence. Many postmodernist epistemologies would balk at this "humanist" stricture, since for them fantasy, dreams, reigning epistemes, unspoken intentions, buried delusions, and all manner of mental furniture are as much grist for the analytic mill as Weber's prosaic notion of *soziale Handeln* ("social action"). And even though "virtual communities" through computer connections are said to be increasingly important to people's lives (for those who can afford them), they will never supplant face-to-face interaction as the principal source of pleasure and pain in human experience. There remains, then, something essential to Weber's humble model (borrowed at least in form from legal reasoning), since it does make available for comparative, analytic inspection a range of human behavior which the more esoteric versions common to our era do not. It offers a foundational expression that summarizes social action as a meaning-ridden, interpretable set of phenomena, without which it becomes increasingly difficult to imagine what a "social science" might do to justify its existence, unless it would be content to track computerized "interactions" as a surrogate for what previously was termed "social life."

Under "Methodological Foundations"—"not intended to be *read* in the ordinary sense," says Roth (p. 57, n. 4)—Weber goes through 11 numbered sections (pp. 4-22), which deal roughly with the following:

1. Two types of meaning
2. Meaning, "becoming Caesar," and recapturing experience
3. Interpretation, *Evidenz*, the analytic uses of empathy
4. Human conditions devoid of meaning as such, e.g., demographic changes
5. Two kinds of understanding
6. The interpretative grasp of meaning of three types (historical, mass phenomena, ideal types)
7. Motives and interpretative "adequacy on the level of meaning"; causality versus statistical regularities
8. Uninterpretable phenomena
9. The subjective meaning-complex of action and the goal of sociology; reified social elements; collective behavior; "organicism"; ethnology and ethology; the limits of rationalist explanations for action and meaning
10. Gresham's Law and the "purely rational pursuit of an end"
11. Typology, causality, analytic adequacy, casuistry, irrationality, and the goals of sociology.

The immediate questions which push themselves to the fore are why Weber numbered these unequal sections at all, as if the numerals added up to something cumulative, and why they are creatively repetitious and redundant of one another—why they overdetermine his conceptual work. Could it be that he was trying to persuade himself of the way that sociology ought to be practiced, since he realized that he was as much arguing against a dozen possible positions within the academy of his day as he was in favor of another half-dozen? He was well aware of what he later called "the apparently gratuitous tediousness involved in the elaborate definition of the above concepts" (ibid.: 44), yet he did little to relieve this discomforting catalogue of concepts and definitions. It becomes obvious as one goes through these passages carefully that the apparent reasonableness of the prose proper, the almost Solonian calm which its author adopted, papers over a great cognitive struggle. Much, though surely not all, of this internal war turns around the question of how successfully the social sciences could hope to rationalize, via a proper lexicon of linked notions, the fundamentally irrational nature of humankind at its least well-behaved (a topic I have treated elsewhere at length: Sica, 1988). By adopting the marginal utility model of social action as the norm against which ordinary human behavior could be measured as "deviations" from pure rationality, Weber threw in his lot with other adventurous analysts of his day who regarded rational action as the necessary companion to modernization. But what gave Weber's work its peculiar piquancy, of course, were the dour conclusions he drew from this change, one which shook up even his innate sobriety of character.

Returning to the text: Weber immediately takes on the question of "meaning" as the necessary prelude to everything that follows. Much sociology, especially in the U.S. (now a full century after Weber's trip to the St. Louis), has dispensed with "meaning" as a useful or achievable tool or goal for research. Survey questions in particular are blunt instruments for discovering what truly constitutes "meaning" for social actors. This is not only because of the intrinsic, practical limitations of questionnaires and the people who administer them (usually by phone), but also because the subjects who are questioned, even if the questions are "open-ended," very likely lack enough self-reflexive capacity and/or the language that goes with it to state unambiguously and accurately what does or does not create meaning in their lives—at least at a level that would satisfy Weber's intentions. Yet for Weber, this was not nearly so much of a problem as I am here making out, perhaps because he was more used to dealing with extremely self-aware people of his own social caste in Germany, or, even more likely, because what I have called "video-cretinization" had not yet diluted ordinary people's linguistic capacity for self-expression. This is no trivial matter when social science hopes to ascertain and then categorize meaningful components of people's lives. If Dilthey, Gadamer, Ricoeur, and other hermeneutic theorists are right in saying that language is the quintessential human gift, and that meaning without language is literally inconceivable, and if, contiguously, critics of mass media harp quite correctly on the progressive dimi-

nution of functional literacy among the throngs who define and rede-
fine their lives through the behavioral prescriptions given to them by TV
and movies, then Weber's sanguine use of "meaning" poses real problems for a *verstehende Soziologie* of the kind he was proposing in 1919.

We might set aside all these reservations temporarily, and listen to
Weber's opening gambit in defining "meaning":

> "Meaning" may be of two kinds. The term may refer first to the actual
> existing meaning in the given concrete case of a particular actor, or to the
> average or approximate meaning attributable to a given plurality of ac-
> tors; or secondly to the theoretically conceived *pure type* of subjective mean-
> ing attributed to the hypothetical actor or actors in a given type of action"
> (ibid.: 4).

Clearly, things are becoming less clear. How does one unambiguously establish the "actual existing meaning" for a social actor in a
"given concrete case"? Sociologists and anthropologists can either ask
or watch, and demographers can count events after the fact, but in the
wake of psychoanalysis, it is impossible to believe that social actors will
answer honestly or completely when asked, or that they would even
know with real certainty what constitutes "meaning" as a part of everyday life. Often enough it is remarked that meaning, like Minerva's owl,
can be known only post facto, following a grave loss of opportunity,
companionship, or physical mobility. I would not for a moment believe
that Weber was unaware of everything I have brought up in the preceding couple of paragraphs, so the question for rhetorical analysis is this:
given that Weber almost surely knew of the limitations of his model for
meaning-analysis, why did he portray it in such brisk, straightforward,
apparently untroubled terms?

If one compares, for instance, Husserl's tortured examination of
"meaning" in *Ideas* around 1913 (the precursor of which was published
in *Logos*, as was Weber's *Kategorienlehre* at nearly the same time), one
would either have to assume that Weber was practicing willful ignorance or that he believed Husserl's work could not be put to good use in
social analysis (cf. Husserl, 1962, section 124). Of course, Alfred Schutz
gave the lie to any such notion in 1932 with his *Der sinnhafte Aufbau der
sozialen Welt* (literally, "The meaningful construction of the social world")
wherein he joined Husserl's sense of meaning with Weber's typology of
social action in order to produce a phenomenological sociology that
bore most fruit during the 1960s and 1970s. Schutz's long meditation
on "The Constitution of Meaningful Lived Experience" has generally
been viewed for decades as a necessary enlargement, if not outright
corrective, to Weber's rudimentary formula for meaning-analysis in
Economy and Society (Schutz, 1967: 45-96). So assuming that Weber was

aware that Husserl and others were straining to bring "meaning" within their ken, which I think is entirely reasonable, then why did he elect to express himself in such, shall we say, "unreflective" terms? A phrase like "the average or approximate meaning attributable to a given plurality of actors" makes literally no sense in either Husserl's, Scheler's, or Schutz's vocabulary. One answer would be that, brushing aside philosophical considerations and hesitations, Weber insisted on a less subtle but more patently useful mode of expression because he thought that social science could escape some of the more trying experiments of philosophy (including Rickert's) if it cast itself within an intentionally naive frame of reference. If sociology spoke through the ingenuous voice of the utilitarian child, it could avoid the hamstrung condition into which philosophy and some branches of psychology had gotten themselves beginning in the late nineteenth century by adopting a tone of the world-weary sophisticate. Put another way, one can choose to view the world as Vico did, full of historically imaginative re-creations and all the troubles that arise from them (Sica, 2002), or as Voltaire did when speaking through Candide's mouth—with an artificial but useful clarity and simplicity. Thus, the "ideal type."

It should be apparent by now, gauged by my snail-like progress through Weber's opening sentences, that the first part of *Economy and Society* is what literary critics for some years have called a "rich text"— hardly surprising given the protracted, anxious labor that produced it. A full-blown hermeneutic appraisal would obviously require hundreds of pages, and even though such an undertaking would be valuable from the point of view of redefining a specifically "Weberian" sociology and clearing up its muddled legacy to date, this is not the place to do it. Yet before bringing my abbreviated venture down this road to a close, there are a few more passages from within the first eleven numbered sections of the "Basic Sociological Terms" that might repay examination, even if in an unperfected form.

Section 3 is enormously interesting and important, for here Weber considers what "interpretation of meaning" is, how it should be carried out, and what forms it takes in the face of that dazzling array of data that faces the researcher no matter where one looks. Just prior to this section, he explains that:

> "recapturing an experience" is important for accurate understanding, but not an absolute precondition for its interpretation. Understandable and non-understandable components of a process are often intermingled and bound up together.
>
> All interpretation of meaning, like all scientific observations, strives for clarity and verifiable accuracy of insight and comprehension. The basis for certainty in understanding can be either rational, which can be further

subdivided into logical and mathematical, or it can be of an emotionally empathic or artistically appreciative quality. Action is rationally evident chiefly when we attain a completely clear intellectual grasp of the action-elements in their intended context of meaning. Empathic or appreciative accuracy is attained when, through sympathetic participation, we can adequately grasp the emotional context in which the action took place. The highest degree of rational understanding is attained in cases involving the meanings of logically or mathematically related propositions; their meaning may be immediately and unambiguously intelligible. . . .With a lower degree of certainty, which is, however, adequate for most purposes of explanation, we are able to understand errors, including confusion of problems of the sort that we ourselves are liable to, or the origin of which we can detect by sympathetic self-analysis.

On the other hand, many ultimate ends or values toward which experience shows that human action may be oriented, often cannot be understood completely, though sometimes we are able to grasp them intellectually. The more radically they differ from our own ultimate values, however, the more difficult it is for us to understand them empathetically. (Pp. 5-6)

These loaded passages once again declare Weber's divided loyalties and allegiances, part of him perfectly willing to follow the Schleiermacher-Dilthey tradition of "empathetic participation" in another's experience in order to categorize what humans do, the other part still vainly holding onto the requirement for scientific clarity and rigor, and the pursuit of "rational action" wherever it might lurk. His belief that certain actions are transparently knowable—"their meanings may be immediately and unambiguously intelligible"—probably applies to a very small proportion of social behavior, even if this fraction grows as societies leave *Gemeinschaft* for *Gesellschaft* at ever increasing speed. Yet his real interest, documented in studies of religion, lies elsewhere.

As much as I sympathize with his goals, I cannot imagine how his program would work today, even if it would have functioned fairly well during his lifetime. "Worldviews" are now so enormously varied, so it seems, even within one nation-state's borders, that to presume the ability to exercise "emotional empathy" or "sympathetic self-analysis" with other social actors who live far beyond the borders of one's own status or ethnic group no longer seems possible, even if still entirely commendable in principle. Can a devout Baptist sociologist of the family in Texas teaching at a church-sponsored school expect to stretch his empathetic powers enough to appreciate the experience of a lesbian couple in San Francisco (or Denmark) who wish to adopt children born in the Philippines and to raise them as a "normal American family"? Nevertheless, Weber's prescription continues to make sense in an ideal way. As difficult as it might well be in many specific, "concrete cases" called up for analysis, there is still no better ultimate guide for social research that deals with human meaning than Weber's axioms. They may seem less and less "do-able," but they are no less valuable as guides for being so. What they call for in a social researcher is cross-cultural sensibility, historical imagination, self-realizing experience in the world's ways, and a tolerant skepticism about self-serving rationalizations that usually clothe tales about motivation.

Another frequently quoted passages lies nearby, and gives particular strength to the hermeneutic wing of Weberians: "The more we ourselves are susceptible to such emotional reactions as anxiety, anger, ambition, envy, jealousy, love, enthusiasm, pride, vengefulness, loyalty, devotion, and appetites of all sorts, and to the 'irrational' conduct which grows out of them, the more readily can we empathize with them." But what he gives with one hand, he retrieves with another, for in the following paragraph comes his most famous dictum, and one which on its face seems to contradict in part the very intention of what preceded it: "For the purposes of a typological scientific analysis it is convenient to treat all irrational, affectually determined elements of behavior as factors of deviation from a conceptually pure type of rational action" (p. 6). Convenient, to be sure, but wholly unrealistic to boot, as he himself was fond of pointing out again and again, for example, "That there is, however, a danger of rationalistic interpretations where they are out of place cannot be denied. All experience unfortunately confirms the existence of this danger" (p. 7). Yet he was willing to take the risk of dealing in unrealities for the sake of fleshing out his growing inventory of ideal-types. The unspoken question here revolves around defining suitable limits to heuristics, to adjustments made by the analyst to the empirically knowable world in order to extend the application of one's preferred model of actions and reactions. The character of Weber's rhetoric here helps explain what so irritated Leo Strauss on the Right when he produced his corrosive response to Weber's apparent unwillingness to stand behind any absolute value system (Strauss, 1953: 36-78), but it equally infuriated Herbert Marcuse on the Left, for it seemed to play endlessly with Kantian antinomies which in the praxis of real life demand resolution, except when pertaining to the insulated bourgeoisie for whom praxis could become a merely theoretical exercise (Marcuse, 1972).

As we have seen, these opening pages are packed with programmatic statements, including several that define the "science" of "sociology" (a term he often put into quotation marks, indicating its tentative existence as a serious academic field). He believed that "the specific task of sociological analysis or of that of the other sciences of action" should principally be "the interpretation of action in terms of its subjective meaning" (p. 8). But when he got as close to the real nub of the matter as he could, his prose began to waver under qualifications and imagery which has managed to confuse many of its readers (even experts, e.g., Eliaesen, 2002, who comments repeatedly about the ambiguity of Weber's message). This paragraph is typical:

> Every interpretation attempts to attain clarity and certainty, but no matter how clear an interpretation as such appears to be from the point of view of meaning, it cannot on this account claim to be the causally valid interpretation. On this level it must remain only a *peculiarly plausible hypothesis*. In the first place the "conscious motives" may well, even to the actor himself, conceal the various "motives" and "repressions" which constitute the real driving force of his action. Thus in such cases even subjectively honest self-analysis has only a relative value. Then it is the task of the sociologist to be aware of this motivational situation and to describe and analyze it, even though it has not actually been concretely part of the conscious intention of the actor; possibly not at all, at least not fully. This is a borderline case of the interpretation of meaning. (Pp. 9-10; emphasis added)

On the next page he advises that a *"striking rational plausibility* of the hypothesis [Eduard Meyer's famous hunch about the effects of ancient warfare on Greek and European culture] must here necessarily be relied on as a support." One's interpretation must be "adequate on the level of meaning," that is, "a complex of subjective meaning which seems to the actor himself or to the observer as adequate ground for the conduct in question" (p. 11; emphasis added).

As I have pointed out above, all of this makes eminently good sense and is sound advice for socal analysis so long as researchers exhibit extraordinary knowledge and skill, and can also count on a certain level of cultural homogeneity which would prevent various perplexing behaviors from erupting that confound the well-intentioned observer— particularly one who is keen to find a deviation from the pure type of rational action that serves as Weber's perpetual baseline. (As I write, another replay of the Crusades seems to have begun in the Middle East, with Western interests trying to dictate ultimate values to Muslims, neither side having much understanding of what the other values most in life and is willing to die for. In such contexts, "empathic understanding" must fall short of its desired end.) The phrases "peculiarly plausible hypothesis" and "striking rational plausibility" are rhetorical stretches into darkened terrain and can carry the argument only to the extent that the reader already agrees with the Weberian project of action analysis, and is therefore willing to give its author the benefit of the doubt; if, in short, the reader will concede that Weber's program seems "peculiarly plausible." I myself find it easy to accept, but that others could reasonably take strong exception also has about it "striking rational plausibility" for reasons that Weber knew quite well, yet here was trying to dodge.

What have we learned from this truncated conversation with Weber's prose? If Strauss and Marcuse were famously outraged by Weber's endpoint in terms of ultimate societal values, such passionate concerns now seem somewhat beside the point given the nature of contemporary sociopolitical culture, and the role of social sciences in the construction of same. Such fundamental objections aside, the reason Weber's prose *as a coherent performance* continues to be studied, reprinted, cherished, and argued over has less to do with the originality of his ideas per se—which, he was the first to admit, were already in the air by the time he codified and embellished them in 1919—than with his delivery of them to an audience which seems to grow with each new generation of social scientists. It was not so much that he took a "complex, middle-of-the-road position" and thereby escaped censure from either side of a given methodological divide (cf. Eliaeson, 2002: 18), although it's clear that he does equivocate when it suits him. What he seems to be able to do better than practically any theorist before or since is to present in workmanlike fashion both sides of an antinomic pair of concepts, problems, or points of view, and then speak on behalf of each with equal force and persuasiveness, finally alighting in his own zone of analytic comfort, all the while making a strong case for its adoption by others. This, of course, is the mark of the master rhetorician, something Weber would have learned in his teens when he studied Cicero's speeches—even if they irritated him at the time because of Cicero's game-playing with the truth.

Reconsider, for instance, his remarks about functionalism and reification:

> How far in other disciplines this type of functional analysis of the relation of "parts" to a "whole" can be regarded as definitive, cannot be discussed here . . . For purposes of sociological analysis two things can be said. First this functional frame of reference is convenient for purposes of practical illustration and for provisional orientation. In these respects it is not only useful but indispensable. But at the same time if its cognitive value is overestimated and its concepts illegitimately "reified," it can be highly dangerous." (P. 15).

In very few choice words, Weber anticipates most of what Parsons spent years trying to clarify and legitimate through his structural-functionalist model, and also argues concisely about its promise and limitations. His modifiers—"convenient," "provisional," "indispensable," "overestimated," "highly dangerous"—bring the passage to life and show that he was no dogmatic friend of any position, the weaknesses of which he could so handily visualize. That he understood a very wide range of ideas about how social science ought to be carried out is indubitable, and that he furthermore was able to "compare and contrast" in ways that left even his brightest colleagues far behind seems to me equally important to keep in mind as we continue measuring Weber's utility to the new century.

Marx, Durkheim, and Freud seem dogmatic and undialectical by comparison, yet theorists who came after Weber lacked his historical and legal knowledge, as well as his theoretical creativity that rested partly on his superhuman capacity for assimilation of economic, cross-cultural, and religious information. This is what gives his voice its unique Siren-like quality and so much distinguishes it other classical theorists'. He could argue any point with authority and therefore chose his antinomies carefully as he restructured them, tamed them, and brought them within his rhetorical power—even if some of the demands he therefore made on sociology now seem overweening. As he said, "for sociology. . . the object of cognition is the subjective meaning-complex of action" (p. 13), which is just tantalizing enough, while shrewdly ambiguous, to inspire loud followers and detractors alike. What Weber does with these kinds of remarks is give his most alert colleagues something essential to talk about, which is the highest achievement of the rhetor, and a role for theorizing that is no longer so skillfully practiced as it was in his day.

References

Adair-Toteff, Christopher 2002: "Max Weber as Philosopher: The Jaspers-Rickert Confrontation." *Max Weber Studies*, 3:1 (November), 15-32.

Arendt, Hannah and Karl Jaspers 1992: *Correspondence, 1926-1969*. Ed. by Lotte Kohler and Hans Saner; tr. Robert and Rita Kimber. New York: Harcourt, Brace, Jovanovich.

Atoji, Y. 1984: *Sociology at the Turn of the Century: On G. Simmel in Comparison with F. Tönnies, M. Weber, and E. Durkheim*. Tokyo: Dobunkan Pub. Co.

Baier, Horst, M. Ranier Lepsius, Wolfgang J. Mommsen, Wolfgang Schluchter 2000: "Overview of the Text of *Economy and Society*" by the Editors of the *Max Weber Gesamtausgabe* (tr. A. Harrington). *Max Weber Studies*, 1:1 (November), 104-114.

Barzun, Jacques 2000: *From Dawn to Decadence: 1500 to the Present: 500 Years of Western Cultural Life*. New York: HarperCollins.

Baumgarten, Eduard 1957: "The 'Radical Evil' in Jaspers's Philosophy." Pp. 337-368 in P. A. Schilpp (ed), *The Philosophy of Karl Jaspers*, LaSalle, IL: Open Court Pub. Co.

Beer, Gillian 1985: Darwin's Reading and the Fictions of Development. Pp. 543-588 in David Kohn (ed), *The Darwinian Heritage*. Princeton: Princeton University Press.

Bruun, H. H. 1972: *Science, Values and Politics in Max Weber's Methodology*. Copenhagen: Munksgaard.

Cahnman, Werner 1995: *Weber and Toennies*. Ed. by J. Maier, J. Marcus, and Z. Tarr. New Brunswick, NJ: Transaction Publishers.

Cantor, Norman 1991: *Inventing the Middle Ages*. New York: Morrow.

Chalcraft, David 1994: Bringing the Text Back in: On Ways of Reading the Iron Cage Metaphor in the Two Editions of *The Protestant Ethic and the Spirit of Capitalism.* Pp. 16-43 in Larry Ray and Mike Reed (eds.), *Organising Modernity*, London: Routledge.

_____ 1999: Love and Death. Weber, Wagner, and Max Klinger. Pp. 196-213 in Sam Whimster, 1999.

_____ 2002: "Max Weber on the Watchtower: On the Prophetic Use of Shakespeare's Sonnet 102 in 'Politics as a Vocation.'" *Journal for the Study of Pseudoepigrapha*, vol. 43, 253-270.

Condren, Conal 1985: *The Status and Appraisal of Classic Texts: An Essay on Political Theory, Its Inheritance, and the History of Ideas.* Princeton, NJ: Princeton University Press.

Dilthey, Wilhelm 1961: *Pattern and Meaning in History.* Trans. by H. P. Rickman. New York: Harper and Row.

_____ 1989: *Selected Works: Volume 1, Introduction to the Human Sciences.* E d . by Rudolf Makkreel and Frithjof Rodi. Princeton, NJ: Princeton University Press.

Eliaeson, Sven 2002: *Max Weber's Methodologies.* Oxford: Polity Press.

Faught, Jim 1985: "Neglected Affinities: Max Weber and Georg Simmel." *British Journal of Sociology*, 36:2, 155-174.

Frisby, David 1984: "The Ambiguity of Modernity: Georg Simmel and Max Weber." Pp. 422-433 in Wolfgang Mommsen and Jürgen Osterhammel (eds.), *Max Weber and His Contemporaries*, London: Allen & Unwin.

Gadamer, Hans-Georg 1975: *Truth and Method.* New York: Seabury Press.

Gerth, Hans H. and C. Wright Mills (eds. and trans.) 1946: *From Max Weber: Essays in Sociology.* New York: Oxford University Press.

Goldman, Harvey 1988: *Max Weber and Thomas Mann: Calling and the Shaping of the Self.* Berkeley: University of California Press.

_____ 1992: *Politics, Death, and the Devil: Self and Power in Max Weber and Thomas Mann.* Berkeley: University of California Press.

Gottl, Friedrich 1901: *Die Herrschaft des Wortes: Untersuchungen zur Kritik des nationalökonomischen Denkens.* Jena: G. Fischer.

Green, Bryan S. 1988: *Literary Methods and Sociological Theory: Case Studies of Simmel and Weber.* Chicago: University of Chicago Press.

Hennis, Wilhelm 2000a: *Max Weber's Central Question.* 2nd ed. Tr. Keith Tribe. Newbury, Berks, UK: Threshold Press.

_____ 2000b: *Max Weber's Science of Man: New Studies for a Biography of the Work.* Tr. Keith Tribe. Newbury, Berks, UK: Threshold Press.

Henrich, Dieter 1987: "Karl Jaspers: Thinking with Max Weber in Mind." Pp. 528-544 in Wolfgang Mommsen and Jürgen Osterhammel (eds.), *Max Weber and His Contemporaries*, London: Allen & Unwin.

Honigsheim, Paul 2000: *The Unknown Max Weber.* Ed. and with an introduction by Alan Sica. New Brunswick, NJ: Transaction Publishers.

Husserl, Edmund 1962 [1931]: *Ideas: General Introduction to Pure Phenomenology.* Tr. W. R. Boyce Gibson. New York: Collier Books.

Jameson, Fredric 1974: "The Vanishing Mediator: Narrative Structure in Max Weber." *New German Critique*, 1:1 (Winter), 52-89.

Jaspers, Karl 1921: "Max Weber": Address at the Memorial Service arranged by the students of the University of Heidelberg, July 17, 1920. (27 pp.) Tübingen: J. C. B. Mohr.

_____ 1928: *Max Weber: Deutsches Wesen im politischen Denken, im Forschen und Philosophieren.* Oldenburg i. O.: G. Stallings.

_____ 1963 [1913]: *General Psychopathology.* [7th German ed.] Tr. J. Hoenig and Marian Hamilton. Chicago: University of Chicago Press.

_____ 1964: *Three Essays: Leonardo, Descartes, Max Weber*. Tr. Ralph Manheim. New York: Harcourt, Brace, and World.

_____ 1969: *Philosophy, Volume 1*. Tr. E. B. Ashton. Chicago: University of Chicago Press.

_____ 1989: *On Max Weber*. Tr. Robert Whelan, ed. J. Dreifmanis. New York: Paragon House.

Johnston, William M. 1967: "Karl Marx's Verse of 1836-1837 as a Foreshadowing of His Early Philosophy." *Journal of the History of Ideas*, 28:3(April-June), 259-268.

Käsler, Dirk 1988 [1979]: *Max Weber: An Introduction to his Life and Work*. Tr. by Philippa Hurd. London: Polity Press.

Kennedy, James G. 1973: *Herbert Spencer*. Boston: Twayne.

Kölwel, Eduard 1962: *Von der Art zu Schreiben: Essays über philosophische und dichterische Ausdrucksmittel*. Halle a.S., at 130-166.

Lichtblau, Klaus 1991: "Causality or Interaction? Simmel, Weber, and Interpretive Sociology." *Theory, Culture, and Society*, 8:3 (August), 33-62.

Manasse, Ernst Moritz 1957: Max Weber's Influence on Jaspers. Pp. 369-392 in P.A. Schilpp (ed.), *The Philosophy of Karl Jaspers*, LaSalle, IL: Open Court Pub. Co. (augmented edition, 1981).

Marcuse, Herbert 1972: "Industrialization and Capitalism in the Work of Max Weber." In Otto Stammer (ed.), *Max Weber and Sociology Today*, New York: Harper and Row, 133-151.

Meinecke, Friedrich 1950: *The German Catastrophe*. Tr. by Sidney Fay. Cambrdige: Harvard University Press. (Reissued Boston: Beacon Press, 1963).

Mitzman, Arthur 1973: *Sociology and Estrangement: Three Sociologists of Imperial Germany* [Sombart, Tönnies, Michels]. New York: Alfred A. Knopf.

Mommsen, Wolfgang 2000: Max Weber's "Grand Sociology": The Origins and Composition of *Wirtschaft und Gesellschaft*. Soziologie. *History and Theory* 39:3 (October), 364-383.

Mommsen, Wolfgang and Jürgen Osterhammel (eds.) 1987: *Max Weber and His Contemporaries*. German Historical Institute/London: Allen and Unwin.

Moreno, Joshua Levy 1934: *Who Shall Survive?: A New Approach to the Problem of Human Interrelations*. Washington, DC: Nervous and Mental Disease Publishing Co.

_____ 1943: *Sociometry and the Cultural Order*. New York: Beacon House.

Nietzsche, Friedrich 1984 [1878]: *Human, All Too Human: A Book for Free Spirits*. Tr. Marion Faber, with Stephen Lehmann. Lincoln: University of Nebraska Press.

Oakes, Guy 1988: *Weber and Rickert: Concept Formation in the Cultural Sciences*. Cambridge, MA: MIT Press.

_____ 2003: "Max Weber on Value Rationality and Value Spheres." *Journal of Classical Sociology*, 3:1 (March), 27-45.

Parsons, Talcott 1937: *The Structure of Social Action*. New York: McGraw-Hill Book Company.

Paxton, Nancy L. 1991: *George Eliot and Herbert Spencer: Feminism, Evolutionism, and the Reconstruction of Gender*. Princeton, NJ: Princeton University Press.

Proust, Marcel 1992: *In Search of Lost Time, Volume 1, Swann's Way*. Tr. C. K. Scott Moncrieff and Terence Kilmartin; revised by D.J. Enright. New York: Modern Library.

Reynolds, Michael 1981: *Hemingway's Reading, 1910-1940*. Princeton, NJ: Princeton University Press.

Rickert, Heinrich 1986: *The Limits of Concept Formation in Natural Science.* Ed. and tr. by Guy Oakes. Cambridge: Cambridge University Press.

Roth, Guenther 1968: Introduction to Max Weber, *Economy and Society,* pp. xxvii-cv. New York: Bedminster Press.

_____ 2001: *Max Webers deutsch-englische Familiengeschichte, 1800-1950. Mit Briefen und Dokumenten.* Tübingen: J C B Mohr.

Schilpp, Paul Arthur (ed.) 1981: *The Philosophy of Karl Jaspers,* augmented edition (Library of Living Philosophers). LaSalle, IL: Open Court Publishing Co.

Schutz, Alfred 1967: *The Phenomenology of the Social World.* Tr. G. Walsh and F. Lehnert. Evanston, IL: Northwestern University Press.

Sica, Alan 1988: *Weber, Irrationality, and Social Order.* Berkeley: University of California Press.

_____ 2002: The Two Neapolitan Titans: Croce's Redefinition of Vico." Pp. ix-xxxiii in Benedetto Croce, *The Philosophy of Giambattista Vico,* New Brunswick, NJ: Transaction Publishers.

Simmel, Georg 1977: *The Problems of the Philosophy of History: An Epistemological Essay.* Tr., ed., and intro. by Guy Oakes. New York: Free Press.

_____ 1978: *The Philosophy of Money.* Tr. Tom Bottomore and David Frisby. (2nd ed., 1990). London: Routledge.

_____ 1980: *Essays on Interpretation in Social Science.* Tr., ed., with an intro. by Guy Oakes. Totowa, NJ: Rowman and Littlefield.

Spencer, Herbert 1973 [1852-1857]: *Literary Style and Music.* Port Washington, NY: Kennikat Press.

Stammler, Rudolf 1896: *Wirtschaft und Recht nach der materialistischen Geschichtsauffassung: eine sozialphilosophische Untersuchung.* Leipzig: V e i t and Co.

Strauss, Leo 1953: *Natural Right and History.* Chicago: University of Chicago Press.

Swedberg, Richard 1998: *Max Weber and the Idea of Economic Sociology.* Princeton, NJ: Princeton University Press.

Tönnies, Ferdinand 1971: *On Sociology: Pure, Applied, and Empirical. Selected Writings.* Ed. and intro. by W. Cahnman and R. Heberle. Chicago: University of Chicago Press.

_____ 2001: *Community and Civil Society.* Ed. Jose Harris; tr. Jose Harris and Margaret Hollis. Cambridge, UK: Cambridge University Press.

Tucker, Robert C. (ed.) 1978: *The Marx-Engels Reader,* 2nd ed. New York: W. W. Norton.

Turner, Stephen P. and Regis A. Factor 1994: *Max Weber: The Lawyer as Social Thinker.* London: Routledge.

Vandenberghe, Frederic 1999: Simmel and Weber as Ideal-Typical Founders of Sociology. *Philosophy and Social Criticism,* 25:4 (July), 57-80.

Weber, Marianne 1975: *Max Weber: A Biography.* Tr. by Harry Zohn. New York: John Wiley and Sons.

Weber, Max 1936: *Jugendbriefe* [1876-1893]. Tübingen: J C B Mohr.

_____ 1968: *Economy and Society: An Outline of Interpretive Sociology.* Ed. by Guenther Roth and Claus Wittich (many translators). New York: Bedminster Press. (Reprinted in unchanged format by the University of California Press, 1978).

_____ 1972: "Georg Simmel as Sociologist." *Social Research,* 39, 155-163.

_____ 1975: *Roscher and Knies: The Logical Problems of Historical Economics.* Tr. with Intro. by Guy Oakes. New York: Free Press.

_____ 1977: *Critique of Stammler*. Tr. and with Intro. by Guy Oakes. New York: Free Press.

_____ 1981 [1913]: "Some Categories of Interpretive Sociology." Tr. Edith Graber. *Sociological Quarterly*, 22:2 (Spring), 151-180.

Whimster, Sam (ed.) 1999: *Max Weber and the Culture of Anarchy*. London: Macmillan.

Wolff, Kurt (tr./ed.) 1950: *The Sociology of Georg Simmel*. Glencoe, IL: Free Press.

3

Weber in the Public Sphere

On June 8, 2003 the *New York Times* op-ed page, probably the most influential such site for public proclamations of its kind, published Niall Ferguson's "Why America Outpaces Europe (Clue: The God Factor)," which begins:

> It was almost a century ago that the German sociologist Max Weber published his influential essay "The Protestant Ethic and the Spirit of Capitalism." In it, Weber argued that modern capitalism was "born from the spirit of Christian asceticism" in it specifically Protestant form—in other words, there was a link between the self-denying ethos of the Protestant sects and the behavior patterns associated with capitalism, above all hard work. Many scholars have built careers out of criticizing Weber's thesis. Yet the experience of Western Europe in the past quarter-century offers an unexpected confirmation of it. To put it bluntly, we are witnessing the decline and fall of the Protestant work ethic in Europe. This represents the stunning triumph of secularizing in Western Europe—the simultaneous decline of both Protestantism and its unique work ethic. Just as Weber's 1904 visit to the United States convinced him that his thesis was right, anyone visiting New York today would have a similar experience. For in the pious, industrious United States, the Protestant work ethic is alive and well. Its death is a peculiarly European phenomenon—and has grim implications for the future of the European Union on the even of its eastward expansion, perhaps most economically disastrous for the 'new' Europe."

Professor Ferguson, author of *Empire: The Rise and Demise of the British World Order and the Lessons for Global Power*, teaches in the business school at New York University, and also has an appointment at Jesus College (!), Oxford, which is perhaps too appropriate. He is well-known as an academic who writes for a broad audience, and his invocation of Weber is an example of what has become an increasingly ordinary event: the pre-legitimation of a complex argument accomplished by using Weber's name as a battering ram against any possible opposition. He concludes his jeremiad by writing "The loser will be the European economy, which will continue to fall behind the United States in terms of its absolute annual output. The winner will be the spirit of secularized sloth, which has finally slain the Protestant work ethic in Europe—and Max Weber, whose famous thesis celebrates its centenary by attaining the status of verity."

The fact that such writing trivializes Weber's two connected essays on the topic and the thousands of scholarly commentaries that grew out of it, while also simplifying the problems of global economic competition, ecological issues, and the place of labor in a world increasingly orchestrated by monopoly capital, would very likely have amused Weber, and not surprised him at all. For the fact is that Weber was an astute, lifelong student of newspapers, a very frequent columnists and op-ed writer himself in a range of highbrow German *Zeitschriften*, and drew up plans in 1909/10 for empirical studies of the newspaper which only lack of money and time prevented him from carrying out. But before we get to those matters, let us reconsider Weber's continuing role as a theorist and spokesman for a particular socio-political point of view that remains vital today.

A protracted debate has occurred within the social sciences during the last twenty-five years, particularly in scholarly circles whose primary goal is the elaboration of social theory. The question at stake—"Who among the 'holy trinity' of classical theorists will most forcefully propel social analysis into the twenty-first century?"—seems finally to be settled, at least for the foreseeable future. Marx has been consigned by most laypersons and many scholars, perhaps only temporarily, to the same "dustbin of history" he eloquently invoked when criticizing his theoretical forbears or contemporary enemies. The Marxist star was most firmly hitched, properly or not, to the political fortunes of the USSR and its Eastern Bloc satellites. As they failed to construct a workable communist social order and were dragged unwillingly into the capitalist world-system, the relevance of Marxist social analysis seemed, especially to the theoretically uninformed, to have disappeared as quickly as did statues of Stalin and Lenin from the streets of Moscow. Marx's uniquely perceptive analysis of how capitalist accumulation occurs on the corporate or global level will likely regain its pertinence during the next major economic downturn. For the inevitable price of uncontrolled global capitalism, environmentally and otherwise, will require a "rethinking" now that the latest so-called "boom" has exhausted itself, especially in the West, where such "booms" are politically defined for mass consumption. But for now, without a major national government using his name for the purposes of political legitimation, the kind of intellectual supremacy Marx's ideas enjoyed between the mid-1960s and late 1970s, especially in those countries where social sciences flourish, is difficult to foresee.

The case of Durkheim, of course, is entirely different, since his ideas were never overtly attached to government policies beyond the reach of French pedagogical practices. Yet it is probably fair to say that Durkheim's most general ideas have so thoroughly saturated analysis common to the social sciences that it is difficult to speak in any tongue but his, especially regarding the related phenomena of deviance, the division of labor, and religious practices. Oddly, though, even given the ubiquity of "the Durkheimian perspective" or "a Durkheimian conceptualization," his works themselves, when reread carefully, seem increasingly musty and time-bound. Leading today's novices through *Elementary Forms of the Religious Life* or even *Division of Labor* with any real hermeneutic care becomes ever more an exercise in identifying anti- quated debates and forgotten scholars than is the case even with Marx's work, despite its having been written thirty or forty years prior to Durkheim's. The latter's pronounced moralism and his dedication to the cause of making civility into a religion (to borrow from Robert Bellah) will always suit certain mindsets and political situations. Yet his role in the postmodern intellectual environment seems more like that of the visiting uncle from deep within the underdeveloped countryside than as a viable family member whose daily advice is prized for its enduring applicability to modern life. And arguments that there is indeed a "postmodern Durkheim," no matter how creatively posed, do little to ward off the suspicion that he is truly of another era. His principal theoretical concerns, it now seems, spoke more immediately to modes of social organization, and the worldviews that sprang from them, which have weakened in form and force since the First World War—a catastro- phe, it should be remembered, that killed not only Durkheim's only son, but his own spirit to live. Increasingly, I suspect, his works themselves will assume a role in social analysis not unlike that of Hobbes's *Levia- than* in political thought: always cited, seldom read.

One could therefore argue with some confidence that it is Weber who remains the towering figure from the classical period, whose work and person continue to inspire endless emulation, commentary, critique, and utility in empirical or "theory-driven" studies, as well as in less lofty forms of published work where normally the names of social theorists seldom appear. His language is quoted, without irony or embarrass- ment, by everyone from newspaper columnists to philosophers of reli- gion; his principal theoretical and substantive concerns are those which continue to inspire ever-growing bodies of scholarship internationally; his theories and corporeal self seem as much at home in today's cultural and intellectual environment as those of his historical peers do not. There is a distinctly Weberian approach, an almost "Weberian mood," as it pertains to various features of the contemporary social scene for which no apology or second-guessing is required, and which still bears as much analytic power as did Marxism only twenty years ago, or as Durkheim continues to do when applied to more restricted zones of social life.

I make these somewhat contentious observations not out of vague impressions based on haphazard reading, but rather from an "empirical study" of my own devising which has been in process for a decade. Years ago, I was asked to answer in book form what then seemed a simple enough question: "To what extent and in what ways does Weber continue to influence contemporary thought and research?"; or, to mimic Croce's wonderful title regarding Hegel in 1907, *What is Living and What is Dead in the Theorizing of Max Weber?* What began as a casual study of major sources has become over time an obsessive search for materials that speak in Weberian diction, which examine his own works in homage or critique, or somehow enlarge on themes he introduced during his relatively short professional heyday between 1904 and early 1920. What I have learned from this bibliographical study has proved endlessly interesting, not only because so many of Weber's ideas continue to lead researchers into passionate and diverse courses of study, but also due to what has *not* been pursued owing to his implied or explicit directives. Weber's mind and writings become all the more interesting after one recognizes how his particular viewpoint and language necessarily curtailed study that might otherwise have occurred. (My own study of Weber's difficulty with the "problem of irrationality" is one example among an increasing number that look for and try to repair specifiable lapses in his thinking, few though they may have been; Sica, 1988). Some of his metaphors ("the iron cage" is the most famous) and many concepts, like "charisma," are still much with us, as are heated arguments over whether, for example, the "Protestant Ethic thesis" applies to historical formations all the way from Korea to Namibia. Yet as with any supremely talented thinker, "lacunae" are almost as informative as the research topics for which he had a ready affinity and left behind detailed analyses. Thus, his forgetfulness, as it were, becomes ours, just as his enthusiasms infect and inform our own.

In a short chapter it is impossible more than to hint at the vast range of scholarly and sub-scholarly work in English over the last eighty years which clearly bear the Weberian stamp. The bibliography I have assembled currently numbers 4,100 published items (nearly all of it in scholarly as opposed to journalistic outlets) and 410 dissertations, plus hundreds of book reviews directly addressing products of "the Weber industry." There are also ninety individually published English translations of Weber's own writing, with more appearing all the time. In Germany the monumental collected works in German (the *Gesamtausgabe*) moves slowly toward its eventual goal of publishing thirty-three thick, annotated volumes of Weber materials, much of it, particularly the letters, currently unknown. Out of this cornucopia, of course, even more and improved translations will surely be made into all the major languages. (Weber has a particularly strong following in Japan, for example.) Although it would be facile, therefore, to summarize under a few simple topic headings everything that is going on today under the Weberian big top, there are noticeable tendencies which have differentiated themselves to some extent from those that held the attention of scholars in preceding decades.

Very much unlike his peers, Durkheim and Simmel, Weber's works had not been deemed worthy of attention by English-language translators until well into the century. Finally in the 1930s Weber gained some currency in the Anglophone world, but even then he was generally misclassified as an unusually broad-gauged historian of socio-economic change, since only his *General Economic History* (1927) and *The Protestant Ethic* (1930) were the only extant translations for many years after his death. As is well known, the former work was assembled posthumously from sets of student notes taken in a course called "Outlines of Universal Social and Economic History" which Weber gave at Munich in the winter term of 1919-1920, materials he never imagined to constitute a finished work. He offered this course due to student demand, and to counter the perceived aridity of his previous lectures on "conceptual foundations" of social science (which apparently drove away students *en masse*), and it was later issued as Part One of *Economy and Society. The Protestant Ethic*, the much more famous piece, came from revised and augmented versions of two essays Weber published as journal articles in 1904-05, and the voluminous debates they inspired until about 1910 when Weber publicly retired from the argument. To these materials was added a 1920 introduction written for another purpose, plus a foreword by R.H. Tawney, a noted British economic historian. Not until the late 1940s were what became the two warhorses of Weber scholarship available to readers of English, *From Max Weber* (1946) and *The Theory of Social and Economic Organization* (Part I of *Economy and Society*) (1947), which have remained in print continuously ever since. During the 1950s many more Weber works appeared, most notably his comparative studies of world religions, some of his methodological essays, his sociology of law, and the fragmentary sociology of music.

It was at this point that Reinhard Bendix published his *Max Weber: An Intellectual Portrait* (1960), a book which more than any other shaped learned opinion across disciplines about Weber's sociological and political theorizing, and served as a surrogate for those thousands of social scientists for whom the original or translated works themselves proved too much of a burden to absorb. Although a few reviewers, like C. Wright Mills, found Bendix's version of Weber objectionably "bloodless," for the great majority Bendix's interpretation became dogma, and remained so until at least the early 1980s when specialist monographs (there are now dozens) and a few full-scale treatments began to appear which were intentionally constructed around more "nuanced" approaches to Weber's complicated life and work (e.g., Käsler, 1979/1988).

In short, the "Weber industry" has imitated the Dow Jones Average during the last twenty years, so that what was still in the 1960s and 1970s a more or less tractable accumulation of scholarship, either generally inspired by Weber's ideas or directly attentive to his own work, has since then become a mountain too high for any one scholar to climb without losing consciousness. What I want to do in this chapter is give a topographical description of part of this comprehensive, embracing Weberian terrain as seen from an airplane overhead, rather than digging into specific debates at ground level, some of which are so intricate as almost to defy solution (e.g., the precise relationship between Weber's writings and those of the greatest German writer, Goethe; or how exactly was Weber's greatest work, *Economy and Society*, constructed into book form after his death; or, in what ways does the Protestant Ethic thesis apply to farming communities in Wisconsin in the mid-nineteenth century).

Weber and the Journalism of His Time

Thanks to the spadework of Hanno Hardt (1979) and Wilhelm Hennis (1998), we now have a fairly complete picture of Weber's ancillary "career" as a journalist, as well as his two proposals to colleagues that newspapers be studied very carefully, that a "sociology of the press" be developed under their collective guidance. He believed that the new professional association of sociologists that he and his friends founded could legitimate its academic presence if sociology applied itself to ventures such as this, which did not at the time fall within the province of any other discipline. It was only by supplying studies of this practical type, focusing on specific social institutions, and not by concocting yet another "general theory of society" of the sort that were popular in the nineteenth century, that sociology might silence its many critics in history, philosophy, economics, and political science.

His elaborate proposal was made public at the first meeting of the German Sociological Society (October, 1910 in Frankfurt), calling for a thoroughly detailed study of newspapers, not only in Germany, but also in Britain, France, and the U.S. His plan for the empirical study included two parts, one concerning the practical business of publishing newspapers for profit, while the other and theoretically more interesting phase pertained to identifying the mechanisms by which newspapers created and shaped public opinion. This document was included in his collected writings on "sociology and social policy," a volume first published in Germany in 1924. But the report itself was not translated into English until 1976 (then reissued by Hardt in 1979). A draft version was found in the papers of Ferdinand Tönnies and also of Werner Sombart, which, in turn, was finally published in English in 1998. From these sources can be gleaned a good sense of the importance that newspapers held for Weber, not only as a lifelong consumer of politically inspired news stories, but also as a contributor to many debates in a range of publications. Given that his father was an important politico in Bismarck's Germany, careful attention to remarks in the press would have come quite naturally to Max, Jr.

The newspapers with which Weber was affiliated, either as a columnist or in some editorial capacity included the *Frankfurter Zeitung*, *Die Hilfe*, *Die Zeit* (published 1896-1903), *Evangelisch-soziale Zeitfragen* (as editor in 1891), *Neue Preussische (Kreuz-) Zeitung* (editorial writer), *Berliner Tageblatt*, *Berliner Börsenzeitung*, and *Münchner Neueste Nachrichten*. (Many of his columns are collected in Weber's *Gesammelte Politische Schriften*.) Hanno Hardt makes the important point that the level of literary and political sophistication that Weber could count on among readers of these papers was very high (Hardt, 1979: 161), and worlds removed from any newspapers printed today in the U.S. with the possible exceptions of the *Wall Street Journal* and the *New York Times*. The role of newspapers in creating what Weber thought of as "modern man" fascinated and troubled him. In his proposal for research on the "new" media, he wondered aloud to his distinguished colleagues about a range of issues, from the purely mundane to the most elevated. For instance, it interested him that newspapers were a unique capitalist production in that too many customers could pose a financial dilemma unless advertising revenues kept up, thereby controlling per/copy production costs. Newspapers were unique in requiring just the right balance between paying readers and paying advertisers, but if too many readers wished to buy individual copies, it could pose a threat to the paper's survival as a capitalist firm. At the other extreme, Weber wondered about the role of journalists viewed cross-culturally. In Britain the most esteemed journalists entered Parliament and were knighted, and in France they could also become important political actors, but in Germany they were often treated as lackeys of the powers-that-be or of special interests, therefore regarded by the upper crust as slightly disreputable, if necessary, acquaintances. Similarly, Weber observed that French newspaper readers expected highly opinionated writing, full of baroque rhetoric and strongly argued positions, whereas British and German readers seemed to look more for "objective" reporting. American news readers, however, demanded "strictly the facts," believing that each person was capable of evaluating the news for themselves and was not in need of being told what to think. Finally, and in keeping with his sustained interest in the phenomenon of "charisma," he asked to what extent newspapers could create celebrities out of whole cloth, and thereby direct public perception and policy through the flimsiest connection to "real" life. Weber goes through all these issues and many more in his proposals for a "sociology of the press," which makes these two short pieces unique in the literature of classical social theory. From all this it becomes obvious that Weber anticipated a great many issues that came to worry media critics in succeeding decades, from the sublime meditations of Walter Lippmann in the 1920s to the most recent research in media studies programs that have proliferated throughout U.S. universities.

Weber was so entranced with the business of newspapers and their effects on a growing mass culture that during the last few months of his life, he told his wife he would become a full-time political journalist himself, or a publisher, should the need arise:

> "*Make money*"? Yes, but how? That is the question for me. Instead of playing professor, I would have to go to work for a newspaper or a publisher *here* [Munich], and to do this I would have no objection. After all, I can do such administrative work better than this academic gabbing [*Kolleg-Schwätzerei*], which *never* gives me spiritual satisfaction." (Marianne Weber, 1975: 692-93)

The polarity implied in his letter to Marianne, between the robust existence of the journalist versus the effete remove from the everyday rough-and-tumble that German mandarins preferred, parallels Weber's dual, divided, even tortured commitment to large-scale social research (that used questionnaires and other ordinary means of study) in contrast to his probing philosophical ruminations about the ultimate direction and meaning of Western culture. Put more simply, journalism kept him in touch with "real life" in ways that academic "*Schwätzerei*" could not, and he needed both.

Though it is not feasible here to capture even the main drift of Weber's ideas regarding the press, a few of his remarks are worth reproducing in order to convey a sense of his concern for the project, and for understanding the meaning of mass media in rapidly democratizing societies:

> 1. "Newspapers which certainly do not collect the most sublime examples of literary culture, however, cement the masses together quite effectively."

2. "So-called 'public opinion' under the conditions of mass-democracy is a communal activity born of irrational 'feelings' (*Gefühl*) and normally stage-directed by party leaders and press.

3. "We must examine the press to this end: What does it contribute to the making of modern man? Secondly, how are the objective, supra-individual cultural values influenced, what shifts occur, what is destroyed and newly created of the beliefs and hopes of the masses: of the *Lebensgefühle*—as they say today—, what is forever destroyed and newly created of the potential point of view?"

4. "Gentleman, as we know, there has been an attempt to examine the effects of the press on the human brain, the question about the consequences of the fact that before he leaves for his daily work modern man has become used to absorbing a journalistic hotch-potch which forces him on a hurried trip through all areas of cultural life, from political to the theatre, and many other subjects. That this makes a difference is obvious. . . One will have to start with the question: what is the effect of newspapers on the kind of reading habits of modern man? On this all kinds of theories have been constructed. There was also the argument that the book is being replaced by the newspapers."

5. "The press is involved in making what are, without doubt, tremendous changes in reading habits, and immense changes of the character and of the manner in which modern man absorbs the external world. The constant change . . . rest[s] with an enormous weight upon the uniqueness of modern man. But how? This we must examine. We must examine the press first to this end: what does it contribute to the making of modern man? Secondly: how are the objective, supra-individual cultural values influenced, what shifts occur, what is destroyed and newly created of the beliefs and hopes of the masses?

Marianne Weber reported that after a couple of years and failing to raise the 25,000 Marks needed for the study, Weber withdrew. He had sued a newspaper for publishing demeaning remarks about his wife's work as a feminist publicist and author, so he thought he could not simultaneously study newspapers and be in court against one. With all this in mind it becomes fascinating to wonder how Weber would respond to seeing the use of his own name in the global media market today, and how he would have proposed that we study this and related phenomena.

Weber and His Image in Today's Popular Press

The formerly sharp demarcation between "serious" thought and the discourse of mass media, particularly of the printed form, has lately become blurred at points almost beyond distinction, following closely Marshall McLuhan's predictions of forty years ago. So before attending, however briefly, to the mountain of scholarly contributions that are clearly Weberian in nature, it might be useful to consider, as a micro case-study in the sociology of public knowledge, how Weber's name and reputation are currently exploited in the mass media. Put another way, why has the descriptor "Weberian" begun to be recognized among ever-larger numbers of readers with the same facility that "Freudian" has been known since the 1930s? (I speak here only of English-language cultures, since his name has long been better known in Europe among well-educated readers for a variety of reasons, partly to do with a different division of labor there between academics and journalists). It is fair to say that prior to the 1980s or so, his name was scarcely known to journalists, but as the cadre of "public intellectuals" or quasi-intellectuals themselves became more widely educated as a group, and as the labor market for their talents pushed them out of universities and into magazine or newspaper production, Weber became not only a historically recognizable and intriguing person, but an icon of sorts.

Probably the most important sign that Weber had crossed from the seminar room into public discourse was his central importance in Allan Bloom's *The Closing of the American Mind* (Bloom, 1987), a semi-scholarly polemic that sold in the hundreds of thousands and was serialized in daily newspapers (e.g., the *Kansas City Star*). By using a caricatured argument first put forth by his beloved teacher, Leo Strauss (Strauss, 1953: 36-78), Bloom's international bestseller argued somewhat preposterously that Nietzsche and Weber, in a combined assault upon so-called "Western cultural values," had themselves led the "youth movement" of the 1960s down the road of axiological nihilism. This dire development, Bloom argued forcefully, had in turn helped cause a Spengler-like "decline" in civility, educational standards, sexual morality, and associated features of cultural decomposition. This extraordinary contention was widely reported, reproduced, and apparently accepted by numbers of readers whose familiarity with Weber's own works seemed to go no further than Bloom's misuse of them. (The Bloom publishing and public relations phenomenon has been immortalized in Saul Bellow's notorious novel, *Ravelstein*, wherein the author, Bloom's close personal friend, explains in explicit terms just how and why Bloom/Ravelstein chose to condemn trends in contemporary culture which flew in the face of his own aesthetic and intellectual penchants, and which appeared to Bloom to be the Mephistophelian work of Weber and Nietzsche. Bellow writes: "Ravelstein... quoted Schiller to the same effect: 'Live with your century but do not be its creature'" [Bellow, 2000: 82].)

In another book, while eulogizing Strauss, Bloom observed that "Strauss recognized the seriousness and nobility of Max Weber's mind, but he showed that he was a derivative thinker, standing somewhere between modern science and Nietzsche, unable to resolve their tensions" (Bloom, 1990: 238). There is no room here to investigate the flourishing debate over the strengths and weaknesses of Strauss's rationalist political philosophy. But it is important only to note that the joint effect of Strauss having declared that Weber's thought was "derivative," stranded between scientism and nihilism, plus Bloom's broadcasting this view to the world at large (very few ordinary readers ever having heard of Leo Strauss) established in "popular consciousness" a straw man of Weber, and one that only recently has begun to diminish in the mass media. For the record, Weber never claimed for an instant to be an "original thinker." His modesty, however, did not prevent one of Germany's most original philosophers of the twentieth century, Karl Jaspers, from characterizing Weber as "the greatest German of our era" (Jaspers, 1989: 31), an epithet that has become famous since he wrote it in 1958. But that aside, if there is any truth to Whitehead's claim that "In Western literature there are four great thinkers....These men are Plato, Aristotle, Leibniz, and William James" (Whitehead, 1938, p. 2), or, as he is often quoted, "Western philosophy is a footnote to Plato," then being "derivative" seems a universal fate. The real question, one could argue, is which writers are "more or less" derivative.

The more important issue is Bloom's charge that Weber's cultural influence has been pernicious, an accusation that still remains in place among literate non-theorists, largely owing to Bloom's posthumous influence and that of his imitators and students. One way of answering Bloom, though too briefly, is to remind his believing readers that Weber never held a brief for a particular set of values, epistemological or otherwise, unless he was writing an explicitly political tract. He simply reported what he uncovered using historical and contemporary data, in the most objective and value-free terms he could muster. And what he saw within Western culture at the fin-de-siécle provoked in him grave forebodings about the future of Europe and all those countries which imitated its general model of social organization. Now needless to say, these misgivings were fully borne out in the forty-five years following Weber's unforgettable imagery at the close of the two essays (1904-05) which became known in English as *The Protestant Ethic and the Spirit of Capitalism*.

In [Richard] Baxter's view the care for external goods should only lie on the shoulders of the "saint like a light cloak, which can be thrown aside at any moment." But fate decreed that the cloak should become an iron cage.

> Since asceticism undertook to remodel the world and to work out its ideals in the world, material goods have gained an increasing and finally an inexorable power over the lives of men as at no previous period in history.

. . .In the field of its highest development, in the United States, the pursuit of wealth, stripped of its religious and ethical meaning, tends to become associated with purely mundane passions, which often actually give it the character of sport.

No one knows who will live in this cage in the future, or whether at the end of this tremendous development entirely new prophets will arise. . . . For of the last stage of this cultural development, it might well be truly said: "Specialists without spirit, sensualists without heart; this nullity imagines that it has attained a level of civilization never before achieved." (Weber, 1930, pp. 181-182; for the possible origin of the famous final quotation, see Sica, 1985)

I do not repeat these honored passages from Weber's most quotable book because they are unknown, but because they have recently come under re-examination for reasons Weber would never have imagined. This is one of Weber's charms, if I may put it that way.

He crafted the final paragraphs of his book with a burst of uncharacteristic rhetoric, a flurry of human sentiment, which he normally excluded from his "scientific" writing. The reason his words proved prescient and, if correctly read today, illustrate the inaccuracy of Bloom's charges against Weber (conflated somewhat with Nietzsche) is because his hopes for human liberation in the twentieth century lay not with regimentation and "rationalization processes," but with their opposite. He never renounced the national-liberal tradition in which he was reared, never underestimated the significance of the nation-state in global politics, or the necessary harshness of *Realpolitik*. But he believed, as did Leo Strauss, that certain, definable human values were preservative of global society, and others wholly destructive. The difference between them, and therefore with Bloom, lay in Weber's highly skeptical view of modernity, in his unwillingness to believe that the machinery of bureaucratized production and government would relinquish its iron grip on well-meaning individuals, and allow them to pursue the philosophically virtuous lives that Strauss and Bloom recommended. Weber's "sin," does not lie in promoting destructive values for the twentieth century, but in believing that the era of individual righteousness had ended for macro-structural reasons—with the invention of the machinegun, barbed wire, poison gas, and high explosives (my own expression, and not Weber's).

Bloom's student, friend, and beneficiary, Francis Fukuyama, exploded onto the highbrow popular culture scene in 1992 with *The End of History and the Last Man*, the first of three books that borrowed heavily from "serious" social and political theory and applied these ideas to contemporary concerns. Most recently he addressed the "literate middle class" in one of their favorite organs, the *Atlantic Monthly*, with a cover story designed to encourage Americans who had wearied of the social initiatives begun in the 1960s and now shown, so he claims, to be at the root of today's major forms of social disorganization (Fukuyama, 1999a). Once again Weber's name appears in multiple contexts, but usually under the same general theme: the dark, brooding, Germanic presence whose dread of modernity's apparent direction seems unduly fearsome to more optimistic spirits, like Fukuyama. It is unnecessary to recount the main argument to his first book, nor the subsequent two of the series (Fukuyama, 1995; 1999b), other than to say that their general proclamation of "glad tidings" plays very well among victims of a shaken world-order, yet would have been given short shrift by Weber, I suspect. The very virtues that Karl Jaspers saw in Weber—incorrigible honesty and acute insight, realism, and a refusal to indulge in mystical escape from painful truths—are missing or highly diluted in books like Fukuyama's. Part of being a Weberian lies in the responsibility to bear up under the weight of bad news without being rendered helpless by it, and this central ingredient of Weber's worldview seems always to be lacking in popularizations purporting to solve world problems through inspirational rhetoric. In short, "New Age" philosophy and Weberian thinking are antonymous.

Weber's name and his image, of the hyper-serious, brooding Teuton, are appearing more regularly in the popular press than ever before, according to the data that have come my way. In a *New York Times* review of John Diggins's *Max Weber*, the political theorist Alan Ryan concludes his remarks by observing "[The book's] purpose is an essentially uncomfortable one. It is to get readers to take Weber's distaste for the brashness, vulgarity and general foolishness of modern democratic societies as seriously as he, John Patrick Diggins, takes it. In that he is rather successful, not in showing that Weber's distaste was right, but in demonstrating that Weber made a case that needs to be answered—and today, surely, more urgently than ever" (Ryan, 1996). Ryan, as a renowned political philosopher, speaks with considerable authority, while other writers usually refer to Weber (far more often than actually quoting him) to validate some broad generalization they seek to make. But occasionally a truly interesting connection to Weber's influence is made, as in another recent *Atlantic Monthly* piece about today's re-evaluation of Confucius: "Zhang Binglin used the cultural-evolutionary theories of Weber and Herbert Spencer to recast Kongzi ["Master Kong," i.e., Confucius] as a secular quasi-modern, China's first rationalizer of a superstitious indigenous tradition" (Allen, 1999: 83). This quotation manages to include a range of Weberian concerns: the role of the traditional intelligentsia in either promoting or retarding "modernization" ("rationalization") processes, the importance of charisma in a cultural or political leader, and the routine redefinition of cultural heritages in the face of societal evolution. In fact, the author might well have had a hard time even conceptualizing the quoted sentence without an awareness of the Weberian viewpoint regarding Confucian ethics and its role in Chinese economic history (as explained in Weber, 1951).

Numerous other citations to Weber's ideas or his person have become available in sub-scholarly publications during the recent past. A few examples might give the general flavor of uses to which the Weberian heritage is now being put, for good or otherwise. Restricting ourselves to the last three years, one can find an abundance of references to Weber from the global press, not all of them mere grace notes to a given text's larger theme. Andrew Porter in the *New York Times Book Review*, evaluating a major book by the historian David Landes, observes:

> Landes's list of false prophets with misguided diagnoses is long. It includes dependency theorists; the new economic historians, who neglect older findings and dismiss any such thing as the Industrial Revolution; econometricians in pursuit of numbers, however unreal; multiculturalists irrelevantly quibbling over the terminology of European "discovery" of the rest of the world; ethnologists denying that there are grounds for criticizing or detecting weaknesses in another culture. By contrast, he admires the champion of the Protestant ethic Max Weber, and Karl Wittfogel, the outstanding student of what he calls "Oriental despotism." "If we learn anything from the history of economic development, it is that culture makes all the difference," Landes says. (Porter, 1998: 15)

This use of Weber, particularly as a polemical weapon, is important in this context since Landes is a distinguished historian (especially of Egyptian economic history, and of timepieces), and the enclaves he is attacking by means of Weber have been for some time in the seat of academic power, especially in the U.S. It is instructive that the reviewer is British. That Weber is made out to be "the champion" of the Protestant Ethic, of course, is a distorting simplification, as clearly indicated by the quotation above from the closing pages of that essential book. But his identification with that ever-growing stream of research on the relationship between religious impulses and socio-economic action in some ways resembles Freud's connection in the "popular mind" with "id, ego, and superego," terms which in his own work are far from crystalline.

Mortimer Zuckerman, editor-in-chief of *U.S. News* called upon Weber similarly in the context of "Creators of Our Prosperity," a paean to Bill Gates: "However, the predominant view of entrepreneurs is pejorative, and the vocabulary is one of selfishness, greed, and self-interest. As George Gilder has written, it is as if 'our wealth springs from some Faustian pact: a deal with the devil by which we gain material benefits in exchange for succumbing to the sin of avarice,' while millions of worthy poor go hungry. Such a negative perception goes back a long way. Max Weber commented on it in *The Protestant Ethic and the Spirit of Capitalism*: "A flood of mistrust, sometimes of hatred, above all of moral indignation, regularly opposed itself to the first innovator" (Zuckerman, 1998: 64; quotation is from Weber, 1930: 69). Linking Gilder and Weber falls under the heading of journalistic license, but the quotation from *PE* is a good one, and not often seen, even in the scholarly literature. Zuckerman claims that "American capitalism" managed to "confirm Weber's insight" by employing innovative trade practices and invention rather than hiding behind trade tariffs. The fact that this seriously distorts not only the record of American innovation proper, but also Weber's intensely nationalist appreciation for German trade barriers does not detract overmuch from the good use made here of his major ideas. Along with Lester Thurow, Weber is the only scholar named in Zuckerman's strongly worded endorsement of Gates' entrepreneurial "spirit." Thus, when an opinion-maker of high visibility such as Zuckerman chooses to speak of capitalist creativity, he turns without many alternatives (Sombart now being forgotten) to Weber.

This is only one step lower on the intellectual ladder from theologian Michael Novak's apologias for capitalist "ethics," including *The Spirit of Democratic Capitalism*, *The Catholic Ethic and the Spirit of Capitalism* and *Business as a Calling: Work and the Examined Life*, all of them clearly imitating Weber's conceptual lead. As a winner of the stupendous Templeton Prize, Novak became an official spokesperson for what might be called "Christian business practices," if such a phrase were not at base oxymoronic. He, too, often quotes Weber while trying to legitimate worldwide predatory capitalist practices (e.g., Novak, 1996: 80-81, 119-120.) That Weber would almost surely regard Novak's "casuistry"— precisely the right word for Novak's thinking, and one which Weber applied even to himself—as subtle capitalist propaganda does not detract from the fact that without Weber's ideas, writers like Novak would only be able to construct a much less coherent argument. The same can be said for a British columnist who begins an op-ed piece in the *Guardian* (London) thus: "Passivity and fatalism used to be regarded as oriental failings by Rudyard Kipling and his like. These characteristics were often attributed, no doubt falsely, to the influence of oriental religions compared with the capitalist-oriented Protestantism celebrated by Max Weber" (Holtham, 1998: 17). This smattering of learning is typical in the higher echelons of the British press, once again setting up a straw man to which is attached the label "Max Weber."

A staff writer from the European office of the *Wall Street Journal* took another route down the Weberian linguistic path while reviewing a philosophy book: "...illegitimate application of scientific reasoning tends to shrink our world, to 'disenchant' it, in Max Weber's famous term" (Pollock, 1998). The German term, *Entzauberung*, means literally to remove magic, to "de-magicalize," for which "disenchantment" is not a wholly satisfactory translation, particularly given the cultural background to Weber's particular use of the word. Nevertheless, it has become a readily recognizable term in the Weberian language of cultural criticism, though one whose prominence today would probably surprise and annoy Weber since it seems to make of him an epigone of Nietzsche (reminiscent of Bloom's accusation). Still another Weberianism (if I may coin a term) appears in a review of Daniel P. Moynihan's *Secrecy*: "As noted by historian Richard Gid Powers in his trenchant introduction, Moynihan's most formidable insight (borrowed from Max Weber) is that secrecy is a form of regulation in which bureaucrats hoard secrets like assets" (*Kirkus Reviews*, 1998). It is interesting that this rather minor point in Weber's definitive analysis of bureaucratic behavior, as intriguing as it is given today's post-Watergate political culture, should be "Moynihan's most formidable insight," apparently rediscovered by the senator ninety years after Weber first made it part of his encompassing theory of organizational functioning. Yet as is so often the case, the anonymous reviewer nodded toward Weber primarily in order to indicate that Moynihan's analysis of Washington's political life is more "serious" and "theoretically grounded" than the run-of-the-mill D.C. memoir.

Within a month of Holtham's piece in the *Guardian*, a columnist for the *Wall Street Journal* made use of still another chestnut from the Weber lexicon: "Death and enemies drive dictators from power, but notable democratic leaders have fallen time and again at the hands of electorates whose gratitude has worn thin under the grind of politics; sociologist Max Weber called this phenomenon 'routinization of charisma.' Weber held that a leader can keep his job only by repeatedly demonstrating his specialness" (Steinmetz, 1998). It becomes clear, then, that as one proceeds through a range of more or less highbrow organs of mass culture, a briskly formed familiarity with Weber's ideas becomes discernible, as key phrases appear regularly: Protestant Ethic thesis, iron cage of bureaucratized life, transformations of charismatic authority to fit modern politics, and so on. What is lacking, of course, is any contextual or elaborated understanding of what exactly Weber intended by these terms, and to which historical configurations he intended them to be applied. Still another gambit, particularly popular since 1989, is to announce that "Max Weber has triumphed over Karl Marx" (MacShane, 1998). Given that during Weber's first year of teaching, he led his students through Marx's *Das Kapital* with painstaking thoroughness, and that his comments on Marx's work were invariably respectful, remarks of this order substitute the crass political symbols "Marx" and "Weber" for the scholars known by the same names.

The most amusing popular use of Weber during 1998 appeared in the *Observer*, where Simon Caulkin described him under the rubric of the "Guru Guide" of the week, apparently a regular feature of the paper. Scanning the formulaic categories "Age," "Claim to fame," "Biography," "Achievement," and "Said," the busy modern reader can "get the gist" of Weberian theory in only 276 words. One of his alleged "claims to fame" is "co-draughtsman of the constitution of the Weimar Republic," an odd and insupportable remark when the details of the case are studied carefully; in fact, Weber's most cherished ideas and suggestions were jettisoned by the constitution's real author, Hugo Preuss (Mommsen, 1984: 332-389; Halperin, 1946: 154-167). Nevertheless, Caulkin admirably captures what I referred to above as "the Weberian mood":

> Although Weber is ridiculed [by whom?] for his description of the ideal bureaucracy as "the most rational means of carrying out imperative control over human beings," history has the last, and darker, laugh. Today's call-centres and fast-food outlets do nothing to dispel Weber's thesis of a society increasingly alienated by formal rationality; nor his insight that formal rationality often has irrational consequences (such as the dehumanisation of work). Weber also wrote tellingly about hierarchy, leadership and authority. Neo-Weberians, of which there are many, sometimes suggest that Scott Adams, creator of Dilbert, is their man in disguise.

I do not know any neo-Weberians who have made the connection in print between Dilbert and Weber's theorizing—perhaps because it is too obvious to merit mention—though for years I have indeed pointed to this confluence in my lectures to undergraduates. What is most intriguing about Caulkin's précis of Weber's ideas is that it appears on the "*Observer* Work Page," presumably for the edification of the busy executive who might want to know the serious background to Dilbert's black humor.

The final entry of popularized Weberianism from 1998 is a brief but dense article in the less ordinary venue, *Management Today*. Borrowing from a 1967 polemic against psychological theory by Arthur Koestler, the author entitles his comment "The Ghost in the Machine." Stuart Crainer quotes lightly from Parsons's 1947 translation of *Wirtschaft und Gesellschaft* (Part One), arguing that "The man saddled with the reputation of being the founding father of the mechanistic world view is Max Weber." The bureaucratic "machine" was to work efficiently, as Weber described it, and human "needs" (of the kind Marx wrote about) became irrelevant. "But this does not mean that Weber advocated the bureaucratic system. He simply described it...In many ways the bureaucratic world mapped out by Weber is similar to Orwell's *1984*: a nightmare scenario rather than a prediction. In some respects, the nightmare has come to pass. Henry Ford echoed many of Weber's thoughts in his faith in strict demarcations and a fervently mechanistic approach to business. Ford preferred science to art. 'How come when I want a pair of hands, I get a human being as well?' he lamented" (Crainer, 1998: 87). While linking Orwell and Weber has become a standard ploy among cultural critics, the tie with Ford is less plausible, since his unapologetic, aggressive capitalism shared very little with Weber's humanistic values. Though granting that the machine "metaphor" (here falsely attributed to Weber) has now been replaced with those of "fractals and amoebas—elusive and ever-changing rather than efficient and static," Crainer ends his piece in a way that has become standard fare for journalists who exploit Weber's larger ideas: "Even so, Max Weber remains important. . . Weber's bureaucratic model stands as a constant reminder of what could be. Aspects of the bureaucratic model remain alive in many organisations. Weber's world lives on and not only in our nightmares" (ibid.).

Weber's name, often attached to some of his best-known ideas, continued to appear in the mass media dozens of times in 1999 and 2000. There is no room here to analyze carefully even the most provocative samples of this peculiar, relatively new form of transplantation—moving material from texts of the most densely systematic social thought into those which suit the facile needs of everyday journalism. A dozen items from 1999 exhibit an even wider range of usages than those from the preceding year. From the subcontinent, a letter to the *New Statesman* quotes Weber's "insightful" *Religion of India* in order to buttress a subtle argument regarding today's caste system (Sarbadhikari, 1999). Another uses Ritzer's "McDonalization thesis," as an extension of Weber's rationalization theory, to explain why modern tourism has become "a version of being at home" (Boddy, 1999). A feature story in *Lingua Franca* characterizes Roberto Unger's recent utopianism as "a fusion of Christian romanticism, Max Weber, and the Marquis de Sade," surely an improbable amalgam, and one that would probably have perplexed even Weber (Press, 1999). At the other extreme, a British historian nominates Weber as an "overrated author" in the *Sunday Telegraph* (London): "It is a sign of a truly overblown reputation when one is referred to rather than actually read. Weber's theory that the industrious culture of capitalism evolved from the ascetic culture of Puritanism is well known. But who has actually waded through *The Protestant Ethic*... Anyone who bothers will be dismayed by the discrepancy between Weber's huge assertions and the tiny empirical basis on which they rest... There is no denying that Weber had big ideas" (Ferguson, 1999). (Apparently, Professor Ferguson had a change of heart between 1999 and 2003, since he—you will recall from the opening of this chapter—relies faithfully upon Weber's argument to support the drift of his latest op-ed piece in the *New York Times*, which deals precisely in these issues.) This is a standard dismissal, particularly from Catholic writers, but given that no fewer than two new English translations of *The Protestant Ethic* have recently been published, with another promised, and that serious re-analysis of Weber's "thesis" continues apace, assertions like those of Ferguson's seem futile. In fact, the opposite viewpoint was expressed within several months in the *Daily Telegraph* (London) under the heading "Weber was Right": "Max Weber's theory about the correlation between Protestantism and progress may be discredited by many of your readers (letters, July 3), but it is alive and thriving in South America. During the past two decades, many South Americans have abandoned 'Marxist' Catholicism for the unashamedly capitalist fervour of the growing evangelical Protestant churches throughout Brazil, Argentina, and Mexico. In Brazil the evangelical Protestants are transforming the urban poor into a new entrepreneurial class. They have formed a separate political group in parliament and are doing for Brazil what Methodism did for Britain during the early stages of the industrial revolution" (O'Grady, 1999). Philip Jenkins has recently published an entire book that validates and expands on O'Grady's insight (Jenkins, 2002).

The use of Weber's name as a cultural "icon" further illustrates that even for those millions who will never "wade through" *The Protestant Ethic* or *Economy and Society*, his larger ideas—or the popularized surrogates for the actual ideas themselves—somehow "resonate" with today's cultural themes. In one whimsical article, Max Weber is claimed to form a so-called "mondegreen" (i.e., the mishearing of popular song lyrics, slogans, or sayings) for the words "Las Vegas" (Carroll, 1999). In another, serious article from the *New York Times* about software and human thought, the puzzling observation is made that "Academic critics echo the arguments made by Max Weber and Marshall McLuhan ("the medium is the message") that form has a critical impact on content" (Zuckerman, 1999). Linking Weber and McLuhan might be feasible in some contexts, but this instance is ingenuous, first, because the observation attributed to both men is a platitude, and second, because to my knowledge Weber never wrote anything about this general topic. At a higher level, but in the same zone of rhetorical impertinence, a reviewer of a scholarly book about ancient Athens begins with, "To possess the capacity to be amazed by the world, Max Weber wrote, is a prerequisite of all unbiased inquiry. The Classical Athenians had this capacity in abundance..." (Stace, 1999). Here it is enough, so the reviewer apparently believes, to invoke Weber's name in order to set the correct tone of high seriousness for what follows. With less solemnity, the *Independent* (London) offered this "Thought for the Day": "The experience of the irrationality of the world has been the driving force of all religious revolution," attributed to "Max Weber, German sociologist" (the *Independent*, 2000). One wonders what the newspaper's readers made of this decontextualized observation since Weber specialists are still debating its precise meaning.

Weber's name seems to spark imaginations across the globe, at least in the higher reaches of print journalism, especially as a handy device for grabbing the reader's attention. Closer to home, a reviewer in the *Washington Post* opens an essay with "It was the roaring '90s—the 1690s—and British investors were swept up in a passion for new technologies, emerging markets and new theories of the discounted value of future earnings. Initial pubic offerings were the rage, new financial derivatives were invented, and ordinary citizens invested as never before. Centuries later, the era's commercial zeal was even elevated to philosophical heights *by no less* than Max Weber, who declared the robust capitalism of the age an extension of the Enlightenment and evidence of the triumph of rationalism (Mufson, 1999, emphasis added). That this is almost entirely wrong regarding Weber's ideas—*not* the Enlightenment but the Reformation, not "rationalism" but "rational action"—is beside the point. What matters in this context is that the words "Max Weber" when used in concert have become part of the lingua franca of "civilized discourse," a shorthand notation covering a range of socio-cultural concerns which even a decade ago would not have seemed plausible. When a Scottish journalist writes, "Take away or undervalue these things [cultural values] and we reduce teachers to what Max Weber called specialists without spirit, soulless technicians constructing machines rather than forming persons," he efficiently situates his argument in a proud polemical lineage against the mediocre and overly rationalized (Reilly, 1999). Other recent linkages to Weber were forged regarding the St. Louis Exposition of 1904, which Weber attended (Tolson, 1999), the relationship of Hans Kelsen, the great legal theorist, to Weber as explained by a celebrated German novelist and jurist (Schlink, 1999), and Mother Teresa's "indefinable quality that Max Weber called charisma" (Johnson, 2000).

During the first part of 2000, Weber has even been used for academic humor: "Refusing to be hemmed in with a 'career,' Ralf Gothoni, the Finnish pianist-conductor, echoes Max Weber, the German founder of modern sociology, who once complained, 'I do not have a field because I am not a donkey'" (Binaghi, 2000). It seems that Weber's sentiments are now entering the realm of the apocryphal. Competition between journalists to cite Weber even hints at mild plagiarism, for example, an editorial from the *Economist* begins "Max Weber once described politics as a struggle between bureaucracy and charisma" (*Economist*, 2000), when from India only four weeks later a similar piece opens thus: "Max Weber once described politics as a struggle between charisma and bureaucracy" (Pande, 2000). Other works within the same few months allude to Weber's distinction in "Politics as a Vocation" between those who live "for politics" versus "from politics" (Martinez-Saenz, 2000), or Weber's ideas about how historical causality should be established (Mclynn, 2000). And in the opening pages of a popular book, *Bobos in Paradise* about today's nouveau riche, the author comments, "Finally, a word about the tone of this book. There aren't a lot of statistics in these pages. There's not much theory. Max Weber has nothing to worry about from me" (Brooks, 2000). Of all the names Brooks could have chosen to distinguish his chatty social analysis from "theory" proper, Weber's apparently seemed to him the most austere or authoritative.

The most important recent comparison between Weber and another social analyst has occurred in the British press, where Manuel Castells's latest, essentially cheery pronouncements about globalization and the internet-driven economy have pointedly been compared to the otherwise unrivalled Weber. For example, "Castells will be ranked by future generations as comparable in breadth and stature to Max Weber or Emile Durkheim" (Taylor, 2000), or "[Castells's book] *The Information Age: Economy, Society, and Culture* [is] a work which, in one admiring view, does for the internet economy what Max Weber's *The Protestant Ethic*...did for the industrial age a century. Like Weber, Castells is European... He is also a social theorist." The author later wisely observes that "Castells's internet is also a deeply unsentimental place, as underdeveloped socially as it is overdeveloped technologically. Weber would recognise it at once. Thus it excludes unwanted elements as ruthlessly as it embraces what's valued" (Caulkin, 2000). A comparison of Castells's work with Weber's along the lines suggested here will likely be carried out by some enterprising graduate student eventually, but one wonders what exactly such a study would yield. In a way, of course, Castells's 1,000-page "three decker" is precisely *not* what the "global libertarian hacker culture" needs or wants from its social theorists—to the extent this "culture" (essentially young males) is aware that such work even exists. If Castells is right about the socially "underdeveloped" nature of globalized electronic "culture," the role of literacy-based social theory of the kind Weber and Durkheim pioneered is thrown entirely into question, in much the same way that classical music has been ousted from the hearts of ordinary people by popular forms ever since World War II. Who can now believe that the Metropolitan Opera radio broadcasts of the 1930s and 1940s were then considered "popular culture"? The reason that Caulkin's premonition about Castells's eventual status as a rival to Weber in the realm of social theory seems far-fetched has less to do with

Castells's abilities than with the nature of reasoned social analysis in a post-literate, image-driven society. Weber chose from an abundance of texts to analyze, and the specific historical groups who tried to live by them. What materials can Castells draw on of comparable intellectual density? And even if they could be shown to exist, to have been created by analogously self-conscious social entities—in ways that resemble the role of Richard Baxter's or John Calvin's writings as part of the Protestant transformation of Europe and the U.S.—where is an audience of the kind who have been studying *The Protestant Ethic* unremittingly for nearly a century?

Lastly, from the plethora of popular references to Weber, several which verge on the absurd: a popular book called *Charisma: Seven Keys to Developing the Magnetism that Leads to Success* (Alessandra, 1998), the advertisement for which reads "Now Tony Alessandra explores the most crucial element in gaining success in every phase of your life. It's the power, mysterious, unstoppable force called...*Charisma*....Breaking down charisma into its key ingredients—the ability to talk, to adapt, to listen, to speak, and to persuade. Using self-quizzes and power examples of charisma in action, Tony offers you a step-by-step program of 'charisma basics.'" Presumably Jesus, Confucius, Luther, Mao Zedong, and others of that ilk would have done even better in their "careers" had they studied this book before "deciding" to become charismatic. A full-page magazine ad for a line of bedding called "Charisma" features a "headshot" of Marilyn Monroe at her most photogenic, with the caption "Some People are Born with Charisma; Others Just Buy It." The Mendel Group, part of "BioMed Management Systems" offered online in 1997 something called the "Rationalization Grid," a term which they copyrighted, that "applies a matrix-based approach to the standard licensing process. Products are selected based on more objective, customized criteria which incorporate rapid screening, classification, and priority ranking of in-licensing candidates based on preset parameters." The language is ersatz Weberian, but the aim seems to revolve around the selection of medical treatments based on a "multi-dimensional matrix" of "pre-set criteria." But surely the most charming "use" of Weber's theoretical insight comes from the cattle-breeding industry. In 1998 a bull named Foreplay, at 2,345 pounds, with suitably impressive scores on both "Frame" and "Scrotal," was described as having fathered calves which brought large prices, from $6K to $22K each: "These calves reflect Foreplay's extreme thickness, moderate frame, whistle front, uncanny style, and *abundance of charisma*. Foreplay has been used successfully on heifers due to the light birth weight of his calves" (SEK Genetics, 1998). Perhaps his owners read Alessandro's book on "how to become charismatic" to the bull when he was young.

It could be argued, and not facetiously, that the proliferating appearances of Weber's name and ideas in the printed mass media are much more important as a contribution to "globalization" than is his perennial popularity among academic scholars. It is often claimed that one defining quality of cross-cultural postmodern culture is the breakdown of barriers between regions, religions, and the finer distinctions of quality that previously held sway. If this is true, then one knowing reference to Weber's ideas, say, about the rationalization process in the *Economist* or the *Washington Post* is surely "worth" a hundred articles in "refereed journals" with readership numbering in the hundreds rather than hundreds of thousands or millions. Though impossible to analyze adequately here, it would seem that this fairly new phenomenon—the "popularization of Weberianism"—will probably itself become a subfield within the "Weber industry" or the sociology of culture in the not too distant future. Such a phenomenon is precisely the sort of pursuit Weber would likely build into a contemporary "sociology of the press" were he still here to carry it out, for it deals directly with an interest that grew ever larger for him as the young twentieth-century unfolded: to what extent the "democratization of culture" (to use Karl Mannheim's term, itself inspired by Weber) would make esoteric knowledge impossible to transmit or use in the public sphere.

Academic Directions of Weberian Scholarship

A distinction could be made, and probably should be, between so-called "substantive" works that are explicitly inspired by one or another of Weber's "big ideas" (e.g., the charismatic nature of the "Founders" of the American Republic) and theoretically motivated writings which probe, expand upon, or truncate an idea or set of notions which Weber offered the social science community during his most fertile creative period. The comprehensive bibliography I have assembled naturally contains far more works of the former type than of the latter. This is because—as evidenced in the journalistic literature—it has become de rigueur for scholars of all kinds to invoke Weber's concepts in order to lend luster to their work, or to clarify a thorny point that crops up in their data that seems otherwise intractable. Yet the number of theorists who have come to know Weber's work thoroughly enough and with sufficient subtlety to expand upon it, or to clarify some notion of his which appears insufficiently lucid in the original, has remained relatively small. Such so-called "hard-core Weberians," despite their pedantic tendencies, play a vital role in clarifying the original texts from semi-philological or purely conceptual points of view. Selected works by Roth (2000), Roth and Schluchter (1979), Mommsen (2000), Hennis (1988), Scaff (1989), Kalberg (1994, 1997), Oakes (1988), or Burger (1976) typify this sort of work, which is as indispensable to a precise understanding of Weber as it is generally unknown to most other researchers who simply utilize one or another of Weber's ideas as it suits their projects.

Yet Weber's ideas have come to "infect" and affect so many realms of scholarship that it would be difficult even to list them all. To take but one typical example, a serious battle of wits has consumed the energies of historians for some time in trying to ascertain the validity of "the Protestant ethic thesis" (in addition to other Weberian notions) when applied to Colonial and Federalist America. Applications of Weber's ideas within the context of American history (which are detailed in chapter 5) are as various as his substantive and theoretical innovations were far-flung. Even while disparaging the "merely theoretical" (see Burke, 1992: 1-11), historians have plundered Weber's ideas when it suited them, even when only half understanding the meaning of his work (for an exception, see Jäger, 1991). Weber's theorizing remains appealing for even skeptical historians, probably because his generalizations always grew directly from contact with historical data of his own collecting, and because he strove to solve substantive problems by means of theoretical innovation, rather than using historical data to legitimize theoretical fantasy.

Perhaps needless to say, many historians have evaluated American Presidents and other leaders in terms of their "charisma" or lack thereof (e.g., Schwartz, 1987 on Washington and Schwartz, 2000 on Lincoln), and scores of additional studies have relied upon Weber's allied explanation of "charismatic domination" (e.g., Lindholm,1990; Spencer, 1980; Peacock, 1989; and Schweitzer, 1984). As mentioned above, the "Protestant ethic thesis" is a longtime favorite for polemics which turn on innovative uses of new data, by now numbering in the thousands. There are numerous subtleties to these arguments, one of which is that Weber did *not* hold that shrewd business practices had never existed in non-Protestant countries. His story instead is that capital accumulation and rational accounting procedures had never found such fertile ideological ground on which to grow as that provided by Reformation theology and the sects which grew out of it. One of Weber's favorite concepts, *Beruf* (vocational dedication or calling), is pivotal to this argument. Important Americanist studies of the connection between devout religiosity and economic prosperity are many (e.g., Axelrad, 1978; Bailyn, 1955; Bier, 1970; Buck, 1993; Cooke, 1994; Henretta, 1991; Johnson, 1971; Kolbenschlag, 1976, and Tolles, 1948), and even if they diverge in subtle details from Weber's original statement (see Lehmann and Roth, 1993; also Hudson, 1988), the centrality of the *PE* thesis cannot be overlooked.

Other important streams of scholarship are connected to the Protestant Ethic debate in the context of American history. The sociologist and historian, Dorothy Ross, has shown that "modernization theory" also springs from Weber's work, as well as that of his colleague and friend, Ferdinand Tönnies (Ross, 1998: 93). These ideas occupy a special place in American culture because they served American political interests during the Cold War as a weapon against revolutionary Marxism. The "psychologizing" for which modernization became famous (and infuriating to some scholars in the developing countries) naturally grew from Weber's portrait of rationalization processes at the micro and macro levels. As such "modernization theory" strongly affected American foreign policy and theories of global economic life, much of which owes its origins to Weber's *Economy and Society*. If imperialism as an economic or political policy is impossible to comprehend without reference to Marx, modernization theory must necessarily be tied to Weber's conceptualization of the global market, and the violent struggles that typically occur when "traditional" societies are confronted by those committed to "rational action," particularly along economic lines (e.g., Wiebe, 1967).

The full range of historiography regarding U.S. culture which has been helped by reference to Weber's ideas is too large to canvass here, but a sense of its magnitude is revealed in studies like those by William Green (1993), Earl Hamilton (1929), H. Stuart Hughes (1960), Ronen Shamir (1993), Kennedy (2000), Marsh (2000), and Joerges (2000). There are also monographs that seek to connect Weber with actual U.S. conditions during his lifetime (Eileen Leonard's unusual dissertation [1975], and Jonathan Imber [1996]). American historians beginning at the turn of the twentieth century with Charles Beard have puzzled about "objectivity" in the transmission of historical knowledge, and Weber's writings have of course been given careful study in this regard, especially "Science as a Vocation" (1917) and "Politics as a Vocation" (1919). Weber's ideas about the proper roles of objectivity and commitment have been subjected to endless critique (e.g., Haskell, 1998: 15-19, 337-45, *passim*, and Novick, 1988).

This abbreviated excursus into Weberian modes of American historiography suggests that by using my bibliography as a database, one could continue, as I have begun here, and divide the bulk of empirical or substantive studies into a range of plausible categories that illustrate Weber's continuing influence among not only scholars, but also journalists. Useful categories could include power, legitimation, cross-cultural meanings of the Protestant Ethic thesis, ideal-types and related methodological problems, rationalization processes, changes in bureaucratic procedures, the role of the press, the sociology of music, or global geopolitics, to name a few. But such an undertaking must await another occasion. Meanwhile, it is enough to observe that Weber's significance seems to grow daily, as scholars try to understand the contemporary socio-economic and political world by means of analytic devices and categories he devised more than ninety years ago.

References

Part I: Selected Works by Max Weber in English Translation:

Weber, Max 1927: *General Economic History*, tr. by Frank Knight. London: Allen and Unwin; reissued in 1981 by Transaction Publishers.
_____ 1930: *Protestant Ethic and the Spirit of Capitalism*, tr. by Talcott Parsons. London: Allen and Unwin; reissued in 1995 by Roxbury Publishing Co.
_____ 1946: *From Max Weber: Essays in Sociology*, tr, ed., and intro. by Hans H. Gerth and C. Wright Mills. New York: Oxford University Press.
_____ 1951: *Religion of China: Confucianism and Taoism*, tr. and ed. by Hans H. Gerth. Glencoe, IL: Free Press.
_____ 1952: *Ancient Judaism*, tr. and ed. by Hans G. Gerth and Don Martindale. Glencoe, IL: Free Press.
_____ 1968: *Economy and Society: An Outline of Interpretive Sociology*, ed. by Guenther Roth and Claus Wittich, 3 vols. New York: Bedminster Press; reissued in 1978 in 2 vols. by the University of California Press.
_____ 1976: *The Agrarian Sociology of Ancient Civilizations*, tr. by R. I. Frank. London: NLB.
_____ 1994: *Weber: Political Writings*, ed. by Peter Lassman and Ronald Speirs. New York: Cambridge University Press.
_____ 1995: *The Russian Revolutions*, tr. by Gordon C. Wells and Peter Baehr. Oxford: Polity Press.
_____ 1998: "Preliminary Report on a Proposed Survey for a Sociology of the Press" [1910] . *History of the Human Sciences*, 11:2 (May), 111-120.

Part II: Works about Weber or Using His Ideas:

Allen, Charlotte 1999: "Confucius and the Scholars." *Atlantic Monthly*, 283:4 (April), 78-83.
Alessandra, Tony 1998: *Charisma: Seven Keys to Developing the Magnetism that Leeds to Success*. New York: Warner Books.
Axelrad, Allan M. 1978: "The Protagonist of the Protestant Ethic: Max Weber's Benjamin Franklin." *Rendezvous*, 13:2, 45-59.
Bailyn, Bernard 1955: *The New England Merchants in the Seventeenth Century*. Cambridge, MA: Harvard University Press.
_____ (ed.) 1965: *The Apologia of Robert Keayne: The Last Will and Testament of Me, Robert Keayne, All of It Written With My Own Hands and Began by Me, MO: 6: I: 1653, Commonly Called August*. New York: Harper and Row.
Bellow, Saul 2000: *Ravelstein*. New York: Viking (Penguin/Putnam).
Bendix, Reinhard 1960: *Max Weber: An Intellectual Portrait*. New York: Doubleday; reissued in 1998, London: Routledge.

Bier, Jesse 1970: "Weberism, Franklin, and the Transcendental Style." *New England Quarterly* 43:2, 179-192.

Binaghi, Claudia 2000: "Dark Horse Likes to Gallop Free" [Letter to the Editor]. *Financial Times* (London), May 15, p. 24.

Bloom, Allan 1987: *The Closing of the American Mind*. New York: Simon and Schuster.

_____ 1990: *Giants and Dwarfs: Essays 1960-1990*. New York: Simon and Schuster.

Boddy, Kasia 1999: "Travelling as a Version of Being at Home." *Independent* (London), February 26, p. 7.

Brooks, David 2000: *Bobos in Paradise: The New Upper Class and How They Got There*. New York: Simon and Schuster.

Buck, Robert Enoch 1993: "Protestantism and Industrialization: An Examination of Three Alternative Models of the Relationship between Religion and Capitalism." *Review of Religious Research*, 34:3, 210-224.

Burger, Thomas 1987: *Max Weber's Theory of Concept Formation: History, Laws, and Ideal Types*. Expanded edition. Durham, NC: Duke University Press.

Burke, Peter 1992: *History and Social Theory*. Ithaca, NY: Cornell University Press.

Carroll, Jon 1999: "More, Yes, More of Mondegreens." *San Francisco Chronicle*, April 13, p. B10.

Caulkin, Simon 1998: "Guru Guide: Max Weber." *Observer* (London), October 4, p. 8 (The *Observer* Work Page).

_____ 2000: "Seer of Cyberspace Symbols." *Observer* (London), June 18, p. 9 (The *Observer* Business Pages).

Cooke, Timothy R. 1994: "Uncommon Earnestness and Earthly Toils: Moderate Puritan Richard Baxter's Devotional Writings." *Anglican and Episcopal History* 63:1, 51-72.

Crainer, Stuart 1998: "The Ghost in the Machine." *Management Today*, December, p. 87.

Economist, The 2000: "Striking Back at the Empire." February 26.

Ferguson, Niall 1999: "Millenium Reputations: Which are the Most Overrated Authors, or Books, of the Past 1,000 Years?" *Sunday Telegraph* (London), March 14, p. 15.

Fukuyama, Francis 1992: *The End of History and the Last Man*. New York: Free Press.

_____ 1995: *Trust: Social Virtues and the Creation of Prosperity*. New York: Free Press.

_____ 1999a: "The Great Disruption." *Atlantic Monthly*, 283:5 (May), 55-80.

_____ 1999b: *The Great Disruption: Human Nature and the Reconstruction of the Social Order*. New York: Free Press.

Halperin, S. William 1946: *Germany Tried Democracy: A Political History of the Reich from 1918 to 1933*. Chicago: University of Chicago Press.

Hamilton, Earl J. 1929: "American Treasure and the Rise of Capitalism (1500-1700)." *Economica*, 9:27 (November), 338-357.

Hardt, Hanno 1979: *Social Theories of the Press: Early German and American Perspectives*. Beverly Hills, CA: Sage Publications.

Haskell, Thomas L. 1998: *Objectivity is Not Neutrality: Explanatory Schemes in History*. Baltimore, MD: Johns Hopkins University Press.

Hennis, Wilhelm 1988: *Max Weber: Essays in Reconstruction*, tr. Keith Tribe. London: Allen and Unwin.

_____ 1998: "The Media as a Cultural Problem: Max Weber's Sociology of the Press." *History of the Human Sciences*, 11:2 (May), 107-110.

Henretta, John A. "The Weber Thesis Revisited: The Protestant Ethic and the Reality of Capitalism." Pp. 35-70 in John A. Henretta, *The Origins of American Capitalism: Collected Essays*. Boston: Northeastern University Press, 1991.

Holtham, Gerald 1998: "Debate: Lie Back, Think of South Korea." *Guardian* (London), August 3, p. 17.

Hudson, Winthrop S. 1988: "The Weber Thesis Reexamined." *Church History* 57 (Supplement), 56-67.

Hughes. H. Stuart 1960: "The Historian and the Social Scientist." *American Historical Review*, 66:1 (October), 20-46.

Imber, Jonathan 1996: "'Incredible Goings-On': Max Weber in Pennsylvania." *American Sociologist*, 27:4 (Winter), 3-6.

Independent, The (London) 2000: "Thought for the Day." January 14, p. 3.

Jäger, Friedrich 1991: "Culture or Society? The Significance of Max Weber's Thought for Modern Cultural History." *History and Memory* 2:2, 115-140.

Jaspers, Karl 1989: *On Max Weber*. Ed. by John Dreijmanis. New York: Paragon House.

Jenkins, Philip 2002: *The Next Christendom: The Coming of Global Christianity*. New York: Oxford University Press.

Joerges, Christian 2000: "Rationalization of Law and Bureaucratic Rationality in The EU: Legitimacy Problems of European Governance in the Light of Weberian Concepts." Presented at the *Economy and Society*: Max Weber in 2000 conference, Madison, Wisconsin, September 22-24.

Johnson, Benton 1971: "Max Weber and American Protestantism." *Sociological Quarterly* 12:4 (Autumn), 473-485.

Johnson, Daniel 2000: "Mother to the Unborn Child." *Daily Telegraph* (London), February 19, p. 24.

Kalberg, Stephen 1994: *Max Weber's Comparative-Historical Sociology*. Oxford: Polity Press.

_____ 1997a: "Max Weber's Sociology: Research Strategies and Modes of Analyses." Pp. 208-241 in Charles Camic (ed.), *Reclaiming the Sociological Classics: The State of Scholarship*, Malden, MA: Blackwell Publishers.

Käsler, Dirk 1988: *Max Weber: An Introduction to His Life and Work*. Tr. by Philippa Hurd. Oxford: Polity Press.

Kennedy, Duncan 2000: "Weber's 'Logically Formal Rationality': A Genealogy and an Assessment of Current Status." Presented at the *Economy and Society*: Max Weber in 2000 conference, Madison, Wisconsin, September 22-24.

Kirkus Service 1998: Review of Daniel Patrick Moynihan, *Secrecy: The American Experience* [Yale, 1998]. July 1, 1998.

Kolbenschlag, Madonna Claire 1976: "The Protestant Ethic and Evangelical Capitalism: The Weberian Thesis Revisited." *Southern Quarterly* 14:4, 287-306.

Lehmann, Hartmut and Guenther Roth (eds.) 1993: *Weber's Protestant Ethic: Origins, Evidence, Contexts*. Cambridge: Cambridge University Press/German Historical Institute.

Leonard, Eileen 1975: "Max Weber and America: A Study in Elective Affinity." Unpub. Doctoral Dissertation (Sociology). New York: Fordham University; 511 leaves.

Lindholm, Charles 1990: *Charisma*. Cambridge, MA: Basil Blackwell.

MacShane, Denis 1998: "Can We Adapt to the Third Way?" [a review of Anthony Giddens' *The Third Way*.] *Independent* (London), September 16, p. 5.

Martinez-Saenz, Miguel 2000: "Whose Interests are Being Represented?" *Tampa Tribune*, March 25, p. 17.

Marsh, Robert 2000: "Weber's Misunderstanding of Traditional Chinese Law." Presented at the *Economy and Society*: Max Weber in 2000 conference, Madison, Wisconsin, September 22-23.

Mclynn, Frank 2000: "When the Past Changes Direction." *Independent* London), June 3, p. 10.

Mommsen, Wolfgang J. 1984 [1959/1974]: *Max Weber and German Politics, 1890-1920*. Tr. by Michael Steinberg. Chicago: University of Chicago Press.

_____ 2000: "Max Weber's 'Grand Sociology:' The Origins and Composition of *Wirtschaft und Gesellschaft*, Sociology." Paper delivered at the Economy and Society: Max Weber in 2000 conference, Madison, Wisconsin, September 22-24, 2000.

Mufson, Steven 1999: "Great Expectations" [review of Edward Chancellor, *Devil Take the Hindmost: A History of Financial Speculation*]. *Washington Post*, September 12, "Book World," p. X06.

Novak, Michael 1982: *The Spirit of Democratic Capitalism*. New York: Simon and Schuster.

_____ 1993: *The Catholic Ethic and the Spirit of Capitalism*. New York: Free Press.

_____ 1996: *Business as a Calling: Work and the Examined Life*. New York: Free Press.

Novick, Peter 1988: *That Noble Dream: The "Objectivity Question" and the American Historical Profession*. Cambridge: Cambridge University Press.

Oakes, Guy 1988: *Weber and Rickert*. Cambridge, MA: MIT Press.

O'Grady, Bernard 1999: "Weber was Right." *Daily Telegraph* (London), July 6, p. 25.

Pande, Mrinal 2000: "Budget Talks and Ballot Boxes." *The Hindu*, March 19.

Peacock, James L. 1989: "Calvinism, Community, and Charisma: Ethnographic Notes." *Comparative Social Research* 11, 227-238.

Pollock, Robert L. 1998: Bookshelf: Review of Robert Scruton, *An Intelligent Person's Guide to Philosophy*. *Wall Street Journal*, June 29.

Porter, Andrew 1998: "The Gap" [review of David S. Landes, *The Wealth and Poverty of Nations*, W.W. Norton.] *New York Times Book Review*, March 15, p. 15.

Press, Eyal 1999: "The Passion of Roberto Unger." *Lingua Franca*, March, 44-54.

Reilly, Patrick 1999: "Why You Might as Well Look for God Through a Telescope." *Herald* (Glasgow), November 29, p. 15.

Ross, Dorothy 1998: "The New and Newer Histories: Social Theory and Historiography in an American Key." Pp. 85-106 in Anthony Molho and Gordon S. Wood (eds.), *Imagined Histories: American Historians Interpret the Past*, Princeton, NJ: Princeton University Press.

Roth, Guenther and Wolfgang Schluchter 1979: *Max Weber's Vision of History*. Berkeley: University of California Press.

Roth, Guenther 2000: "Max Weber's Anglo-German Family History." Translated extract from *Max Weber's Anglo-German Family History*, Tübingen: Mohr Siebeck, 2001 (in German)]. Delivered at the "Economy and Society: Max Weber in 2000" conference, Madison, Wisconsin, September 22-24, 2000.

Ryan, Alan 1996: Review of John P. Diggins, *Max Weber: Politics and the Spirit of Tragedy*, New York: Basic Books, 1996. *New York Times Book Review*, August 4, p. 14.

Sarbadhikari, Atanu 1999: "Dalit and Conversion" (Letter to the Editor). *The Statesman* (India), February 20.

Scaff, Lawrence 1989: *Fleeing the Iron Cage: Culture, Politics, and Modernity in the Thought of Max Weber*. Berkeley: University of California Press.

Schlink, Bernhard 1999: "Best Lawyer, Pure Law" [Hans Kelsen]. *New York Times (Magazine)*, April 18, Section 6, p. 100.

Schwartz, Barry 1987: *George Washington: The Making of an American Symbol*. New York: Free Press.

_____ 2000: *Abraham Lincoln and the Forge of National Memory*. Chicago: University of Chicago Press.

Schweitzer, Arthur 1984: *The Age of Charisma*. Chicago: Nelson-Hall.

SEK Genetics 1998: Website advertisement for the breeding bull, Foreplay": *http://www.pitton.com/~sekgen/w14.htm*.

Shamir, Ronen 1993: "Formal and Substantive Rationality in American Law: A Weberian Perspective." *Social and Legal Studies*, 2, 45-72.

Sica, Alan 1985: "Reasonable Science, Unreasonable Life: The Happy Fictions of Marx, Weber, and Social Theory." In Robert Antonio and Ronald Glassman (eds.), *A Weber-Marx Dialogue*. Lawrence: University Press of Kansas.

_____ 1988: *Weber, Irrationality, and Social Order*. Berkeley: University of California Press.

Spencer, Olin 1980: "The Oneida Community and the Instability of Charismatic Authority." *Journal of American History* 67:2, 285-300.

Stace, Christopher 1999: "Goodbye to Sepulchral Bury" [review of Christian Meier, *Athens*]. *Daily Telegraph* (London), July 3, p. 3.

Steinmetz, Greg 1998: "Democracies Bestow a Fleeting Blessing on History's Greats." *The Wall Street Journal*, September 2, Section A, Page 1, Column 1.

Strauss, Leo 1953: *Natural Right and History*. Chicago: University of Chicago Press.

Tolles, Frederick B. 1948/1963: *Meeting House and Counting House: The Quaker Merchants of Colonial Philadelphia, 1682-1763*. New York: Norton/Chapel Hill: University of North Carolina Press.

Tolson, Jay 1999: A Meeting of Minds, with a Nod to Yesterday. *U.S. News and World Report*, June 28, p. 61.

Weber, Marianne 1975: *Max Weber: A Biography*, tr. by Harry Zohn. New York: John Wiley and Sons; reissued in 1988 with a new introduction by Guenther Roth, New Brunswick, NJ: Transaction Publishers.

Whitehead, Alfred North 1938: *Modes of Thought*. New York: Macmillan.

Wiebe, Robert 1967: *The Search for Order*. New York: Hill & Wang.

Zuckerman, Laurence 1999: "Words Go Right to the Brain, but Can They Stir the Heart?" *New York Times*, April 17.

4

Weber and the Meaning of Rationalization

Ever since "branding" became a common term beyond the limits of advertising circles, it has become simpler to recall the importance of various classical social theorists by mentioning their "brand identifiers." By this means even the novice can easily be made to remember that for Auguste Comte there are "the three stages of history, " for Herbert Spencer there is "social Darwinism" (or "biological Spencerianism, " which is more accurate), for Marx, of course, "the dictatorship of the proletariat" or the fact that "all history is the history of class conflict, " and for Durkheim there were "three types of suicide" and constant concern over "social solidarity" or "collective consciousness." For some years the favored tag attached to Weber's overall achievement as a social analyst has been "rationalization, " which has triumphed over the half-dozen other concepts that Weber originated or perfected, for some time memorialized in textbooks. "The iron cage of bureaucracy" (an irreparable but appealing mistranslation) goes along with this idea, as does "the routinization of charisma." All of the "nuances, " as they say, which Weber worked into his analysis of rationalization have been set aside for the most part, except for debates among dedicated Weberians, who for the most part talk quietly among themselves. In the place of Weber's precise qualifiers, one finds a comfortably comprehensible amalgam of Weber's basic notions mixed with random images from Kafka's *The Trial*, Huxley's *Brave New World*, and Orwell's *1984* (both book and film versions of each), plus hundreds of dystopian science fiction novels and movies in which a despotic Regime runs roughshod over the hapless individual's desire for autonomy and freedom. This is not precisely what Weber had in mind since he was too realistic not to appreciate the positive contributions rationalization had made to the advancement of Western societies when contrasted with static "Oriental despotism" and other, earlier forms of social organization and material production. Yet there is indeed in his work a sorrowful edge regarding the likely fate, more baleful than joyous, which would overpower liberalism's Lockean ideal and create of humans an obedient herd of producers, fighters, and consumers who would have seemed repugnant to Weber and all those who shared his fundamental view of life.

All the mixed metaphors and multivalent imagery aside, the basic question which logically precedes them is what precisely Weber meant by "rationalization, " and where in his vast oeuvre one can find the crispest presentation of the linked set of ideas to which it alludes. I will have more to say about this later in the chapter, but for now, it might be useful to establish some basic textual markers. But first a few general statements can serve to guide us into the thicket of Weber's own words. Martin Albrow considers the inevitable conflict between values and rationalization when he writes:

> It is here that the notion of *Eigengesetzlichkeit* [autonomy, inner logic, self-determination] plays a strategic role within his whole account of the rationalisation process. As we examined in our account of rationality, all action for Weber stems from irrational roots in the human being. Rationality always has an irrational base. In talking about action, this did not pose any great problem for Weber. Motives were either rational or irrational, and in the case of rational ones they invariably depended ultimately either on needs (by definition irrational) which were consciously pursued, or on values (which could not be proven). (Albrow, 1990: 239; see n. 13 below for full bibliographical details about this and all other sources)

I do not think Albrow has penetrated this conundrum—that is, the relation for Weber between the rational and irrational—so satisfactorily as he seems to believe, but he has brought up an essential point. Rationalization processes are fated to crash into the irrational roots of action and its manifold justifications, and modern society's perpetual struggle is to bring its desire for conformity, predictability, and order into alignment with the explosive, disorderly tendencies of people acting on their own volition and in accordance with pre-rationalized or non-rationalizable values.

Writing from a less agitated viewpoint, Dirk Käsler offers a helpfully succinct summary of what the concept entails in his notable Weber primer:

> Rationalization, as the "fate of our age, " was the common formula for those *component processes* which he, in turn, calls bureaucratization, industrialization, capitalist development, specialization, secularization, objectivization, demystification and dehumanization. Weber's research into the "validity" of this hypothesis led him both into areas of historical reality, for which a rational approach was expected (like technology, science, economy, and law), but also (and here we detect his special interests) into areas which would otherwise be perceived as "irrational"—such as religion, ethics, music, art, and culture. (Käsler, 1988: 172; see n. 13 below for full bibliographical details about this and all subsequent sources).

This is a very broadly sketched account of what Weber was trying to accomplish by using this term, but at least it demonstrates the gigantic reach this set of ideas gave Weber, and the challenges it posed to him in exploring ever-wider sources of data.

More precisely, Ferdinand Kolegar claimed forty years ago in a noted article that "the most concise historical account of modern rationalization from Weber's pen is to be found in his *General Economic History*. . . Chapters 29 ["The Rational State, " pp. 338-351] and 30 ["The Evolution of the Capitalistic Spirit, " pp. 352-369]" (Kolegar, 1964: 364n26; see n. 13, below, for bibliographical details on this and all subsequent basic sources). Kolegar also made the important point, one of few commentators to have done so in such persuasive terms, that "The decisive moment in Weber's analysis of rationality is his perception of the fundamental ambivalence of rationality and his realization that rationalization, especially when pursued most systematically and with a singleness of purpose, engenders irrationality. The most striking fact with which Weber is confronted in his investigation of modern capitalism, a fact which at first appears as unintelligible and 'absolutely irrational' to him, is 'the calling of making money, ' the orientation of the entire life to the 'earning of more and more money' which is increasingly thought of as an end in itself, indeed as an 'ultimate purpose of. . . life.'" Furthermore, "The process of 'intellectual rationalization, ' having undermined the belief in absolute values, brings in its wake relativization of values and sharpens the 'irreconcilable conflict' between the various value spheres" (Kolegar, 1964: 364-65, 368). There is considerable wisdom in Kolegar's remarks, particularly his realization that for Weber, rationalization could be thought of in no other way than as a truly Faustian bargain, and that conflicting values of a fundamental kind— like those currently going on between the West and the Middle East, Christendom and Islam, secular and sacred societies—would never be resolved through tidy processes of rationalization, either intellectual, religious, or military.

As to Kolegar's highlighting two chapters in *General Economic History*, it is no accident that these should be the most straightforward portrayals of rationalization that Weber wrote, since they and the rest of the book were reconstructed after his death from students' notes. This was his last course, taught in the winter term, 1919-1920, but does not represent his finest work; rather, he gave the students what they wanted: a thumbnail sketch of a topic about which he claimed no special expertise. The fact that it was his first work translated into English (1927) would have pained him no end, since it was also his least perfected. (This did not prevent Frank Knight from beginning his "Translator's Preface" to the book with "Max Weber is probably the most outstanding name in German social thought since Schmoller.") And yet the tortured, philosophically attuned flavor of his other commentaries wherein he lays out his notion of how rationalization has affected Western civilization (e.g., in the *Zwischenbetrachtung*, the sociology of music, the sociology of law, and most memorably, in "Science as a Vocation" and "Politics as a Vocation"), is not allowed in this history of economic life to smother the countless facts of the case which Weber wanted to convey to his students as efficiently—as "rationally"—as possible. Flying through the historical material, Weber explains how the "rational state" and "rational law" grew hand-in-hand, how Roman and canon law were fruitfully joined through a form of rationalization, how mercantilism swept aside pre-capitalist formations, how Puritanism helped spur capitalist development, and how "the capitalist spirit" was blocked among the ancient Jews, Chinese, and Indians, while becoming the reigning ideology of Northern Europe and England, thereby displacing magic by means of an efficiency-driven asceticism.

Many parts of *Economy and Society*, especially in chapter two of part I (pp. 63-211), while not very pleasant to read, include a great many comments about rationalization procedures. One section, "The Conditions of Maximum Formal Rationality of Capital Accounting" (161-164), is typical. Here Weber suggests that all the "irrationalities" of pre-capitalist relationships must be jettisoned if rational capitalism is to succeed. He explains:

> The following are the principal conditions necessary for obtaining a maximum of formal rationality of capital accounting in production enterprises: (1) complete appropriation of all material means of production by owners and the complete absence of all formal appropriation of opportunities for profit in the market; that is, market freedom; (2) complete autonomy in the selection of management by the owners, thus complete absence of formal appropriation of rights to managerial functions; (3) complete absence of appropriation of jobs and of opportunities for earning by workers and, conversely, the absence of appropriation of workers by owners. This implies free labor, freedom of the labor market, and freedom in the selection of workers; (4) complete absence of substantive regulation of consumption, production, and prices, or of other forms of regulation which limit freedom of contract or specify conditions of exchange. This may be called substantive freedom of contract; (5) complete calculability of the technical conditions of the production process; that is, a mechanically rational technology. (Pp.161-62)

He continues in this vein for several pages, and even though the material seems chronically lifeless, it is in fact loaded with sociological meat, for what he's saying is that "humanness" as defined in all pre-capitalist societies must be cast out in order for rationalized capitalist relations of production to succeed.

In a passage from his "sociology of religion" that appears much later in the book, he once again explains how religious modernization, ever-increasing incursions by capitalist relations, inevitably diminish the power of sacred ties, between the supernatural and humans, and among humans themselves:

> We may note that every economic rationalization of a barter economy has a weakening effect on the traditions which support the authority of the sacred law. For this reason alone the pursuit of money, the typical goal of the rational acquisitive quest, is religiously suspect. Consequently the priesthood favored the maintenance of a natural economy (as was apparently the case in Egypt) wherever the particular economic interest of the temple as a bank for deposit and loans under divine protection did not militate too much against a natural economy.
>
> But it is above all the impersonal and economically rationalized (but for this very reason ethically irrational) character of purely commercial relationships that evokes the suspicion, never clearly expressed but all the more strongly felt, of ethical religions. For every purely personal relationship of man to man, of whatever sort and even including complete enslavement, may be subjected to ethical requirements and [be] ethically regulated. This is true because the structures of these relationships depend upon the individual wills of the participants, leaving room in such relationships for manifestations of the virtue of charity. But this is not the situation in the realm of economically rationalized relationships, where personal control is exercised in inverse ratio to the degree of rational differentiation of the economic structure. There is no possibility, in practice or even in principle, of any caritative regulation of relationships arising between the holder of a savings and loan bank mortgage and the mortgagee who has obtained a loan from the bank, or between a holder of a federal bond and a citizen taxpayer. . .The growing impersonality of the economy on the basis of association in the market place follows its own rules, disobedience to which entails economic failure and, in the long run, economic ruin. (Pp. 584-85)

Weber believes that "caritative regulation" must be forbidden in market relationships, that the same "caritas" which Heidegger (and others) have held to be humankind's most distinctive and vital positive attribute must be discarded at the first hint of a business relationship. As rationalization of the economy takes over, "the ethic of brotherliness, " as Weber called it in another context, will always be given short shrift, and in due course becomes an historical relic.

In addition to covering in detail the effects of rationalization upon religious ethics, economic relations, and the administration of complex organizations, Weber wrote at length about the rationalization of law, not only because he knew a great deal about law as a practicing attorney, but because he thought it most clearly embodied the distinction between premodern and modern societies. He explains how this works on several levels:

A body of law can be "rational" in several different senses, depending on which of several possible courses legal thinking takes toward rationalization. Let us begin with the seemingly most elementary thought process, viz., generalization, i.e., in our case, the reduction of the reasons relevant in the decision of concrete individual cases to one or more "principles, " i.e., legal propositions. (P. 655)

The older forms of popular justice had originated in conciliatory proceedings between kinship-groups. The primitive formalistic irrationality of these older forms of justice was everywhere cast off under the impact of the authority of princes or magistrates (*imperium*, ban), or, in certain situations, of an organized priesthood. With this impact, the substance of the law, too, was lastingly influenced, although the character of this influence varied with the various types of authority. (P. 809)

From a theoretical point of view, the general development of law and procedure may be viewed as passing through the following stages: first, charismatic legal revelation through "law prophets"; second, empirical creation and finding of law by legal honoratiores, i.e, law creation through cautelary jurisprudence and adherence to precedent; third, imposition of law by secular or theocratic powers; fourth, and finally, systematic elaboration of law and professionalized administration of justice by persons who have received their legal training in a learned and formally logical manner. (P. 882)

One might note that premodern legal systems produced substantively rational outcomes during adjudication of cases by reference to norms and customary behavior patterns that were widely known and discussed among members of the given society. "Justice" was the goal in these matters, whereas today "legality" is the *summum bonum*, and justice is often quite intentionally left to one side, thought of as beside the point. Pre-rationalized legal practices had to deliver substantively satisfying results more often than not, or else they would be replaced or disregarded. Weber was aware of this anomaly, for as much as he valued the sophistication of Western legal philosophy and practice, he understood all too well from his own experience how unjust its proceedings could often become. Once again over-rationalization could produce "irrational" results.

Besides the numberless passages concerning rationalization processes which Weber built into his treatises on comparative religion, law, bureaucracy, and methodology of the social sciences, he also made it the centerpiece of his fragmentary work on musicology, known in English as *The Rational and Social Foundations of Music*. This work is not much studied by social scientists because it requires knowledge of music theory in order to be understood properly, and also because the only English translation, now forty-five years in print, is not entirely reliable. Weber's arguments in this work—an unfinished part of what would have been a comprehensive sociology of culture—turn around his observation that Western music is structured so as to exclude "irrationalities" that are common to musical forms that originated in the Middle and Far East. He explained his argument in terms of harmony and its relation to melody, how the Western "rationalized" scale system grew out of and diverged from Eastern musical notation, musical solutions to problems having to do with polyvocality and polysonority, and how certain musical instruments (notably the piano) contributed to musical rationalization. A student and close friend of Weber's, Paul Honigsheim, has written about Weber's sociology of music from a uniquely personal vantage point:

> Max Weber was himself tremendously musically minded. As in regards to so many other things, I did not always agree with his musical judgments, so that we often ended up arguing intensely. Anyway, he was fully familiar with musical theory, mastering the theory and structure of the instruments of all human history and knowing what they sounded like. He died too early to be able to publish on it. It may well be that I am the only one who knows about some of his ideas, because he nevertheless told them to me. He pointed in this direction: Christianity is almost the only culture that has produced purely instrumental compositions of such large scale and importance. In other cultures instrumental music is somehow less important, more of an introduction to something else. But it is the Christian world that has produced symphonies and similar things. Is there some connection to the structure of Christianity? (Honigsheim, 1973: 35)

Weber's work in this area does not make for transparent reading. For example, in trying to explain the origin and role of fourths and fifths within Western tonality, Weber gives these particulars, which are in keeping with the rest of this short, dense, remarkable book:

> If Collangettes is right, in the thirteenth century both fourths were rationalized by the theory in such a way that one, also to be discussed more completely later, retained the third contained next to it. In each fourth was contained, likewise, one irrational second, which was separated from it by a pythagorean tone step. Moreover, the intervals between these neutral and pythagorean relations were reduced to the range of residual pythagorean intervals. Thus they were included in the scheme of tonal formation by the numbers 2 and 3. The lower of both fourths now contained the following tones (reduced to c): pythagorean d-flat, irrational d, pythagorean e-flat, irrational e, pythagorean e, f, with six distances of: limma, limma, apotome, limma, apotome minus the limma, limma. The rational d was cancelled. One did not yet dare to exclude the harmonic fifth g. The upper fourth, on the contrary, contained the following tones. . . (P. 57)

And with this slim volume, Weber invented the sociology of music, or what might more fully be termed the sociological account of the rationalization of musical forms. It is not the clearest of his expositions of the concept, but is surely the most innovative.

Current Uses of Weber's Rationalization Theme

As suggested by the preceding, then, the complex, multi-layered, perhaps unidirectional set of phenomena known to social theorists as "rationalization processes" would seem to be a sturdy device for appraising Weber's primary historical and analytic achievements. It is superior to other possible choices (charisma, value-freedom, ideal-types, status groups, bureaucratization), because Weber's best working years were spent exploring it. In addition, this key set of linked processes, unlike other phenomena he studied in detail, still seems to be enlarging its range of meaning in contemporary societies rather than becoming a part of inessential history. Paradoxically, rationalization might also be viewed as the simplest to understand of all Weber's principal innovations to social and economic thought. His discovery, if it can be so called, held that modern societies are forever striving to order what in its "natural" state is less ordered or even randomly occurring. Where people once noisily milled about, now they are put in rows or ranks of quiet obedience; where fiscal accounting was done from memory and rough approximation, now it is taken to the hundredth of one percentage point, or beyond; where music was the work of a single minstrel inventing melodies and lyrics as he strolled, now it requires an orchestra that plays perfectly in unison from a printed score, willful deviation from which is a cardinal sin. Weber realized that the organization of thought and action into regimented forms had virtually replaced religion as the unquestioned, motivating creed across much of "advanced civilization." And while he recognized in these developments a range of admirable achievements, particularly in the steady production of material goods, the undeniably related seedbeds of pathology that affected individuals as much as the hyper-rationalized societies in which they struggled, vainly he thought, to maintain their individuality and freedom, were also quite evident to him.

For Weber, rationalization processes were ubiquitous and inconquerable—even if he refused to assign the concept any inevitability or evolutionary irreversibility. He did not care to join either the Spencerian or Hegelian parades—nor the newer one headed by Spengler—because he refused to accept determinism in any formal sense. So powerful is the rationalization theme, more so even than his other major ideas, that it readily lends itself to popular expression in a number of forms. For example, some version of it has inspired a sequence of memorable formulations as cinema. In 1973 when George Lucas was twenty-nine—long before he bequeathed lasting images to the iconography of popular culture via his *Star Wars* movies, the Indiana Jones trilogy, and *Tucker*—he wrote, directed, and edited the futurist anti-romance, *THX 1138*. In this moody, understated entry into the dystopian literature genre, the protagonist (Robert Duvall), for reasons unclear even to himself, cannot manage to ingest State-required quantities of daily sedatives. In this emotionless world of Lucas's devising, owing equal parts to *Brave New World* and the film, *2001: A Space Odyssey*, passion is illegal, and interpersonal attachment quite literally unthinkable. When Duvall's character inconveniently wishes to maintain a longer involvement with his "computer-selected mate" than the State condones, paranoidal chase scenes and authoritarian terrorism bring the movie to an inevitably (and by now predictably) bleak ending. The film's audience—even if unaware of Huxley, Kafka, or Orwell as novelists—has become thoroughly familiar with the principal motif: substantive irrationality accompanying cruel rationalization of social behavior, portrayed not only in *THX 1138*, but in numerous sister films, for example, *Brazil*, the Mad Max series, and *Kafka*. The lone hero, constitutionally incapable of long-term obedience, rails against a social system that combines incomprehensibility, mean-spiritedness, and maddening benevolence of a purely cosmetic nature. But rebellion almost always fails, as state-sponsored order maintains its iron grip upon those whose desire for autonomy conflict with its demand for predictable and standardized social action.

In the slower but broader world of print, Weber's ideas about rationalized processes have been drawn upon in endless forms, sometimes almost in caricature. This was demonstrated twenty years ago when George Ritzer in a short statement introduced his audience to the "McDonaldization" of social relations, [1] his inspiration being Weber. By invoking this term for sociological purposes, Ritzer hoped to show that practices common to U.S. "fast food" chains had taken the rationalization of restaurant work to a previously unknown extreme. That his remarks grow ever more pertinent was demonstrated not long ago in three Associated Press stories. The first explained that with 20, 160 U.S. McDonald's restaurants operating as of September, 1996, having fed 95 percent of the nation's people at least once, almost no town of any size has escaped this company's version of culinary delight. [2] More intriguingly, a sister story revealed that political scientists have noted a correlation between the opening of McDonald's restaurants abroad and the beginnings of peaceful life in previously unruly societies. The "Golden Arches Theory of Conflict Prevention" reflects the restaurant's presence in 102 countries, along with its having achieved for the first time more worldwide brand recognition than Coca-Cola. In order to "qualify" for McDonald's presence, a nation must provide a steady supply of safe beef, reliable labor, construction companies of merit, and a lack of governmental red tape, all geared to the same, rationalized end: "McDonald's understands that its success lies in delivering consistency." And while the company is losing market share and profitability in the U.S., it is fast improving its balance sheet abroad (thus imitating the tobacco industry).[3]

Even more Weberian than these hamburger tales is the new development in the U.S., where McDonald's is trying to survive by lessening the time it takes to order and receive one's food. By using an array of robots, computers, and associated equipment, the restaurant can guarantee delivery of an order within ninety seconds at rush hour, or forty-five seconds at calmer moments, in those sixty-four experimental outlets where the technology is in place. The underlying assumption behind this extraordinary capital investment—that speed of delivery is more important to consumers than the nature of what is delivered—does not receive mention either by the journalist, nor the company's officials.[4] Perhaps unsurprisingly, there are still other serious students of "McDonalization" who view the entire enterprise as a form of cultural fascism, which implants corrosive behavior and demand patterns, especially among children, that would be the envy of any authoritarian regime, for example, "The benign nature of capitalist production portrayed by McDonaldland and Ronald McDonald is a cover for a far more savage reality."[5]

Even if the unblushing Americanization of Weber's global concept that is embodied in so-called "McDonaldization"—said to be interpreted abroad as a credible snapshot of and totem for extant U.S. culture—lacks the profundity and breadth typical of Weber's own writing, it nevertheless has its uses (perhaps as "Weber lite"). For it points toward a cognate set of events and developments which first took hold in Western societies, but has since overspread the globe, particularly among the richer countries. Like no other coherent grouping of changes in behavior, the rationalization of social and economic life has made the world a different place than it was before the process became entrenched, affecting every aspect of private and public life for anyone who cannot or will not escape its grasp. Weber, of course, did not discover this all by himself, but he put the process under a special, comparative lens that only he knew how to grind to proper dimensions. The changes he saw with some alarm through this cultural microscope, then just developing (particularly in the U.S. in 1904), we have come to accept practically without thought. The losses he lamented we can no longer even remember as such.

The range of alterations associated with rationalization is nearly synonymous with the most telling changes in world history over the last two centuries. The way war is waged, business is carried out, learning codified, and personal life experienced, then evaluated—to begin what could easily become an endless list—have endured a transformation so thorough that picturing a pre-rationalized world becomes ever more a feat of imagination granted only to the most gifted historians, novelists, and filmmakers. One way to visualize this is to examine antique college yearbooks, or, better yet, stroll through a vintage gymnasium, finding the hall of fame where yellowed photographs of yesterday's athletic heroes are mounted—say, those from around the turn of the century— and then to study their bodies carefully. They are leaner, of course, often taller, and more muscular than was normal at the time. Yet very few look anything like the "sculpted" bodies expected within athletic programs today, where height, weight, body fat, muscularity, and all sorts of internally measured variables are analyzed by computer in order to find the "ideal" for any given athlete and the position they wish to play on a specific team.

In fact, one of Weber's other gifts to theoretical terminology, the "ideal-type, " finds almost perfect expression in the idealized model against which the individual athlete's physical condition and appearance are measured. Sports medicine, kinesiology, and all manner of related specializations, themselves only recently "rationalized" as suitable for educational and professional credentialing, aim to protect, repair, and improve the athletic body—to produce a physical specimen impossible to better. Taken together, they amount to a rationalization of the haphazard in an almost pure form. Sports in the last century—in collegiate or family settings, whether for aristocrats or the lower orders, and for which one either had a "knack" or did not, therefore pursued mainly for sociability and pleasure—are now entirely altered into global business opportunities, underwritten by electronic mass culture. And the professionals in charge of shaping bodies suitable for the highest level play, or of designing equipment that can speed up the game (e.g., wooden versus composite tennis rackets), had some time ago reached the status of quasi-science, all in pursuit of that winning millisecond, and the hoped-for profits that may come with this tiny competitive edge.

In like manner, those actions which since Ovid and Sappho were regarded as the "irrational" pleasures of sexual activity have lately found their sports analogues in the rationalized business that supplies therapists, instructional materials, and talk-groups, wherein one's inability to reach "the perfect game" are attacked frontally. The underlying assumption to this form of rationalization holds that golf strokes and sexual movements are both kinesiological phenomena, thus equally susceptible to deliberate analysis and improvement. The "mental aspect" of each, much harder to dissect and explain, eludes complete rationalization, but this, it is argued, is merely a temporary setback in the pursuit of complete understanding and inevitable perfectibility. The notion that in principle *any* human activity by its nature should be resistant to thoroughgoing rationalization has become both repugnant and fantastic to the minds whose unrelenting goal is victory over the haphazard or accidental. This worldview would hold, for example, that the skill which allowed John Keats to write "Ode to a Nightingale" (the holograph of which indicates that he wrote it in a single draft and with one small alteration) ought to be decomposed into its constituent parts and then taught to anyone who cares to learn.

All of this, oddly enough, points toward something first noted in 1744 by the great iconoclast, Vico, in his *New Science*. As Momigliano explains: "The basic difference between Vico and Gibbon was, of course, that Vico was interested in barbarism as the root of civilization itself and studied barbarism not as a problem of degeneration but as the matrix of language, poetry, law, and ultimately of reason. Conversely he realized—the first to do so—that too much reason could lead back to barbarism: there was such a thing for him as the *barbarie della reflessione*, " which, he believed, did not affect "the mind of the pagan *bestioni*" as it did the more civilized folk. "Vico did not dream of preferring barbaric law to Roman law. But reason was insufficient to keep control beyond a certain point. Barbaric laws had come as an unavoidable *ricorso*." [6] This foreshadows by centuries Karl Mannheim's observation (borrowed from Weber) that an excrescence of the formally rational, whether in social organization or in thinking, always leads to substantive irrationality. [7] Or, as acutely expressed by a former graduate student who studied Weber with Lawrence Scaff and myself, after spending six months in the 'real world' of bureaucracy: "I'm beginning to think that George Orwell was the greatest prophet who ever lived." [8] If these juxtapositions— modern sports fetishization, Vico's concern about the *ricorso* to barbarism, interpersonal fascism in today's soft-voiced bureaucracy—seem forced or confusing, let us reduce the apparent lack of fit by viewing them through the conceptual apparatus which Weber built while he combined historical phenomena even more (apparently) incommensurable.

Weber's Ideas Themselves

The conventional wisdom about Weber, and those myriad textbook treatments which purvey and sustain it, argues that analyzing and describing "the rationalization process" inspired and organized his lifework, and therefore should serve as the master key to the treasure chamber of the Weberian castle. One particularly strong version of this argument was first announced in Germany by Tenbruck, then distributed in the Anglophone market by others (e.g., Kalberg; Casanova). [9] Yet some noted Weber scholars (e.g., Hennis; Roth; Schluchter[10]), while disagreeing about much else, concur that this is not the best or most "correct" reading of Weber, especially if an evaluative theory of history is attached to what Weber actually wrote. So the first question to resolve regarding Weber and "the problem of rationalization" is to discover to what extent knowing about this idea leads directly into Weber's theoretical core, or whether it is perhaps one of several crucial notions around which he created a chaotically brilliant portrait of social life, historical and contemporary.

One way of approaching this pivotal question is to retrace our steps to that graceful and lucid map of the Weberian continent drawn by the Alsatian scholar, Julien Freund. His geographical birthright—equal facility in Germanic density and French style—served him well while explaining Weber to the outside world. His concise summary of the rationalization process from "Weber's Vision of the World" is worth quoting, in part:

> Weber's rationalization is not to be confused with the notion of the rationality of history, which professedly directs human evolution on a course of universal progress. . . . It is, rather, the product of the scientific specialization and technical differentiation peculiar to Western culture. . . sometimes associated. . . with the notion of intellectualization. It might be defined as *the organization of life through a division and coordination of activities on the basis of an exact study of mens' relations with each other, with their tools and their environment, for the purpose of achieving greater efficiency and productivity.* Hence it is a purely practical development brought about by man's technological genius.
>
> Weber also described rationalization as a striving for perfection. . . as an ingenious refinement of the conduct of life and the attainment of increasing mastery over the external world. . . . he analyzed its evolution in all major branches of human activity—religion, law, art, science, politics, and economics—while being careful not to go beyond the limits of what is objectively ascertainable. . .[11]

This is unobjectionably accurate and, when joined to other passages Freund dedicates to the topic, lands the naive reader generally in the right sector. Yet a look at Freund's sources within Weber's works illustrates one of the first problems confronting those who seek unambiguous familiarity with Weber's idea. Like most other exegetes, including many less talented than himself, Freund drew on a couple of famous passages in *From Max Weber*, unspecific reference to *The Rational and Social Foundations of Music* (though only regarding painting!), a minor speech Weber gave in 1910 about technology—and his exposition was ended! The approach to the question is unique only in Freund's sure grasp of the fundamentals and an extraordinary style, but his light reference to the original materials has become all too common among most writers trying to describe Weber's pivotal concept. And, to be sure, short of a full-scale intellectual biography, the fulcrum of which would be "rationalization, " it is impossible tell the whole story of how a political-economist and lawyer (1889-1897) converted himself into the foremost comparativist of his time (1904-1920). Yet perhaps within these few pages, we can make a practical start.

Attempts to explain, put to use, expand upon, correct, or reject Weber's rationalization thesis are legion, and when culled from a complete bibliography of Anglophone Weberiana that I compiled for another occasion, [12] it is easy to name dozens of valuable treatments, quite diverse in approach, intention, and subject matter.[13] One reason for this abundant work is that in some ways, this topic rivals the "Protestant ethic thesis" as a favored route toward coming to grips with Weber at his most contentious and intriguing. Yet everyone who comments with scholarly authority on rationality and the behaviors which are, in historical hindsight, now thought to be its product, agrees on at least one point: Weber was inconsistent in his technical use of terms, and there is no firmly delineable *locus classicus* to which the reader can turn for an unambiguous statement of Weber's global intentions.[14]

If one undertakes an "empirical" examination of the texts to which a range of Weber specialists has referred when offering their interpretations of the rationalization process, certain of his works, major and minor, do receive mention more than once. Yet this may be more an artefact of received wisdom or scholarly habit than a true measure of where one might go to find Weber's clearest, most embracing, or most mature formulation. This, at least, is what I have concluded after pedantically marching through representative treatments by Aron, Brubaker, Collins, Giddens, Habermas, Parsons, Löwith, and Ritzer, noting the Weberian sources of their stories.[15] There apparently being no consensually agreed upon textual sites to which all committed Weberians can turn in order to learn what he meant by the set of related events we call "rationalization, " a measure of hermeneutic flexibility must be entertained that might be put to good use. One unusually fruitful text was quoted by Reinhard Bendix in his fusillade against Marcuse thirty-five years ago, and comes from the famous "Technical Superiority of Bureaucracy" section of *Economy and Society*, chosen (and translated) by Bendix because it illustrates the consequences of rationalization in the everyday world of industrialized life. Opening with Weber's observation that "the second element mentioned, calculable rules, is the most important one for modern bureaucracy, " the argument is developed thus:

> Bureaucracy in its fullest state of development also comes in a specific sense under the principle of *sine ira ac studio* (impartiality) [literally: *without anger and also devotion to a person*]. Its specific character, welcomed by capitalism,

develops all the more completely the more it is "de-humanized." By "more completely" is meant, the more this specific character, which is seen as a virtue, succeeds in eliminating from all official business love, hate, all purely personal and all irrational elements of feeling, elements defying calculation. [The standard translation adds: "This is appraised as its special virtue by capitalism"; p. 975.] Instead of gentlemen of the old order, inspired by personal interest, favour, grace, and gratitude, modern culture requires, for the external apparatus which supports it, the more complicated and specialised it becomes, the less humanly concerned, strictly "practical *expert*."[16]

Despite obvious syntactical problems typical of Weber's fractured prose, the ideas are clear enough. But there are other routes toward understanding Weber's ideas in this general realm of theorizing.

Given the right semi-formal occasion, Weber could temporarily set aside his mandarin German and assume a bluntness of delivery that even today succeeds in animating his abstract arguments. A famous, biting example, first translated forty years ago by J.P. Mayer in *Max Weber and German Politics*, is this set of stenographically recorded remarks which Weber delivered to colleagues in the *Verein für Socialpolitik* at their Vienna meeting in 1909 (which Mayer titled "Max Weber on Bureaucracy"):

> . . . the forward progress of bureaucratic mechanization is irresistible . . . When a purely technical and faultless administration, a precise and objective solution of concrete problems is taken as the highest and only goal, then on this basis one can only say: away with everything but an official hierarchy which does these things as objectively, precisely, and "soullessly" as any machine.

> The technical superiority of the bureaucratic mechanism stands unshaken. . . Imagine the consequences of that comprehensive bureaucratization and rationalization which already to-day we see approaching. Already now, throughout private enterprise in wholesale manufacture, as well as in all other economic enterprises run on modern lines, *Rechenhaftigkeit*, rational calculation, is manifest at every stage. By it, the performance of each individual worker is mathematically measured, each man becomes a little cog in the machine and, aware of this, his one preoccupation is whether he can become a bigger cog. . . it is strikingly reminiscent of the ancient kingdom of Egypt, in which the system of the "minor official" prevailed at all levels. . . we are proceeding towards an evolution which resembles that system in every detail, except that it is built on other foundations, on technically more perfect, more rationalized, and therefore much more mechanized foundations. . . it is still more horrible to think that the world could one day be filled with nothing but those little cogs, little men clinging to little jobs and striving towards bigger ones. . . The passion for bureaucracy...is enough to drive one to despair. It is as if in politics the spectre of timidity—which has in any case always been rather a good standby for the German—were to stand alone at the helm; as if we were

deliberately to become men who need "order" and nothing but order, who become nervous and cowardly if for one moment this order wavers, and helpless if they are taken away from their total incorporation in it. . . but what can we oppose to this machinery in order to keep a portion of mankind free from this parcelling-out of the soul, from this supreme mastery of the bureaucratic way of life. . . I only wish to challenge the unquestioning idolization of bureaucracy.

As Weber had become well aware, individuals, organizations, and societies at large, in their pursuit of private goals, profits, or predictability of performance, have come to trade efficiency and precision for human warmth and due regard for the personally unique. Or, as Benjamin Nelson observed at the same occasion in 1964 that inspired Bendix's pointed remarks:

Professor Marcuse's insistent forthrightness in blaming so many of the ills of recent times on the "rationalism" which Weber, in his view, espoused in so undialectical a fashion, underscores a little known fact: Weber's renowned comparative studies from his *Protestant Ethic* (1904-05) to his *Wirtschaft und Gesellschaft* have yet to be understood in their true light. They are much more than they seem or are generally understood to be, comparative sociological investigations against a background of the history of Western civilization and culture. In a sense which many overlook, they are prophecies and warnings—prophecies about the menacing shape of things to come, warnings against the further expansion of the domain of conscienceless reason, even in the name of the most noble ideals. . . . The noblest impulses only too often gave rise to the most baleful consequences. Thus the disenchanted world order of contemporary industrial "capitalist" society has been spurred on its fateful course by. . . high-minded altruistic religious impulses.[17]

The connections between Nelson's astute penetration of Weber's deepest motives and a host of related theoretical developments, some of them apparently quite distant from Weber's original concerns (e.g., Merton's famous argument about "unanticipated consequences of social action") are perhaps too obvious to require elaboration. But they do testify to the fertility of Weber's undemarcated "philosophical anthropology" as his ideas have circulated among serious social thinkers during this century.

Another astonishingly useful passage appears in a work to which none of the other specialists referred when handling the topic. "Parliament and Government in Germany under a New Political Order, " which Weber wrote for a quasi-popular audience, first appeared as a set of five *Frankfurter Zeitung* articles between April and June in the anxious year of 1917. Weber was then being urged to participate in postwar German politics, and this essay reveals not only a topical study of problems facing his ruined country in the new, post-monarchical environment, but also manages to include some fairly dense theoretical pronouncements. I quote at length from the consolidated essay because within this thick passage there appear most all of the truly important ingredients that went into Weber's rationalization schema:

> Historically, too, "progress" towards the bureaucratic state which adjudicates in accordance with the rationally established law and administers according to rationally devised regulations stands in the closest relation to the development of modern capitalism. The main inner foundation of the modern capitalist business is *calculation*. In order to exist, it requires a system of justice and administration which, in principle at any rate, function in a *rationally calculable* manner according to stable, general norms, just as one calculates the predictable performance of a *machine*. By contrast, it finds quite uncongenial what is popularly called "cadi [*khadi*] justice, " where judgements are made on each *individual* case according to the judge's sense of fairness, or according to other irrational means of adjudication and principles which existed everywhere in the past and still exist in the Orient today. Equally uncongenial to capitalism is the patriarchal form of administration based on arbitrary decision and grace, but otherwise operating according to binding, holy but irrational tradition, such as one finds in the theocratic or patrimonial associations of rule (*Herrschaftsverbände*) in Asia and in our own past. The fact that this form of "cadi justice" and the type of administration that corresponds to it are very often *venal*, precisely because of their irrational character, allowed a certain form of capitalism to come into existence (and often to flourish luxuriantly thanks to these qualities), that of the trader and government contractor and all varieties of the *pre*-rational capitalism that has been in existence for four thousand years, specifically the adventurer and robber capitalism which was tied to politics, war, administration as such. *Nowhere* in such irrationally constructed polities, however, did or could there emerge the *specific* feature of *modern* capitalism that distinguishes it from those ancient forms of capitalist acquisition, namely the strictly rational *organization of work* on the basis of *rational technology*. These modern types of business, with their fixed capital and precise calculations, are far too easily damaged by irrationalities of justice or administration for them to have emerged under such circumstances. They could only emerge where law was practiced in one of two ways. *Either*, as in England, the practical shaping of law was in fact in the hands of advocates who, in the service of their clientele (men with capitalist interests), devised the appropriate forms for conducting business, and from whose ranks there emerged judges who were bound strictly by "precedent, " and thus to *calculable* schemata. *Or where*, as in the bureaucratic state with its rational laws, the judge is a kind of legal paragraph-machine, into which one throws the documents on a case together with the costs and fees so that it will then spit out a judgment along with some more or less valid reasons for it; here again, the system works in a more or less *calculable* way.[18]

Careful hermeneutic analyses of these three excerpts, two from Weber, plus Nelson's, would constitute a small monograph—especially if carried out in line with the interpretative principles laid down by virtuosi such as Gadamer, Betti, de Man, Hirsch, George Steiner, Harold Bloom, and others who specialize in such labors.[19] Even without this ideal rigor, however, Weber's pointedly delivered vocabulary—a mixture of icy science and prophetic passion—leads the studious reader to several realizations that figure centrally in his overall understanding of rationalization.

From the beginning of Weber's realization that the Faustian bargain constituting modern Western science and industrialization dazzled as well as blinded its beneficiaries—a lesson he may well have learned directly from Goethe during his enthusiastic boyhood reading[20]—his analysis had taken two antipodal forms. Nelson openly admitted, Bendix often obscured, and Marcuse joyfully exploited this well-known "tension" in Weber: on one hand, a clear-eyed portraiture of a civilizational condition from which he could not picture a likely escape, yet on the other a strong-voiced denunciation of those "de-humanizing" tendencies which were already well in place 100 years ago. Marx and many lesser thinkers offered utopian plans that promised redemption from the Faustian bargain—having one's cake while eating it, rendered in social theoretical language. In contrast, Weber understood precisely the benefits, political and economic, of rationalized life, and also recognized that this move away from the tailor-made, wisdom-based practices of *khadijustiz* that had served humankind for millennia to the "legal paragraph-machine" judgeships of today could not be reversed, no matter how many miscarriages of "justice" might occur because of hyper-rationalized legal proceedings.

Another element of Weber's theorizing, one that pervades his detailed analyses of music, law, comparative religion, government, ancient history, and the lot, is his obsessively repeated opinion that modern life strains toward rationality at every opportunity, and in so doing leaves behind an irrational or non-rationalizable past of primordial practices which were, until very lately in history, the chief indicators of humanness. Having written about this complex of ideas at length,[21] I will refer here only lightly to what I regard as the central paradox of Weber's rationalization theme, and its continuing importance to social and cultural theory today; and in a way that I think is consistent with Weber's sometimes unvoiced conclusions.

Western, modernized, rationalized humans have become childish in their demands upon each other and upon their environments, social and ecological, as have peoples in other parts of the world who have begun imitating this general model of behavior and social organization. When it suits their private short-term desires, they exhibit "rationality" in the purest economic meaning of the term. Yet after their material and status needs are more or less satisfied, at least temporarily, they turn for relief from regimentation and predictable tedium to those very realms of social life, those zones of solace, wherein rationality has the least play and the least likely future influence. That is, they rush to those few remaining human or animal intimates still available to them, to aesthetic realms of abandon which seem ever more important (perhaps the hallmark of "postmodern culture"), and to a revived yet only half-believed supernatural realm of doctrine and chant that requires, in order to work properly, a suspension of modern scientific principles that educated people find very difficult to manage—except those in dire psychological straits.

Taken together, this package of behaviors is not only schizoid, but also infantile. It requires a regulated, predictable, and unspontaneous "maturity" on the job site that is starkly alien to humanity's past, and rewards this intolerable condition with a range of "after-hours" children's amusements which intelligent adults from earlier times would likely consider imbecilic and demeaning. These are aspects of Weber's thoughts which, had he lived into the film and radio ages, might have formed the next chapter in *Wirtschaft und Gesellschaft*, where he would have been called upon to answer the question: "What is the next step for a culture which has lost its literacy and found its sedatives, both electronic and chemical?"

Weber has been vilified over the years for the carelessness of his prose. In fact, were it not for a team of selfless editors and transcribers headed by his wife, his vast posthumous output in the early 1920s would never have come together, and he would not now be remembered nearly so well. Only occasionally did he bother to work over a sentence or passage until it spoke his true language, one that imitated his apparently riveting lectures. Perhaps the single most famous of his observations— so uncharacteristically poetic that some believe it was inspired by a great writer Weber admired (Goethe, Nietzsche, and Rilke have been proposed)—appears near the end of *The Protestant Ethic*. This concluding flash of brilliant pathos captures Weber's feelings about the rationalized life, and remains his most frequently quoted statement:

> No one knows who will live in this cage in the future, or whether at the end of this tremendous development entirely new prophets will arise, or there will be a great rebirth of old ideas and ideals, or, if neither, mechanized petrification, embellished with a sort of convulsive self-importance. For of the last stage of this cultural development, it might well be truly said: 'Specialists without spirit, sensualists without heart; this nullity imagines that it has attained a level of civilization never before achieved.'[22]

If one still needs to justify the study of Weber these eighty-four years after his death, this single paragraph, and all the theorizing that inspired it, is probably all that is required to make the case.

If there is one criticism to be leveled at Weber's rationalization theme today, it may be that it gives moderns too much credit for seriousness and high-minded concern for their condition. After all, how many today could understand the meaning of Calvin's or Luther's writings?; how many would be troubled by Nietzsche's attack on "philistine" thinking?; how many would stare sleepless into the starry night after reading Goethe's *Faust* for the first time, and realizing there is no "comfortable" way out?

Notes

1. George Ritzer, "The McDonaldization of Society, " *Journal of American Culture*, 6 (1983), 100-107; see also Ritzer's *The McDonaldization of Society* (Newbury Park, CA: Pine Forge Press, 1994), and Ritzer, *Sociological Beginnings: On the Origins of Key Ideas in Sociology* (New York: McGraw-Hill, 1994), 131-157 for an autobiographical account of Ritzer's interest in the problem, and his audience's enthusiasm for it, itself an interesting bit of quasi-Weberian data.
2. Ted Anthony, "McDonald's Moves Into All Segments of Society." Associated Press (July 15, 1997), from Coudersport, PA.
3. Tom Hundley, "It's Been a Proven Fact [*sic*]: Peace Follows Franchise." Associated Press (July 15, 1997), from Kiev, Ukraine.
4. Cliff Edwards, "Back to the McFuture: Technology Creates Faster Service, Tastier Food." Associated Press (July 21, 1997), from Colorado Springs, CO.
5. Michael Raphael, "Professor Argues McDonald's Brainwashes Youth, " Associated Press, August 1, 1997 (State College, PA), reporting on Joe Kinchloe's "McDonald's, Power, and Children: Ronald McDonald (a k a Roy Kroc) Does It All for You, " a chapter in *Kinderculture: The Corporate Construction of Childhood* (Boulder, CO: Westview Press, 1997).
6. Arnaldo Momigliano, "Gibbon from an Italian Point of View" in G.W. Bowersock, John Clive, and Stephen R. Graubard (eds.), *Edward Gibbon and the Decline and Fall of the Roman Empire* (Cambridge, MA: Harvard University Press, 1977), 75-85, at 78-79. See also Momigliano's "Vico's *Scienza Nuova*: Roman 'Bestioni' and Roman 'Eroi, '" in his *Essays in Ancient and Modern Historiography* (Middletown, CT: Wesleyan University Press, 1982), 253-276, as well as Mark Lilla, *G.B. Vico: The Making of an Anti-Modern* (Cambridge, MA: Harvard University Press, 1993), especially pp. 209-217.
7. Karl Mannheim, *Man and Society in an Age of Reconstuction: Studies in Modern Social Structure* (London: Routledge and Kegan Paul, 1940), 39-75, "Rational and Irrational Elements in Contemporary Society"; see also *Rational and Irrational Elements in Contemporary Society*, L.T. Hobhouse Memorial Trust Lectures, No. 4; March 7, 1934 (London: Humphrey Milford/Oxford University Press, 1934).
8. The same former Weber student recently sent me new company guidelines from her redesigned workplace, where transparent cubicles have replaced walled spaces. These hortatory flyers instruct well-educated bureaucrats how to look at each other, how to speak, how to think, how to dress, and how to feel about what they have been instructed to do—all

in the maternal tones of a kindergarten teacher, whose iron fist is gloved in silk, e.g., "If a coworker is too loud, kindly ask them to be sensitive to others in the area. They probably don't realize they are disturbing others..." Workers learn that "the new office design promotes a high-energy, creative team environment, that will allow employees to be more interactive and more efficient. There are many changes to adjust to in our new home, including color and interior design." One key innovation is to play "white noise" (i.e., static) throughout the work areas in order to mask regular office noises and music, but the volume is so high that it has driven workers to seek solace in restrooms, causing headaches and earaches. Orwell, indeed!

9. Friedrich H. Tenbruck, "The Problem of Thematic Unity in the Works of Max Weber, " *British Journal of Sociology* 31:3 (September, 1980), 316-351; Stephen Kalberg, "The Search for Thematic Orientations in a Fragmented Oeuvre: The Discussion of Max Weber in Recent German Sociological Literature, " *Sociology* 13:1 (1979), 127-139, and "Max Weber's Types of Rationality: Cornerstones for the Analysis of the Rationalization Process in History, " *American Journal of Sociology* 85:5 (March, 1980), 1145-1179; José Casanova, "Interpretations and Misinterpretations of Max Weber: The Problem of Rationalization, " in R.M. Glassman and V. Murvar (eds.), *Max Weber's Political Sociology: A Pessimistic Vision of a Rationalized World* (Westport, CT: Greenwood Press, 1984), 141-154.

10. Wilhelm Hennis, "Max Weber's 'Central Question', " *Economy and Society* 12:2 (May, 1983), 136-180; Guenther Roth, "Rationalization in Max Weber's Developmental History, " in Scott Lash and Sam Whimster (eds.), *Max Weber, Rationality, and Modernity* (London: Allen and Unwin, 1987), 75-91; Wolfgang Schluchter, "The Paradox of Rationalization: On the Relation of Ethics and World, " in Guenther Roth and Wolfgang Schluchter, *Max Weber's Vision of History: Ethics and Methods* (Berkeley: University of California Press, 1979), 11-64.

11. Julien Freund, *The Sociology of Max Weber*, tr. by Mary Ilford (New York: Random House, 1968), 18. (Same pagination for paperback edition: New York: Vintage Books, 1969.)

12. Alan Sica, *Max Weber: A Comprehensive Bibliography* (New Brunswick, NJ: Transaction Publishers, 2004), which includes a 4,600-item bibliography of secondary Weberian works in English, in addition to a complete listing of Weber's works in English translations.

13. Representative works that elaborate Weber's notion of rationalization, chosen for their variety of approach, include the following (alphabetized by author): Martin Albrow, "The Application of the Weberian Concept of Rationalization to Contemporary Conditions, " in Scott Lash and Sam Whimster (eds.), *Max Weber, Rationality, and Modernity*, (London: Allen and Unwin, 1987), 164-182; Martin Albrow, *Max Weber's Construction of Social Theory* (London: St. Martin's Press, 1990); Michael Banton, "Mixed Motives and the Processes of Rationalization, " *Ethnic and Racial Studies* 8:4 (October, 1985), 534-547; Reinhard Bendix, "The Cultural and Political Setting of Economic Rationality in Western and Eastern Europe, " in Reinhard Bendix, et al. (eds.), *State and Society: A Reader in Comparative Political Sociology* (Boston: Little, Brown, and Co., 1968), 335-351; Roslyn Wallach Bologh, "Max Weber and the Dilemma of Rationality, " in Ronald M. Glassman and Vatro Murvar (eds.), *Max Weber's Political Sociology: A*

Pessimistic Vision of a Rationalized World (Westport, CT: Greenwood Press, 1984), 175-186; Rogers Brubaker, *The Limits of Rationality: An Essay on the Social And Moral Thought of Max Weber* (London: George Allen and Unwin, 1984); Joseph M. Bryant, "From Myth to Theology: Intellectuals and the Rationalization of Religion in Ancient Greece, " in William Swatos, Jr. (ed.), *Time, Place, and Circumstance: Neo-Weberian Studies in Comparative Religious History* (Westport, CT: Greenwood Press, 1990), 71-85; Bruce Carruthers and Wendy Nelson Espeland, "Accounting for Rationality: Double-Entry Bookkeeping and the Rhetoric of Economic Rationality, " *American Journal of Sociology* 97:1 (July, 1991), 31-69; Randall Collins, *Weberian Sociological Theory* (Cambridge: Cambridge University Press, 1983), especially Chapter 2; Arnold Eisen, "The Meanings and Confusions of Weberian 'Rationality,'" *British Journal of Sociology*, 29:1 (March, 1978), 57-70; Joseba I. Esteban, "Habermas on Weber: Rationality, Rationalization, and the Diagnosis of the Times, " *Gnosis*, 3:4 (December, 1991), 93-115; Ferenc Feher, "Weber and the Rationalization of Music, " *International Journal of Politics, Culture, and Society*, 1:2 (Winter, 1987), 147-162; Franco Ferrarotti, *Max Weber and the Destiny of Reason*, tr. John Fraser (Armonk, NY: M. E. Sharpe, 1982); Ernest Gellner, *Reason and Culture: The Historic Role of Rationality and Rationalism*, (Oxford: Blackwell Publishers, 1992); Andrew Goodwin, "Rationalization and Democratization in the New Technologies of Popular Music, " in James Lull (ed.), *Popular Music and Communication*, 2nd ed. (Newbury Park, CA: Sage Publications, 1992), 75-100; Jukka Gronow, "The Element of Irrationality: Max Weber's Diagnosis of Modern Culture, " *Acta Sociologica* 31:4 (1988), 319-331; Jürgen Habermas, "Max Weber's Theory of Rationalization, " in *The Theory of Communicative Action*, Vol. 1, tr. T. McCarthy (Boston: Beacon Press, 1984), 143-271; Niles M. Hansen, "Sources of Economic Rationality, " in Robert W. Green (ed.), *Protestantism, Capitalism, and Social Science: The Weber Thesis Controversy* (Lexington: D.C. Heath, 1973), 137-149; Heinz Hartmann, "On Rational and Irrational Action, " *Psychoanalysis and the Social Sciences: An Annual*, Vol. 1 (ed. by Geza Roheim; New York: International Universities Press, 1947), 359-392; Soma Hewa and Robert W. Hetherington, "The Rationalization of Illness and the Illness of Rationalization, " *International Journal of Contemporary Sociology* 30:2 (October, 1993), 143-153; Richard A. Hilbert, "Bureaucracy as Belief, Rationalization as Repair: Max Weber in a Post-Functionalist Age, " *Sociological Theory* 5:1 (Spring, 1987), 70-86; Barry Hindess, "Rationality and the Characterization of Modern Society, " in Scott Lash and Sam Whimster (eds.), *Max Weber, Rationality, and Modernity* (London: Allen and Unwin, 1987), 137-153; Paul Honigsheim, *Music and Society: The Later Writings of Paul Honigsheim* (New York: John Wiley and Sons, 1973); Ludger Honnefelder, "Rationalization and Natural Law: Max Weber's and Ernst Troeltsch's Interpretation of the Medieval Doctrine of Natural Law, " *Review of Metaphysics* 49:2 [issue No. 194] (December, 1995), 275-294; H. Stuart Hughes, "Weber's Search for Rationality in Western Society, " in Robert W. Green (ed.), *Protestantism, Capitalism, and Social Science: The Weber Thesis Controversy* (Lexington: D.C. Heath, 1973), 150-169; David C. Jacobson, "Rationalization and Emancipation in Weber and Habermas, " *Graduate Faculty Journal of Sociology* 1:2 (Winter, 1976), 18-31; Aleksandra Jasinska-Kania, "Rationalization and Legitimation Crisis: The Relevance of Marxian and Weberian Works for an Explanation of the Political Order's Legitimacy Crisis in Poland, " *Sociology* 17:2 (May, 1983), 157-164; Bryn Jones, "Economic Action and Rational Organisation in the Sociology of Weber, " in Barry Hindess (ed.), *Sociological Theories of the Economy* (London: Macmillan, 1977), 28-65; Lutz Kaelber, "Weber's Lacuna: Medieval Religion and the Roots of Rationalization, " *Journal of the History of Ideas*, 57 (July, 1996), 465-485; Stephen E. Kalberg, "The Rationalization of Action in Max Weber's Sociology of Religion, " *Sociological Theory* 8:1 (Spring, 1990), 58-84; Dirk Käsler, *Max Weber: An Introduction to his Life and Work* (Cambridge: Polity Press, 1988); Howard L. Kaye, "Rationalization as Sublimation: On the Cultural Analyses of Weber and Freud, " *Theory, Culture, and Society* 9:4 (November, 1992), 45-74; Andrew M. Koch, "Rationality, Romanticism, and the Individual: Max Weber's 'Modernism' and the Confrontation with 'Modernity,'" *Canadian Journal of Political Science* 26:1 (March, 1993), 123-144; Ferdinand Kolegar, "The Concept of 'Rationalization' and Cultural Pessimism in Max Weber's Sociology, " *Sociological Quarterly* 5:4 (Autumn, 1964), 355-373; M.M.W. Lemmen, *Max Weber's Sociology of Religion: Its Method and Content in the Light of the Concept of Rationality*, tr. H.D. Morton (Hilversum: Gooi & Sticht, 1990), 254 pp.; Donald Levine, "Rationality and Freedom: Weber and Beyond, " *Sociological Inquiry* 51:1 (Winter, 1981), 5-25; Karl Löwith [Loewith], "Weber's Interpretation of the Bourgeois-Capitalistic World in Terms of the Guiding Principle of 'Rationalization', " in Dennis Wrong (ed.), *Max Weber* [Makers of Modern Social Science] (Englewood Cliffs, NJ: Prentice-Hall, 1970), 101-122; Valerie Ann Malhotra, "Weber's Concept of Rationalization and the Electronic Evolution in Western Classical Music, " *Qualitative Sociology* 1:3 (January, 1979), 100-120; Gert H. Mueller, "The Notion of Rationality in the Work of Max Weber, " *Archives européennes de sociologie* 20:1 (1979), 149-171; Benjamin Nelson, "Max Weber and the Discontents and Dilemmas of Contemporary Universally Rationalized Post-Christian Civilization, " in Walter Sprondel and Constans Seyfarth (eds.), *Max Weber und die Rationalisierung sozialen Handelns* (Stuttgart: Ferdinand Enke Verlag, 1981), 1-8; Donald A. Nielson, "The Inquisition, Rationalization, and Sociocultural Change in Medieval Europe, " in William Swatos, Jr. (ed.), *Time, Place, and Circumstance: Neo-Weberian Studies in Comparative Religious History* (Westport, CT: Greenwood Press, 1990), 107-122; Raul Pertierra, "Forms of Rationality? Rationalization and Social Transformation in a Northern Philippine Community, " *Social Analysis* #17 (August, 1985), 49-70; George Ritzer, "Professionalization, Bureaucratization and Rationalization: The Views of Max Weber, " *Social Forces* 53:4 (June, 1975), 627-634; Guenther Roth, "Duration and Rationalization: Fernand Braudel and Max Weber, " in Guenther Roth and Wolfgang Schluchter, *Max Weber's Vision of History: Ethics and Methods* (Berkeley: University of California Press, 1979), 166-193; Mahmoud Sadri, "Reconstruction of Max Weber's Notion of Rationality: An Immanent Model, " *Social Research* 49:3 (Autumn, 1982), 616-633; Wolfgang Schluchter, *The Rise of Western Rationalism: Max Weber's Developmental History*, tr. Guenther Roth (Berkeley: University of California Press, 1981); Wolfgang Schluchter, *Rationalism, Religion, and Domination: A Weberian Perspective*, tr. Neil Solomon (Berkeley: University of California Press, 1989); Alfred Schutz, "The Problem of Rationality in the Social World, " in Dorothy Emmet and Alasdair MacIntyre (eds.), *Sociological*

Theory and Philosophical Analysis (New York: Macmillan Co., 1970), 89-114; Thomas W. Segady, "Rationality and Irrationality: New Directions in Weberian Theory, Critique, and Research, " *Sociological Spectrum* 8 (1988), 85-100; Ronen Shamir, "Formal and Substantive Rationality in American Law: A Weberian Perspective, " *Social and Legal Studies* 2 (1993), 45-72; Alan Sica "Reasonable Science, Unreasonable Life: The Happy Fictions of Marx, Weber, and Social Theory, " in Robert Antonio and Ronald Glassman (eds.), *A Weber-Marx Dialogue* (Lawrence: University Press of Kansas, 1985), 68-88; Alan Sica, *Weber, Irrationality, and Social Order* (Berkeley: University of California Press, 1988 [revised paperback edition, 1990]); Joyce S. Sterling and Wilbert E. Moore, "Weber's Analysis of Legal Rationalization: A Critique and Constructive Modification, " *Sociological Forum* 2:1 (1987), 67-89; J.J.R. Thomas, "Rationalization and the Status of Gender Divisions, " *Sociology* 19:3 (August, 1985), 409-420; Bryan S. Turner, "The Rationalization of the Body: Reflections on Modernity and Discipline, " in Scott Lash and Sam Whimster (eds.), *Max Weber, Rationality, and Modernity* (London: Allen and Unwin, 1987), 222-241; Stanley H. Udy, Jr., "'Bureaucracy' and 'Rationality' in Weber's Organization Theory: An Empirical Study, *American Sociological Review* 24 (1959), 791-795; Johannes Weiss, "On the Irreversibility of Western Rationalization and Max Weber's Alleged Fatalism, " in Scott Lash and Sam Whimster (eds.), *Max Weber, Rationality, and Modernity* (London: Allen and Unwin, 1987), 154-163;

14. From the list in note 13, the most pertinent entries include Brubaker, 1984; Kalberg, 1980; Schluchter, 1981; Sica, 1988; to which should be added Randall Collins, *Max Weber: A Skeleton Key* (Beverly Hills, CA: Sage Publications, 1986, 61-80, and Otto Stammer (ed.), *Max Weber Today* (New York: Harper and Row, 1972), especially pp. 154-175, where several eminent Weberians answer Herbert Marcuse's famous attack on Weber's putative view of Western history and politics.

15. Raymond Aron, *German Sociology* and *Main Currents in Sociological Thought*, vol. 2 (New York: Basic Books, 1967), no specific references; Rogers Brubaker, *The Limits of Rationality*, a detailed, unchronological, and eclectic usage, with particular attention to *ES*, and several essays, including "'Author's Introduction' to *The Protestant Ethic*" and "Anticritical LastWord on The Spirit of Capitalism"; Randall Collins, *Weberian Sociological Theory* and *Max Weber: A Skeleton Key*, mostly attending to ES, GEH, and *PE*; Anthony Giddens, *Capitalism and Modern Social Theory*, heavily relying on From *Max Weber, GEH*, and *ES*; Jürgen Habermas, *Theory of Communicative Action*, the most sustained attempt at definitive exploration, putting to use several dozen passages from *ES, From Max Weber*, and *PE*; Karl Löwith, "Weber's Interpretation of the Bourgeois-Capitalistic World..." in Dennis Wrong (ed.), *Max Weber*, the most unusual set of citations, including by far the most references to *The Methodology of the Social Sciences* and other essays regarding method, plus his political writings; George Ritzer, *Classical Sociological Theory*, 2nd ed. (New York: McGraw-Hill, 1996) relying heavily on the essays of Stephen Kalberg and on Brubaker's short book, he cites material from *ES, GEH*, and *PE*, in a standard textbook treatment which is surely seen by more novices than any of the previously mentioned literature.

16. Reinhard Bendix, "Discussion on Industrialization and Capitalism" [in response to a paper by Herbert Marcuse], in Otto Stammer (ed.), *Max*

Weber and Sociology Today (New York: Harper and Row, 1972), p. 159; Bendix translated this from *Wirtschaft und Gesellschaft*, II (Tübingen, 1920), p. 662; for a different and standard English translation, see Weber's *Economy and Society*, p. 975.

17. Benjamin Nelson, "Discussion on Industrialization and Capitalism," in Otto Stammer (ed.), *Max Weber and Sociology Today*, 167-168. 4.

18. Max Weber, *Political Writings*, edited by Peter Lassman and Ronald Speirs (Cambridge: Cambridge University Press, 1994), 147-148, translated by Speirs; all emphases are Weber's own. The standard translation, under the title "Parliament and Government in a Reconstructed Germany: A Contribution to the Political Critique of Officialdom and Party Politics," is in *Economy and Society*, at pp. 1394-1395.

19. For bibliographic details, see Gary Shapiro and Alan Sica (eds.), *Hermeneutics: Questions and Prospects* (Amherst, MA: University of Massachusetts Press, 1988, pb ed), 293-307, 319-320. Especially enlightening in this context are Hans-Georg Gadamer, *Truth and Method* (rev. translation) (New York: Continuum Publishing, 1989/1995); Emilio Betti, "Hermeneutics as a General Method for the Human Sciences," tr. in Josef Bleicher (ed.), *Contemporary Hermeneutics* (London: Routledge and Kegan Paul, 1980); Paul de Man, *Allegories of Reading* (New Haven: Yale University Press, 1979); E. D. Hirsch, *Validity in Interpretation* (New Haven: Yale University Press, 1967); George Steiner, *After Babel* (2nd ed.) (New York: Oxford University Press, 1992); and Harold Bloom, *A Map of Misreading* (New York: Oxford University Press, 1975).

20. For details of Weber's lifelong attachment to the imagery and ideas of Goethe, particularly with regard to Faust and the rationalization theme, see Alan Sica, "Reasonable Science, Unreasonable Life: The Happy Fictions of Marx, Weber, and Social Theory," in Robert Antonio and Ronald Glassman (eds.), *A Weber-Marx Dialogue* (Lawrence, KS: University Press of Kansas, 1985), 68-88.

21. See Alan Sica, *Weber, Irrationality, and Social Order* (Berkeley: University of California Press, 1988; rev. pb ed., 1990), passim.

22. *The Protestant Ethic and the Spirit of Capitalism*, tr. by Talcott Parsons (New York: Charles Scribner's Sons, 1930), p. 182. As explained in note 20 above, I have argued at length that Weber's inspiration for this passage was Goethe.

5

Weber, Historiography, and the U.S. Case

Max Weber's Intellectual Legacy

Since his death in 1920, Max Weber's name has become virtually a synonym for unsurpassed creativity and breadth in social research and theorizing, especially in the U.S. and Europe. His scholarly influence in other parts or the world is extensive as well, principally because he made meticulous studies of social structures and social change concerning ancient Rome, medieval Italy and Spain, ancient Israel, India, China, colonial America, and other locales, thereby perfecting "comparative analysis" of the sort that is now routinely practiced by social scientists. He developed methodological tools for social and historical research, such as the "ideal type," and illustrated their use in dozens of applications, treating everything from ancient Roman land use practices to workplace behavior in his grandfather's textile mill which in 1908 he studied in person. His importance to social and political theory, comparative religion, the sociology and philosophy of law, and the philosophy and method of the social sciences refuses to diminish. Each year scholarly studies and applications of his work appear in greater numbers than before, so that in English alone nearly 4,600 items now fill the largest bibliography of Weberian analysis (see Sica, 2004). In the last several years, a dozen monographs exclusively about Weber have been published just in the Anglophone world, mimicked by similar rates of production in Asia and Latin America.

Additionally, it is now impossible to discuss American social science without quickly coming upon the terms "rationalization," "ideal-type," "unintended consequences of social action," "charismatic authority," "the iron cage of bureaucratic life," and, "the Protestant ethic," to name only a few of Weber's neologisms. All these terms were either of his own making or greatly augmented by his work, and when tied to his "nominalistic" and "value-free" approach to social research, they go a long way toward defining what modern social science has become. In short, if there has been a "Renaissance man" in modern historical and sociological scholarship, Weber comes as close to this polymathic ideal as anyone. His way of going about historical and social research has inspired countless studies in the past, and continues to exert widespread influence today.

Though it is possible to separate Weber's life from his work in considering the latter, it is not advisable, for the same "tensions" (*Spannung*) which he constantly invoked in his writing, whether regarding ancient civilizations or his own, affected his private life profoundly. Born in 1864, Weber was the eldest son of a well-known nationalist political leader who operated comfortably within the harsh realm of *Realpolitik*, and with whom Weber experienced constant, muted struggles, for approval and understanding. But he was much closer emotionally to his devout Pietist mother, for whom every question in life revolved around pressing ethical and moral demands for propriety, issues which arose in letters they exchanged even when he was still quite young. It was this potentially explosive and classical dualism of character and motivation which led, in July, 1897, to Weber's now famous break with his father, never reconciled before the father's sudden death six weeks later. A more classically perfect Oedipal struggle could hardly be imagined. His father, Max, Sr., with a heavy patriarchal hand, had pushed his wife, and Weber's summer houseguest, into an untenable ethical position regarding finances and domestic living arrangements. Max, Jr., violating the unwritten law of Victorian paternal authority, ordered his father to leave his home in order to protect his mother's autonomy, and the resulting rupture remained permanent. The impossibility of reconciliation occasioned by Max, Sr.'s death in August, 1897, led directly to his son's severe encounter with mental illness that lasted in full force for five years, but lingered in its life-changing impact until Weber's own death in 1920. This event and its aftermath have occasioned several monographs and many articles, since it seems to encapsulate many of the positive and negative aspects of *haute bourgeois* existence at the fin de siécle, and Weber's special role within and understanding of that peculiar constellation of cultural forces.

Weber wrote a self-analysis of this disoriented period of his life, and consulted eminent psychiatrists (notably Karl Jaspers), but the documents were destroyed during the Nazi period by his wife, Marianne Weber, for fear they would be used by Hitler's government to discredit him. What we do know is that he experienced insomnia, neurasthenia, hysterical paralysis, almost surely impotence, and perhaps worst of all given Weber's heroic dedication to academic labors, a nearly complete inability to read, write, or lecture for months at a time. That he survived this period without recourse to suicide (which had claimed some of his close relatives) is testimony to his iron will, even in the face of complete emotional and physical collapse. The argument has been made repeatedly by Weber scholars that it was largely in response to these overwhelming sensations of powerlessness, displacement, and pervasive meaninglessness, which he darkly believed saturated and characterized modern life for many modern sophisticates, that Weber began the single largest research task ever undertaken by a solo social scientist, and carried it remarkably far toward completion in his short professional life of about twenty years.

The influence of Nietzsche is apparent in this general point of view, but Weber's response to cultural malaise followed entirely different lines than those of his countryman. He sought to answer several large, interrelated questions, and found that only through rigorous comparative research could he attempt to offer plausible answers. Marx's challenge to conventional historical methods posed itself to all social scientists and historians of Weber's generation, and forced him from the outset to consider the causal relation of ideas to societal change. Among the more dogmatic of Marx's followers, it was generally held that substructural forces ("the means and relations of production") determined in more or less direct fashion the superstructural ideologies that guided human actions, and which supplied ethical, religious, and philosophical justifications for whatever historical events actually transpired. In short, for the intellectual Left, ideas held an epiphenomenal status vis-à-vis forces that churned along in the infrastructural (political-economic) sphere. Weber repeatedly stressed his agreement with the claim that in the last instance, economic interests do guide "consciousness," and not vice versa. One of his most memorable and often-quoted observations spells this out very clearly: "Not ideas, but material and ideal interests, directly govern men's conduct. Yet very frequently the 'world images' that have been created by 'ideas' have, like switchmen, determined the tracks along which action has been pushed by the dynamic of interest. 'From what' and 'for what' one wished to be redeemed and, let us not forget, 'could be' redeemed, depended upon one's image of the world" (Weber, 1946: 280). (The famous "switchmen metaphor" came to Weber in 1913 when he was composing his introduction to the articles that heralded his "sociology of religion," and which reflected his pessimism about the ideological justifications for war clouds that were threatening Europe for the first time since Napoleon.) Thus, his unrivalled historical knowledge and his accompanying sensitivity to the subtleties of historical explanation forced him to accede to the importance of the opposing, "idealist" view. This antinomy, which irreconcilably divided Marxist from "bourgeois" social science, Weber went further in mitigating than anyone before him, specifically through his studies in the "economic ethics of world religions." This gargantuan series eventually included *The Protestant Ethic and the Spirit of Capitalism* (1905), *The Religion of China* (1916), *The Religion of India* (1916/17), and *Ancient Judaism* (1917), plus a study along similar lines regarding Islam which Weber did not live to finish. Each of these works has been judged a prescient masterpiece by generations of scholars who have learned from them, and they continue to be read and debated even today. And it was in carrying out these works that he developed his most famous analytic, substantive, and methodological approaches to the problem of world history.

Yet he had begun much differently, and with more conventional, smaller aims. He had been excellently educated in history and languages prior to university training as were most young men of his caste at the time, learning English, French, Greek, and Latin. One of the privileges attached to being his father's son was the opportunity to eavesdrop on conversations in his home among some of the leading political and intellectual leaders in Bismarck's Germany. Household visitors and friends included Wilhelm Dilthey, Theodor Mommsen, Heinrich von Treitschke, and many family members who were academics or clergymen. At a very early age, Weber wrote essays on "Reasons for the decline of Rome" and similarly weighty topics, surely inspired in part by some of these houseguests. It was during this impressionable period of life that he also began to understand the definitive difference between actions based on political expediency versus knowledge acquired for its own sake, something which he codified and made famous in two paired speeches near the end of his life, "Science as a Vocation [*Beruf*]" and "Politics as a Vocation" (1919). This distinction not only grew from his witnessing of political strategy talks held between his father and his cronies, but also, and more importantly, it systematized a fault line which always existed between his parents' conflicting *Weltanschauungen*. For his father the possession and exercise of political power was an end in itself, but for his religiously devout mother, only unblemished ethical ends should be energetically pursued for their own sake, and no quarter was given for the use of shabby means toward some "higher" goal.

Weber's mature position on these issues, expressed in the two speeches and elsewhere, has become canonical, not only for the social sciences, but for all modern citizens wishing to understand political power on the one hand, and undistorted truth on the other. He bluntly explained that an "ethic of responsibility" in political matters made it essential for political actors sometimes to make use of unsavory techniques in order to nurture their political agendas, whereas the scholar, committed in principle to an "ethic of absolute ends," could never allow himself (or herself) this luxury of "realism" or "instrumental rationality." Weber understood the need to merge both in the personality of the great states-man, but learned through his historical studies how rarely both ethics were optimally conjoined—that difficult balance between effectiveness and propriety. (He also witnessed the failure of grand statesmanship at Versailles in 1919, where he served as a German government expert on constitutional law during the treaty talks.) He followed these dictates literally and thereby sometimes appeared to contemporaries as a genu-inely quixotic figure, for example, when he refused to appear at exami-nations of his own students by other professors as they tried to win beginning academic positions, since he did not want "unfairly" to preju-dice the examiners by his prestige as a scholar.

Yet these developments came late in a hectic professional life. His superb early education in classics, history, and languages while still young provided him with a firm foundation for a number of phenom-enally precocious essays on ancient history and political economy, al-ready displaying both wide learning and remarkable analytic ability. After the obligatory law degree he published a dissertation (1889) on early global trading companies in Italy and Spain, for which he needed to teach himself medieval Italian and Spanish (the tedium of which caused him to complain to his mother in letters home) in order to use the proper archival materials. Quickly he then composed a habilitation on Roman agrarian history and law (1891) using an entirely fresh set of data and methods, thereby winning for himself instant esteem among two entirely separate subfields within German historiography. The ti-tan of Roman history, Theodor Mommsen, then seventy-four, was present at Weber's well-attended public defense of the habilitation, spoken in Latin as by tradition, and when everyone else had weighed in, he asked the young Weber a penetrating question which pitted Mommsen's own view against Weber's regarding the tricky historical relationship of *colonia* versus *municipium*. In characteristic fashion, Weber answered directly and honestly, after which Mommsen uttered the now famous line, "But when I have to go to my grave someday, there is no one to whom I would rather say, 'Son here is my spear; it is getting too heavy for my arm' than the highly esteemed Max Weber" (as reported by Marianne Weber in her *Max Weber*). There could not have been a more auspicious beginning than this to an academic career as a humanist, and Weber had thereby qualified himself to teach and write in two separate areas of historical specialization.

This precocious recognition led to his being invited to oversee a vast empirical study of agrarian workers in Prussia. Though only twenty-eight when this 900-page report appeared, Weber had already adopted a style of conceptualization that stayed with him throughout his career. The specific concern of the sponsoring research organization was to learn what effect Slavic workers would have upon indigenous culture east of the Elbe. They feared that a mighty influx of uneducated agrarian laborers from what is now Poland and Russia would have deleterious effects on "the German character" and, more importantly, on the political economy of the region. But Weber, wishing always to bridge structure and process, to identify the altering power of ideas within political-economic constraints, focused instead on the pull urban "individualism" exercised on traditionally inert rural workers. He combined this social-psychological perspective with treatment of grosser issues concerning the transformation of the Prussian political economy due to revised circumstances and practices of the ruling (*Junker*) class in their new, "anti-traditional" pursuit of capitalist profit. As their private fortunes grew, their commitment to the commonwealth naturally declined. This reordering of priorities was long in evidence among the bourgeoisie, who meanwhile "ennobled" themselves by purchasing landed titles. Taken together these new behavior patterns imperiled Prussian social structure, and hence the nascent German nation-state, whose military strength relied heavily on Prussian cultural practices. Weber took inordinate pains to work up the report, based on thousands of questionnaires submitted to local notables, doing the tabulations himself and by hand, and filling the final report with dozens of tables, which at the time was still a new technique in social research. He thrived analytically on just these sorts of phenomena, since their explanation demanded the shrewd connecting of micro (psychological) with macro (structural) events and processes. Surely without being aware of it, Weber was helping to create a new mode of social research that brought together quantified survey data and high-level cultural and political theorizing, which, once he had illustrated it in practice, became his calling card throughout the rest of his work.

Even more importantly, though, it prompted Weber to reflect on the antinomic relation of ethics peculiar to pre-capitalist life and the totally different focus of action suited to capitalist social organization. Though published much later, after his death (as part of his chaotic masterpiece, *Economy and Society*), his typology of fundamental social action originated here, as he assessed the behavior of social actors moving from one historical structure to the next. For with this structural transformation and steady erosion of ageless traditions, necessarily came rearrangements of personality as people adapted to their new social world. According to Weber's four fundamental types of social action—roughly translated as purpose-rationality, value-rationality, emotional, and traditional—it is most difficult to move from a traditional mode of behavior, characterized in almost pure form by the mindset of agrarian peasant life, to the purpose-rationality that typifies cost-benefit analysis within a capitalist environment. Weber understood as did few others at the time that each of these widely disparate *Weltanschauungen* offered strengths and weaknesses to the people who lived "within" them. And even though capitalist social organization was pushing relentlessly to extirpate traditional and emotional modes of social action, there still lay within these spheres a reservoir of resistance to the cold logic of profit-seeking which caught Weber's interest, and which he studied through a variety of topics, particularly religiously inspired economic behavior.

What Weber explained, at a level of thoroughness and complexity which surpassed everyone coming before him, was that as huge structural transformations began to take hold in Europe and the U.S. in the latter nineteenth century, these necessarily demanded reconfigurations of the individual's character traits. What "worked" for laborers and entrepreneurs in early capitalist society no longer met the requirements of monopoly capital as practiced in the world's industrialized nations. This type of linkage, between the micro-environment of interpersonal life, and the macro-environment of large scale, organizational interaction, could be viewed as Weber's major contribution to social theory and general social science. Yet it is also in some ways the most difficult to understand.

Many modern practitioners see Weber as principally a "structuralist," yet the quintessential Weberian analysis, of the Protestant capitalist, turns more upon social-psychological then organizational dynamics. (This could be said tout court for his theory of "charismatic domination.") For Weber the sociologist must attend not only to character types (the traditional mode of explanation), nor only to the frozen givenness of structure à la crude Marxism, but to a heuristically satisfying synthesis of both. This he did by dividing action into the famous typology of four types mentioned above (see *Economy and Society*, pp. 25ff). The subtleties of this arrangement cannot be pursued here—entire monographs have been written elucidating it—but his overall intention seems clear. To the first two types (traditional and emotional forms of "social action") he ascribed pre-rational, pre-capitalist motivation and the resulting behavior which grew out of it. However, he circumspectly noted, as was his habit in everything he wrote, that none of these four "ideal-types" of action were ever to be found within social life in pure form, and that all four types (including purpose-rationality and value-rationality) played essential roles in modern existence. In fact, they could be seen working simultaneously within certain complex socio-economic interactions, which was all the more reason to separate them *for analytic purposes* while analyzing social change.

That said, however, it became clear as he wrote about the origins of capitalism, in Europe and the U.S., that *homo oeconomicus* had "evolved" to become the core of the last type of action (*zweckrationalische*). To adopt "cold rationality" in economic *and* social calculations as the predominant organizing principle of life seemed to some economists of Weber's generation (and even today) as the definitive indicator that a society's members had "modernized," throwing off the yoke of their traditional past. Weber understood this simplification to be nefarious in its distortion of historical data, as well as in its meaning for the future of industrialized societies. It is undoubtedly the case that purpose-rationality served not only as an empirical reference point for comparison with the other three types of action, but also became for many investigators, noticeably less subtle than Weber, a normative goal toward which contemporary social actors and the collectivities they constituted should aspire. This is an important avenue toward understanding Weber's mature work and its remarkable staying power as a guide for social and historical research. It was as a rigorous, even ascetic proponent of rationality in all social arrangements, and especially in politics, that he most fully recognized the dimensions of the irrational or non-rationalizable aspects of societal existence. To argue he became the Freud of *collective* nonrationality is only a minor exaggeration (while choosing to ignore Gustave Le Bon, Vilfredo Pareto and others who, though once central to this stream of thought, have fallen into eclipse).

Weber always pursued solutions to large questions through comparative research. When he wanted to disentangle the basic ingredients of the earliest capitalist social organization in Western Europe and the United States, he turned to the Orient, rapidly producing masterful analyses of Hinduism, Confucianism, Buddhism, Judaism, and unfinished notes on Islam. Although these monographs reached in scope far beyond the central question which inspired them, the main purpose was to discover why sheer business acumen, even greed, had not produced within these cultures a capitalist form of behavior and organization of the type easily identified in Northern Europe after the sixteenth century. Likewise, when assessing modern bureaucracies and their tendency toward ethical and practical "universalism" (of form and content)— that is, the systematic elimination of nonrationalizable categories of knowledge, advancement, and control—he studied bureaucracies in ancient Egypt, Rome, China, India, and his own Prussia. Similarly, when he wanted to learn the prospects for democracy in his own country, he looked to Russia, and wrote a series of extraordinary studies, in 1905, of the penultimate revolution prior to Bolshevik hegemony in 1917. (To do this, incidentally, be learned to read Russian in about six weeks by hiring emigré tutors then in Heidelberg, so that he could follow news reports in Russian newspapers.)

One should not conclude, however, that because he studied the course of rationalization processes through history, noting its advances and retreats with equal care, that he embraced a rational model of action as an unequivocal good. He was not a crude Benthamite, or what in modern parlance would be a "rational choice theorist." But neither was he Hegelian or romantic enough to overvalue the "organic" pre-rationality of social life prior to industrialism. There were aspects of the latter—personal honor and integrity, historical sensitivity, individual sacrifice for collective well-being—that he strongly admired. But he refused to join the massive chorus of protest against modernity and its values which could then be heard from many German intellectuals (perhaps most notably the poet Stefan George, with whom Weber had several unsatisfactory meetings). Though not an evolutionist, he recognized the irresistible power of rationality as it turned from one social institution to another—to use Hegelian imagery—creating sometimes irritating uniformity and predictability where before had been some measure of uniqueness and chance. Today's celebration of The Other and "difference" were not welcome under the regimen of wholesale rationalization which Weber so carefully documented. The logic of modernization demanded predictability in mechanical as well as personal relations, in addition to consistency of approach, record keeping, and uniform action toward a specified goal. The fruits of this regimenting were obvious to all the celebrants of Victorian, imperialistic Europe, but Weber (along with Nietzsche and a few others) also saw the debilitating nature of profound rationalization, both for the individual and social organization at large. What had begun in the eighteenth century as a "light cloak" of social reorganization had resolutely evolved into an "iron cage," and in some of Weber's most famous lines, he warned: "No one knows who will live in this cage in the future.... For of the last stage of this cultural development, it might well be truly said: Specialists without spirit, sensualists without heart; this nullity imagines that it has attained a level of civilization never before achieved" (*The Protestant Ethic and the Spirit of Capitalism*, 1930: 182). One recalls Marx's prescient remark in his *Early Philosophic Manuscripts of 1844*: "An unobjective being is a *nullity* — an *un-being*." For both theorists, the end result of massive rationalization for the affected individuals was a condition of non-being in its most fundamental sense.

Certain German scholars today argue that Weber was predominantly a moral and political philosopher, and that his summary essays on the sociology of religion should be viewed as his Archimedean point. Yet whether one takes his theory of bureaucracy, his analyses of classical religious dogmas and their social structures, his work on Roman and modern law, his abstract typologies of economic, political, and legal relations, or even his revolutionary "sociology of music," as the central achievement of the man, the reason he continues to lead social theorists and researchers into new paths is because of his informed moral vision and his courage in stating it boldly. What Nietzsche did for philosophy, Weber did for social science, but without the bravado and inaccuracy of long-dismissed authors like Spengler. He continued to believe that rationality, in creating the iron cage, at the same time proved its ability to soften the bars when applied wisely. What he could not find in 1920 was the social group which was skilled, lucky, powerful or faithful enough to do it.

Max Weber and American Historiography

Applications of Weber's ideas within the context of American history are as various as his substantive and theoretical innovations were far-flung. The characteristic aversion most historians are trained to feel for the "merely theoretical" (see Burke, 1992: 1-11 for an enlightened discussion of this condition) has not prevented them from plundering Weber's ideas when it suited them, yet it is clear that many could have strengthened their studies had they known more details about his methods and ideas (for a rare exception, see Jäger, 1991). The unusually high quality of Weber's theorizing probably reflects the fact that his theories always grew out of direct contact with historical data, and his unswerving desire to solve substantive problems by means of theoretical innovation. It should also be remembered that he was never shy about asking for expert help from his friends and colleagues, some of whom numbered among the top scholars in their fields (e.g., Ernst Troeltsch on the history of the Christian church, and Paul Deussen on Eastern religions). Popular uses of his ideas among historians have included treatments of presidents and other leaders who either exhibited "charisma" (Lincoln, both Roosevelts, Kennedy; see particularly Schwartz, 1987 on Washington and Schwartz, 2000 on Lincoln) or lacked this mysterious power over their followers (most of the remaining ones). Weber borrowed Rudolf Sohm's notion of charisma ("gift of grace") from the latter's works in church history (1875), then broadened it to include forms of political, military, or religious leadership that draw on "irrational" sources of attraction for infatuated followers. Hundreds of studies have exploited Weber's explanation of "charismatic domination" (the *locus classicus* for which is in his *Economy and Society*: 1111-14 and 1141-42), including those by Lindholm (1990), Olin (1980), Peacock (1989), and Schweitzer (1984). No one has argued that this relatively small part of Weber's oeuvre can be viewed as an unassailable analytic device, yet its widespread use among historians and other social scientists, even in diluted form, suggests its fundamental strength as a way of interpreting macro-political events.

Many more historians have commented on and otherwise evaluated, often with carefully documented caveats, Weber's perennially fascinating "Protestant Ethic thesis," which has by now occasioned several thousand publications in the international scholarly press. It is unnecessary to recount Weber's argument here, other than to note that its subtleties and qualifications are very often missed, perhaps because most of the data are buried in the forbidding endnotes that make up one half of the printed text. Though tricky, therefore, to summarize, the outline of Weber's complex argument can be laid out easily enough. Just emerging from his five-year emotional crisis in 1903, and on the heels of a pivotally important extensive tour of the U.S. in 1904, Weber turned to the question of why certain cultures seemed to promote capitalist accumulation in its earliest stages, while others either put roadblocks before its progress, or were indifferent to the way it changed their social landscape. In two landmark essays published in 1904/05 in a specialty journal, Weber offered the world what has become one of the most frequently cited (if misunderstood) texts in the history of social analysis. He held that in Northern Europe, Britain, and the U.S., attitudes toward work, savings, and a prohibition against conspicuous consumption (to use Veblen's term, coined in 1900; see Diggins, 1999: 111ff, for a comparison of Weber's and Veblen's theories of capitalist development) all conspired to establish fertile ground in which capitalism could flourish. Southern European (hence, Catholic) countries, as well as those in Asia, did not inculcate in their citizens the requisite virtues of thrift, punctuality, rational accounting, and a fear of luxurious living necessarily linked to ideas of predestination that Weber identified as essential for the wholehearted adoption of capitalist procedures and economic organization.

Weber did not argue that sharp business practices had never existed, say, in China, India, or Italy. Rather, capital accumulation and rational accounting procedures had never found so suitable an ideological basis as that provided by Reformation theology, much of which can be summarized in the unique German concept of *Beruf* (God-given work). One need not look very far in American religious texts to find documentation of this attitude. It was well summarized by Thomas Chalkley, an American Quaker: "We not only have Liberty to labour in Moderation, but... it is our duty so to do. The Farmer, the Tradesman, and the Merchant do not understand by our Lord's doctrine, that they must neglect their Calling, or grow idle in their Business, but must certainly work, and be industrious in their Calling" (Tolles, 1948: 56). Weber's "data" for these conclusions were largely though not exclusively the published texts of important theological writers, from Luther to Calvin to Wesley, augmented by his insightful analysis of religion and economic life in America which he saw first-hand (reported in his "The Protestant Sects and the

Spirit of Capitalism" [1906]; see *From Max Weber*: 302-322), plus his personal knowledge of Protestant businessmen in Europe. Critics have argued that he would have done better to examine "hard" economic data rather than intellectual tracts, but Weber had already in his previous work done exactly this, and believed that the tracts were legitimate guides to the Protestant worldview.

Needless to say, his arguments about this issue, particularly because he used Benjamin's Franklin's *Autobiography* (see inter alia, Axelrad, 1978; Bier, 1970), Richard Baxter's devotional literature (see Cooke, 1994), and other familiar writings as hallmarks of "the Protestant ethic," have been scrutinized in extraordinary detail. And not surprisingly, when particular cases have been considered (e.g., the merchants of seventeenth-century Boston [Bailyn, 1955]), what is taken to be Weber's general prescription for capitalist growth has not always held (see Henretta, 1991: 35-70; also Buck, 1993; Johnson, 1971; Kolbenschlag, 1976; for a sharp critique, see Kolko, 1961; for an intriguing extension concerning presidential rhetoric, see Falk, 1980). Part of this is the result of misinterpretation of what Weber actually claimed (for thorough documentation, see Lehmann and Roth, 1993; also Hudson, 1988), and partly it is because even as good as he was in handling historical data, he could not possibly anticipate every "anomalous case" which researchers would subsequently be able to identify, for example, "The Business Ideology of Benjamin Franklin and Japanese Values of the 18th Century" (Watanabe, 1988).

James Henretta has examined the Weber thesis carefully in terms of the colonial American case (Henretta, 1991), and overall finds considerable support for the argument, even if modifications must be made to accommodate peculiarities of place and time. First of all, it is child's play to find quotations from early Americans, especially in Quaker Philadelphia or Puritan Massachusetts, who wrote testaments of faith that clearly support Weber's portrait of the prototypical capitalist "mentality." As Weber put it, dedication to a calling originated in "rational planning of the whole of one's life in accordance with God's will" (Weber, 1930: 153). Bailyn had already demonstrated the persuasiveness of Weber's view in an early work, by quoting sources like Joshua Scottow of Boston, who, after moving to Maine, declared in 1691 that mercantile Boston had become "a lost Town. We must cry out" and admit "our Leanness, our Apostasy" (Bailyn, 1955: 122-123). Scottow knew that unbridled capitalist activity would spell the end of religious devotion, even as devout practices enlarged capitalist fortunes. Perry Miller (1953) and Frederick Tolles (1948) were early students of this phenomenon, and recognized that "the lives of such Puritans and Quakers were not easy, for this religious doctrine created a major tension in their lives" (Henretta, 1991: 38). As their fortunes grew, the strain within their religiosity, and that of their children, naturally began to tell. Existential contradictions of this type were studied by later historians of the phenomenon, such as Foster (1971) and Ziff (1973), and even though certain clarifications of Weber's claims had to be made, the edifice of his argument held.

The most important alteration sprang from the insight that independent entrepreneurial activity generated substantial friction when set opposite the needs of community, a problem that surfaced very early, as famously documented in *The Apologia of Robert Keayne* (Bailyn, 1965). Keayne, a successful merchant, was punitively fined in 1639 for having practiced what we now call "price-gouging," but his windy self-defense celebrates the virtues of his business practices as part and parcel of his religious devoutness. Joyce Appleby (1984; 1993), Jack P. Greene (1988), Karl Hertz (1991), Daniel Howe (1972), Gary Nash (1984), and Michael Walzer (1963) have elaborated this modification of the Weberian picture, highlighting the economic communalism that was practiced in early American society as opposed to ruthless capitalist practices of the ideal-type. Bruce Mann (1980; 1987) extended this stream of argument from the familiar case of Boston to a Connecticut village, with particular attention to the ways "community norms of equity" controlled profit making (Henretta, 1991:68). Yet even with all such qualifications duly registered, Henretta summarizes his survey with this observation: "The ambiguities of the 'Protestant ethic' carried to New England by John Hull, Joshua Scottow, and John Higginson had achieved a clear definition in the 'capitalist spirit' of the founders of Waltham and Lowell, their religious and biological descendants" (ibid.: 70). Thus, considering early American history without utilizing Weber's ideas seems at this point in scholarly developments almost inconceivable.

A number of tangent scholarly streams can be connected to the Protestant Ethic debate. In a recent publication, Dorothy Ross has shown that "Another kind of new history emerged from efforts to use modernization theory as the narrative and analytical spine of American historiography. Modernization theory descends from ideas of liberal progress that have been powerful since the eighteenth century and from the sociological theories of Ferdinand Tönnies and Max Weber" (Ross, 1998: 93). She enlarges this argument by pointing out that modernization theory served broad American political interests during the Cold War as an antidote to revolutionary Marxism, "casting economic development as the prime motor of progress, to which were linked changes in personality and politics. . . it tended to view modernization as an integrated, deterministic process but allowed for failure, particularly through the semiautonomous sphere of politics." Although historians were "wary of it from the start," modernization theory had a strong impact on American foreign policy and theories of global economic life, much of which owes its fundamental notions to Weber's work in his magnum opus, *Economy and Society*. Just as an understanding of imperialism as an economic or political policy is impossible to understand without reference to Marx's work, so too modernization theory must necessarily be tied to Weber's conceptualization of the global market, and the violent struggles that typically occur when "traditional" societies are confronted by those ideologically and practically committed to "rational action," particularly along economic lines. An important contribution to this neo-Weberian research was Robert Wiebe's *The Search for Order, 1877-1920* (Wiebe, 1967), in which "island communities" were shown over time to be unwillingly amalgamated into a nation-state built on capitalist foundations. Wiebe's version of what happened undercuts naive views of bureaucratization as being seamless, untroubled processes, for in fact, "separate bureaucracies, barely joined in some areas, openly in conflict elsewhere" were more the norm than the exception as the U.S. was being shaped into the mid-century powerhouse it later became (ibid.: 300).

The range of historiography regarding U.S. culture, from its colonial beginnings to its postmodern incarnation, which has benefited from Weber's ideas is much too broad and deep to canvass here. But a sense of this extraordinary scope might be gained by mentioning a few other studies that typify the sort of work that has entered the Weberian canon. General statements that highlight Weber's use to historiographical method include William Green (1993) and H. Stuart Hughes (1960). Earl Hamilton (1929) long ago used a Weberian perspective in showing how riches plundered from the Americas buttressed capitalist development in Europe. One of many such works, Ronen Shamir (1993) contrasted "formal" versus "substantive" rationalization in American legal history, two Weberian notions which are as central to the history of law as "charisma" has become to studies of leadership. There is also a body of work which connects Weber as a political actor or researcher with actual U.S. conditions during his lifetime, including Eileen Leonard's prescient dissertation (1975), and Jonathan Imber's more recent reflections (1996). The history of political theory and practice in the U.S. can also be easily linked with Weber's work, for example, in Stephen Kalberg's studies (1997). And John King's *The Iron of Melancholy* (1983) illustrates how a fresh psychohistorical vantage point can be tied fruitfully to more old-fashioned concerns with conversion processes and religious activity. Such studies are the tip of an iceberg which has not yet been thoroughly analyzed, either by American historians or by Weber scholars.

That said, however, it remains the case that American historians have been less inclined than have their colleagues in the social sciences to incorporate into their work some of Weber's more famous theoretical innovations. Whereas "rationalization processes," "legitimation crises," "the typology of social action," and fine distinctions among "class, status, and party" have suffused a great many scholarly publications within U.S. historiography, it has been others of Weber's neologisms which have seen more use. In addition to issues of charisma and the Protestant Ethic, historians have been concerned at least since the days of Charles Beard with questions surrounding objectivity in the creation of historical knowledge. Weber wrote the seminal works in this regard, delivered as two speeches to large, unsympathetic audiences, "Science as a Vocation" (1917) and "Politics as a Vocation" (1919) (both in *From Max Weber*: 77-156). He insisted that the scholar's job is to tell the truth, no matter what the social costs, and that the politician's is to further the goals of his or her platform, once duly elected. Thus, they cannot be one in the same person, and he who conflates the two roles risks destroying the efficacy of both. This highly contentious argument has been subjected, like so much of Weber's writing, to unwearied critique, most recently by Haskell (1998: 15-19, 337-45, *passim*) and Novick (1988). Yet in any analysis of the political uses to which social knowledge is put, Weber's essays form the bedrock of all subsequent discussion. And the same can be said—and has been with increasing frequency during the last thirty years—for nearly all of Weber's theoretical work in its relation to the most ambitious forms of historical writing and thinking now being carried out, here and abroad. If a fully literate historiography survives both the postmodernist epistemological assault on definitions of "truth," as well as the eradication of printed documents due to the predominance of electronic forms of communication, then Weber's methods, ideas, and scholarly demeanor will surely continue to play an ever-enlarging role within it.

References

Selected Works by and about Max Weber

Bendix, Reinhard 1960: *Max Weber: An Intellectual Portrait*. New York: Doubleday; reissued in 1998, London: Routledge.
Käsler, Dirk 1988: *Max Weber: An Introduction to his Life and Work*. Cambridge, UK: Polity Press.
Mitzman, Arthur 1971: *The Iron Cage: An Historical Interpretation of Max Weber*. New York: Grosset and Dunlap; reissued in 1985, New Brunswick, NJ: Transaction Publishers.
Scaff, Lawrence 1989: *Fleeing the Iron Cage: Culture, Politics, and Modernity in the Thought of Max Weber*. Berkeley: University of California Press.
Sica, Alan 1988: *Weber, Irrationality, and Social Order*. Berkeley: University of California Press.

_____ 2004: *A Complete Bibliography*. New Brunswick NJ: Transaction Publishers (includes 4,800-item comprehensive bibliography of works in English pertaining to Weber).

Weber, Max 1927: *General Economic History*, tr. by Frank Knight. London: Allen and Unwin; reissued in 1981, New Brunswick, NJ: Transaction Publishers.

_____ 1930: *Protestant Ethic and the Spirit of Capitalism*, tr. by Talcott Parsons. London: Allen and Unwin; reissued in 1995, Roxbury Publishing Co.

_____ 1946: *From Max Weber: Essays in Sociology*, tr., ed., and intro. by Hans H. Gerth and C. Wright Mills. New York: Oxford University Press.

_____ 1951: *Religion of China: Confucianism and Taoism*, tr. and ed. by Hans H. Gerth. Glencoe, IL: Free Press.

_____ 1952: *Ancient Judaism*, tr. and ed. by Hans G. Gerth and Don Martindale. Glencoe, IL: Free Press.

_____ 1968: *Economy and Society: An Outline of Interpretive Sociology*, ed. by Guenther Roth and Claus Wittich, 3 vols. New York: Bedminster Press; reissued in 1978 in 2 vols., Berkeley: the University of California Press.

_____ 1976: *The Agrarian Sociology of Ancient Civilizations*, tr. by R. I. Frank. London: NLB.

_____ 1994: *Weber: Political Writings*, ed. by Peter Lassman and Ronald Speirs. New York: Cambridge University Press.

_____ 1995: *The Russian Revolutions*, tr. by Gordon C. Wells and Peter Baehr. Oxford: Polity Press.

Weber, Marianne 1975: *Max Weber: A Biography*, tr. by Harry Zohn. New York: John Wiley and Sons; reissued in 1988 with a new introduction by Guenther Roth, New Brunswick, NJ: Transaction Publishers.

Works Using Weber's Ideas

Appleby, Joyce 1984: "Value and Society." Pp. 291ff in Jack P. Greene and J.R. Pole (eds.), *Colonial British America: Essays in the New History of the Early Modern Era*. Baltimore, MD: Johns Hopkins University Press.

_____ 1993: "New Cultural Heroes in the Early National Period." Pp. 163-188 in Thomas L. Haskell and Richard F. Teichgraeber III (eds.), *The Culture of the Market: Historical Essays*. Cambridge: Cambridge University Press.

Axelrad, Allan M. 1978: The Protagonist of the Protestant Ethic: Max Weber's Benjamin Franklin. *Rendezvous* 13:2, 45-59.

Bailyn, Bernard 1955: *The New England Merchants in the Seventeenth Century*. Cambridge, MA: Harvard University Press.

_____ (ed.) 1965: *The Apologia of Robert Keayne: The Last Will and Testament of Me, Robert Keayne, All of It Written With My Own Hands and Began by Me, MO: 6: I: 1653, Commonly Called August*. New York: Harper and Row.

Baltzell, E. Digby 1979: *Puritan Boston and Quaker Philadelphia: Two Protestant Ethics and the Spirit of Class Authority and Leadership*. New York: Free Press.

Bier, Jesse 1970: Weberism, Franklin, and the Transcendental Style. *New England Quarterly* 43:2, 179-192.

Buck, Robert Enoch 1993: Protestantism and Industrialization: An Examination of Three Alternative Models of the Relationship between Religion and Capitalism. *Review of Religious Research* 34:3, 210-224.

Burke, Peter 1992: *History and Social Theory*. Ithaca, NY: Cornell University Press.

Burrell, Sidney A. 1960: Calvinism, Capitalism, and the Middle Classes: Some Afterthoughts on an Old Problem. *Journal of Modern History* 32: 132 ff.

Cooke, Timothy R. 1994: Uncommon Earnestness and Earthly Toils: Moderate Puritan Richard Baxter's Devotional Writings. *Anglican and Episcopal History* 63:1, 51-72.

Diggins, John Patrick 1999: *Thorstein Veblen: Theorist of the Leisure Class.* Princeton: Princeton University Press. (Originally published as *The Bard of Savagery: Thorstein Veblen and Modern Social Theory*, Seabury Press, 1978.)

Falk, Gerhard 1980: Old Calvin Never Died: Puritanical Rhetoric by Four American Presidents Concerning Public Welfare. Pp. 183-190 in Milton Plesur (ed.), *An American Historian: Essays to Honor Selig Adler.* Buffalo, NY: SUNY Press.

Foster, Stephen 1971: *Their Solitary Way: The Puritan Social Ethic in the First Century of Settlement in New England.* New Haven, CT: Yale University Press.

Green, William A. 1993: *History, Historians, and the Dynamics of Change.* Westport, CT: Praeger Publishers, pp. 107-126.

Greene Jack P. 1988: *Pursuits of Happiness: The Social Development of Early Modern British Colonies and the Formation of American Culture.* Chapel Hill: University of North Carolina Press.

Hamilton, Earl J. 1929: "American Treasure and the Rise of Capitalism (1500-1700)." *Economica*, 9:27 (November), 338-357.

Haskell, Thomas L. 1998: *Objectivity is Not Neutrality: Explanatory Schemes in History.* Baltimore, MD: Johns Hopkins University Press.

Henretta, John A. "The Weber Thesis Revisited: The Protestant Ethic and the Reality of Capitalism." Pp. 35-70 in John A. Henretta, *The Origins of American Capitalism: Collected Essays.* Boston: Northeastern University Press, 1991.

Henretta, John A. and Gregory H. Nobles 1973: *Evolution and Revolution: American Society, 1600-1820.* Lexington, MA:.

Hertz, Karl H. 1991: "Max Weber and American Puritanism." Pp. 86-102 in Peter Hamilton (ed.), *Max Weber: Critical Assessments 2*, London: Routledge.

Howe, Daniel Walker 1972: "The Decline of Calvinism: An Approach to Its Study." *Comparative Studies in Society and History* 14, 317ff.

Hudson, Winthrop S. 1988: The Weber Thesis Reexamined. *Church History* 57 (Supplement), 56-67.

Hughes. H. Stuart 1960: "The Historian and the Social Scientist." *American Historical Review*, 66:1 (October), 20-46.

Imber, Jonathan 1996: "'Incredible Goings-On': Max Weber in Pennsylvania." *American Sociologist*, 27:4 (Winter), 3-6.

Jäger, Friedrich 1991: Culture or Society? The Significance of Max Weber's Thought for Modern Cultural History. *History and Memory* 2:2, 115- 140.

Johnson, Benton 1971: Max Weber and American Protestantism. *Sociological Quarterly* 12:4 (Autumn), 473-485.

Kalberg, Stephen 1997: "Tocqueville and Weber on the Sociological Origins of Citizenship: The Political Culture of American Democracy." *Citizenship Studies*, 1:2, 199-222.

King, John Owen, III 1983: *The Iron of Melancholy: Structures of Spiritual Conversion in America from the Puritan Conscience to Victorian Neurosis.* Middletown, CT: Wesleyan University Press.

Kolbenschlag, Madonna Claire 1976: The Protestant Ethic and Evangelical Capitalism: The Weberian Thesis Revisited. *Southern Quarterly* 14:4, 287-306.

Kolko, Gabriel 1961: Max Weber on America: Theory and Evidence. *History and Theory* 1:3, 243-260.

Leonard, Eileen 1975: Max Weber and America: A Study in Elective Affinity. Unpub. Doctoral Dissertation (Sociology). New York: Fordham University; 511 leaves.

Lindholm, Charles 1990: *Charisma*. Cambridge, MA: Basil Blackwell.

Lucas, Rex A. 1971: "A Specification of the Weber Thesis: Plymouth Colony." *History and Theory* 10: 3, 318-346.

Mann, Bruce H. 1980: "Rationality, Legal Change, and Community in Connecticut, 1690-1740." *Law and Society Review* 14, 196ff.

_____ 1987: *Neighbors and Strangers: Law and Community in Early Connecticut*. Chapel Hill: UNC Press.

Miller, Perry 1953: *The New England Mind: From Colony to Province* Boston: Beacon Press.

Nash, Gary 1984: "Social Development." Pp. 236ff in Jack P. Greene and J. R. Pole (eds), *Colonial British America: Essays in the New History of the Early Modern Era*. Baltimore: Johns Hopkins University Press.

Niebuhr, H. Richard 1929/1957: *The Social Sources of Denominationalism*. New York: Henry Holt.

Novick, Peter 1988: *That Noble Dream: The "Objectivity Question" and the American Historical Profession*. Cambridge, UK: Cambridge University Press.

Olin, Spencer C. 1980: The Oneide Community and the Instability of Charismatic Authority. *Journal of American History*, 67:2, 285-300.

Peacock, James L. 1989: Calvinism, Community, and Charisma: Ethnographic Notes. *Comparative Social Research* 11, 227-238.

Schwartz, Barry 1987: *George Washington: The Making of an American Symbol*. New York: Free Press.

_____ 2000: *Abraham Lincoln and the Forge of National Memory*. Chicago: University of Chicago Press.

Shamir, Ronen 1993: "Formal and Substantive Rationality in American Law: A Weberian Perspective." *Social and Legal Studies*, 2, 45-72.

Spencer, Olin 1980: The Oneida Community and the Instability of Charismatic Authority. *Journal of American History* 67:2, 285-300.

Tolles, Frederick B. 1948/1963: *Meeting House and Counting House: The Quaker Merchants of Colonial Philadelphia, 1682-1763*. New York: Norton/Chapel Hill: UNC.

Walzer, Michael 1963: "Puritanism as a Revolutionary Idea." *History and Theory*, 3, 59-90.

Watanabe, Kishichi 1988: The Business Ideology of Benjamin Franklin and Japanese Values of the 18th Century. *Business and Economic History* 17, 79-90.

Ziff, Larzer 1973: *Puritanism in America: New Culture in a New World*. New York.

6

Weber and Pareto

This chapter deals with a small question in the history of classical theory, but with larger ramifications than might first meet the eye. The issue is one of historical accuracy. We ask ourselves, for instance, based on the interpretation of textual evidence, whether Comte's ideas were lifted in large part from the pioneering genius of Saint-Simon, his employer for several years, and if Saint-Simon's notion of civilizations going through stages of development were not already expressed as such by Condorcet and, in turn, Turgot some years before. But we do know in great detail the ups and downs of the personal relationship between Comte and Saint-Simon because they both left plenty of documentation, as did others who were witnesses. Oddly enough, we have almost no such data when piecing together the relationships, if they even existed, among the founders of classical social theory. One can almost as easily argue, based on the slight available documents, that they knew of each other's existence and writings, or that they did not. My small adventure in the archives addresses one of these imaginable relationships.

Among the consequences of undisciplined growth in sociology and its sister disciplines over the last generation, one of the less fortunate is the widespread reliance upon secondary sources (not to be confused with textbooks proper) that serve to acquaint interested parties with the history of their discipline's theories. Of course, some of the secondary treatments succeed in representing their respective subjects superbly, so much so that they become credible surrogates for the actual texts they analyze. They render the theorist (or school) comprehensible to a modern audience often ill equipped to interpret the original material, particularly if it remains for the most part untranslated. But the very success and approbation these studies gain for themselves may in the end prove a disservice to their audiences. In an atmosphere in which Bendix (1960) became for most readers during the 1960s through 1970s an able substitute for Weber—treated as if synonymous in fact—Lukes (1972) and

LaCapra (1972) became Durkheim, Pickering (1993) is the new Comte, Peel (1971) is Spencer, Hodges (1952) and Makkreel (1975) the stand-in for Dilthey, Remmling (1975) for Mannheim, Miller (1973) and Joas (1985) for Mead, and so on, it is inevitable that over time certain factual errors become concretized into conventional wisdom simply by virtue of being passed from one secondary or tertiary source to another. They are thereafter very difficultly removed from standard discourse, even that of some sophistication. I am not referring here to interpretational (or hermeneutical) errors, which turn heavily upon judgments of taste, perception, and one's often unspecifiable "intellectual aesthetics."[1] For the moment we may leave that aside and look instead to simple statements of fact, which, while individually innocuous, may over time begin to distort in a quiet, yet cumulative way intellectual projects that need not suffer under the burden of misinformation.

In an article dealing with this sort of problem (one of the few of its kind), Edward Tiryakian pointed out that "[t]he social significance of ignorance and ignoring may have important latent functions which are as revealing as positive knowledge" (1966: 330). By using a variety of historical data, he demonstrated with reasonable certainty that Durkheim and Weber had "full awareness of each other," though, as is well known, never referring to one another in print.   Although this finding may interest only specialists in the history of social thought, Tiryakian closes the article with a reflection still cogent, and one that signals a hindrance to interpretive synthesis of classic texts on which the growth of knowledge inevitably depends:

> A more subtle question raised by all this is just what are the criteria used to determine what external stimuli (and by external we can include a different culture or a different perspective) are cognized by a writer or a school as being relevant for their own creative development. Concretely, did Durkheim know of Weber's sociological writings but ignore them because he considered them irrelevant for his own studies and *vice versa*? The practical consequence of this little problem in the intellectual history of sociology is that it can put us on our guards against perpetrating sins of omission—is American sociology, for example, aware of theoretical and substantive developments in French sociology or the latter of developments in say, British sociology? If not, is this due to the fact that mental products are so related to their sociocultural setting that even the towering figures of the same social science may operate from sufficiently different presuppositions concerning social reality and concerning what is socially relevant that they will know of each other without knowing each other? In any case we hope by this paper to have drawn attention to the sociological salience of silence. (1966: 336)

Even though a number of important volumes appeared on the "sociology of sociology" in the decade after Tiryakian's article, thus far little has been written about "the salience of silence" (especially "international silence").[2] This is most obviously the case regarding the preeminent "fathers" of sociology, Marx, Durkheim, and Weber. Given that Weber was putatively doing battle with the "ghost of Marx" (an assumption more often stated as fact rather than explored as an hypothesis), that Weber and Pareto both theoretically confronted "rationality" at almost the same time, that in fact many of the forefathers wrote in *conscious* response to one another—*vide* Durkheim's dismissive use of Tönnies in his *Division of Labor*, plus his impatient review-essay on *Gemeinschaft und Gesellschaft* in an 1889 issue of *Revue philosophique*—perhaps it is time to respond to Tiryakian's suggestion and try to learn *exactly* who knew about whom when, and what was done, or not done, with this knowledge. If nothing else, a more accurate history of the field will result, and from that perhaps a clearer sense of social theory's trajectory.

As a case in point, let us examine Weber and Pareto. The testimony of all the textbooks in print on the history of social thought[3] indicates that the issue was settled long ago. In fact, consensus is so strong that the case seldom occasions any comment at all: Weber and Pareto knew nothing of each other's work, nor of each other's person. Since I have not been able to locate any definitive remarks dealing with this question in an influential work published in English prior to 1937, I am assuming that for most readers, Parsons's *The Structure of Social Action* decided the issue (for so I have been told by any number of theorists):

> Another point strongly in favor of this choice [to use Marshall, Pareto, Durkheim, and Weber as contributors to the development of Parsons's "voluntaristic theory of action"] is that although all four of these men were approximately contemporary, there is with one exception not a trace of direct influence of any one on any other. Pareto was certainly influenced by Marshall in the formulation of his technical economic theory, but with equal certainty not in any respect relevant to this discussion. And this is the *only possibility of any direct mutual influence.* (1937 [1968]: 13-14, emphasis added)

Parsons immediately expands upon this claim by attaching its significance to his own theoretical aims:

> In fact, within the broad cultural unit, Western and Central Europe at the end of the nineteenth and beginning of the twentieth century, it would scarcely be possible to choose four men who had important ideas in common who were less likely to have been influenced *in developing this common body of ideas* by factors other than the immanent development of the logic of theoretical systems in relation to empirical fact. (Ibid.: 14)

Although Parsons parenthetically acknowledges the role that *Wissenssoziologie* can play in situations such as this, the sentiment expressed in this paragraph points toward an idealization of intellectual creation which exaggerates isolated, individual achievements, just as it repudiates the need for study of mutual influences among even the most innovative thinkers. (An interesting and utterly contrary comparison in this regard is the monumental study by Parsons's one-time student, Randall Collins, of how philosophers carefully responded to each other while competing for their publics' attention; Collins, 1998).

Again midway through the work and at the end, Parsons reiter-ates his belief that Durkheim, Pareto, and Weber wrote in absolute isolation from one another: "Weber, being unacquainted with Pareto's work. . ." (1937: 535), and, more crucial for Parsons's own project (which may help explain why he was not anxious to discover actual links among the three):

> That the conceptual elements which have been differentiated in the course of analyzing the work of Pareto and Durkheim really do belong to the *same* theoretical system, and that the work of the two really did converge, is conclusively demonstrated by the fact that it has been possible to show that *all* of them and one other are to be found in the work of Weber. This is true in spite of the fact that Weber's work was entirely independent of that of either of the other two, and that Weber's methodological position was such as seriously to obscure the status of a generalized theoretical system. (1937: 714)

Parsons goes on to reflect how "remarkable" it was that theorists of such different epistemologies (a "German historical economist" versus the "neoclassicist Pareto") "should have come to a *point-for-point* correspondence in the distinctly complex system of structural categories relating to religious ideas, institutions, ritual and value attitudes, with the outspoken positivist Durkheim" (1937: 714).

Parsons's "convergence" theory has endured (or enjoyed) voluminous critique during the ensuing sixty years, but not usually on strictly historical grounds.[4] It has been suggested time and again that the convergence Parsons offered as a pre-existent, accomplished fact is a product of his own imagining, perhaps even a tribute to his theoretical capabilities. But as pure *history* of theory it is something of a failure. A less subtle point has escaped Parsons's battalion of critics: perhaps he was factually wrong; perhaps, for example, Weber and Pareto did indeed compose certain aspects of their theories (or descriptive typologies) in *conscious* response to one another. If this be the case, then Parsons has misled some influential "elder statesmen" whose bailiwick has been for a generation the history of social thought, and whose writings have educated thousands of sociologists.

One of the most successful and fondly read of such treatments, by H. Stuart Hughes, obviously owes a great deal to Parsons, as Hughes himself points out (1958: 33, 186-87, *passim*). Early in the book, Hughes writes:

> In the course of the study I hope to establish that it was Germans and Austrians and French and Italians. . . who in general provided the fund of ideas that has come to seem most characteristic of our own time. Moreover, they often arrived at strikingly similar theories within just a few years of each other. Sometimes this can be explained by personal friendship and intellectual change. More frequently it looks purely fortuitous: the two thinkers were in fact totally ignorant of each other's work. (1958: 13)

Hughes then adds a twist via *Wissenssoziologie* (unsympathetic with Parsons's posture), observing that such "fortuitous" convergence was not actually surprising given that "the countries of the Western and Central European Continent shared institutions and an intellectual heritage. . . that presented their leading social thinkers with a similar set of problems" (1958: 13-14). It is interesting, and also typical, that Hughes perceived the common cultural background of all the "bourgeois" theorists he treats in the book, but fails to note that within the geographically and intellectually compact locus of Central Europe, personal acquaintance and interchange among each nation's intellectual elite seem utterly plausible. Like most others, he has nothing to say about the possibility of a Pareto-Weber connection, which is especially disappointing in that in addition to understanding the German theoretical scene well, Hughes also spent considerable time in Italy, wrote books about Italian politics and thinking, and had a much firmer grasp of its intellectual landscape than have other historians of social thought. He even recalled in his autobiography, "The sociologist Vilfredo Pareto had also lived in Céligny, and I duly paid my respects to his grave, overgrown and neglected in the tiny cemetery" (in 1950) (Hughes, 1990: 218).

Another resource which has gained "classic" status is Lewis Coser's *Masters of Sociological Thought* (1971, 1977). In trying to account for Pareto's apparent theoretical inferiority relative to Weber, Coser is moved to comment:

> . . . Pareto ignored Freud completely so that much of what he had to say inevitably appeared anachronistic to his readers. In a like manner, Pareto managed to ignore not only the work of Max Weber, but the whole German tradition of the social sciences. (Coser, 1977: 422)

Still another agent in acquainting Americans with European social thought, Kurt H. Wolff, reissued an essay on Pareto in 1974 that originally appeared in 1941. In it he introduces a remark without supporting documentation such that one might suppose by the early 1940's it had become established doctrine: "Max Weber, the great sociologist—who had no personal acquaintance with Pareto—uttered the same opinion [concerning the "provisional character of the world of European liberalism"] quite explicitly in 1919, a year before his own death. . ." (1974: 15).

While these three writers are not alone in following Parsons's lead, they are among the most influential, and embody enough elements to call for a revision. Since Parsons did not revise his remarks for the 1968 reprint edition (even though Tiryakian's correction, noted above, was published two years before), Coser's second edition reads the same as the earlier one, and Wolff's reissue is likewise unchanged, it appears that these authors continue believing that Pareto and Weber did not know of each other and made no theoretical concessions to one another's work. There is reason to doubt this belief.

Let us return for a moment to Parsons's assertion that there is "not a trace of direct influence on any one on any other" (1937: 13), with the irrelevant exception of Marshall upon Pareto. If we take this to mean that in none of their works which he used are there references to works of the others, Parsons is correct. Perhaps this is what he intended, but the drift of his paragraph quoted above (1937: 14) suggests a more embracing view. If, on the other hand, one were to understand from this, as I believe most American social scientists have, that among the three theorists there existed total lack of mutual awareness, Parsons is wrong. Tiryakian reports (1966: 332) that he learned from Raymond Aron, himself told by Marcel Mauss, that in Weber's private library in Heidelberg, the latter saw a complete set of Durkheim's journal, the *Année sociologique*.[5] In addition to this "circumstantial" evidence that Weber's isolation from Durkheimian notions was less than pure, Beate Riesterer, a sociologist and former student of Alfred Weber, reported to me that Max was well aware of Durkheim and his work, but chose to ignore it, perhaps for reasons not totally disassociated from nationalistic prejudice of a refined type.[6] It is also known that Durkheim reviewed one of Marianne Weber's works, *Ehefrau und Mutter in der Rechtsentwickelung* [*sic*], in his journal (vol. 11, 1906-09: 363-369) which she wrote in close association with her husband. Durkheim was none too flattering in his appraisal of the work, published in the very journal that Mauss saw in Weber's study: "What this book lacks is, rather, an organizing concept which would set forth the facts according to a methodical plan and take account of the way in which they converge upon the conclusion to which one is led. The order in which questions are approached is rather arbitrary" (Durkheim, 1978: 139). Given Weber's hypersensitivity to matters dealing with his wife's honor, it is very hard to believe that he would not have read what Durkheim had to say in this context. Finally, Sandro

Segre has gone over the available evidence on this score more thoroughly than anyone else, and concluded that Weber was perfectly aware of Durkheim and his importance to social theory, but chose for a variety of reasons not to deal with him in print (Segre, 1986).

Thus Parsons was mistaken in asserting Weber and Durkheim's lack of intellectual commerce, a point Tiryakian rather clearly made thirty-seven years ago by comparing mutual references (or their absence) in "their" respective journals, Durkheim's *Année* and Weber's *Archiv für Sozialwissenschaft und Sozialpolitik*.

Let us consider Durkheim's knowledge of Pareto. It is known that Durkheim was perfectly aware of Pareto, having published a negative review of his *I problemi della sociologia* in 1900, in which, as Lukes explains, "He saw (the early) Pareto as seeking to 'justify the old abstract and ideological method of political economy and wanting to make it the general method of all the social sciences'" (Lukes 1972: 405, n. 78). What is not so widely known is that in 1898, in the premier issue of Julius Wolf's *Zeitschrift für Socialwissenschaft* (*sic*), Pareto published a very harsh review (in French) of Durkheim's *Le Suicide*. This review is one of thirty-four which Pareto published in the *Zeitschrift* between 1898 and 1902. This fact punctures Coser's criticism that Pareto was unaware of "the whole German tradition of the social sciences," since he contributed frequently to a journal in that very tradition. The review begins with Pareto characterizing Durkheim's "reasoning" as "un-fortunate" and lacking rigor (reminiscent of the latter's way of chastising Marianne Weber). He attacks *Suicide* on statistical terms, pointing out that Durkheim manipulated the data to suit his conclusions, and had he followed strict empirical method, he could not have substantiated, for instance, his hypothesis about the aggravation of altruistic suicide among the military. After detailed critique of Durkheim's handling of the data and the empirical conclusions he drew from them, Pareto castigates him further for failing to employ proper methodology, and concludes that Durkheim's study is "not acceptable," for "the discipline of the experimental method." Except for admitting that the study was well written, he has scarcely a kind thing to say.[7]

Thus by 1900, Pareto knew one of Durkheim's most important books well, Durkheim was intimately aware of Pareto's methodology, and conceivably, they each knew of the other's harsh reviews. This, then, is a clear case of "ignoring," for nowhere in Pareto's *Trattato* does Durkheim (or any of his "school") appear, and Durkheim's work is equally free of any Pareto entry. It must be admitted, of course, that this is not unequivical "proof," since, for instance, Croce receives practically no mention in the *Trattato*, yet Pareto had managed already in 1900 to have corresponded at length (through public letters) with Croce, and was well aware of his views on economics and philosophy (see Croce and Pareto, 1953). But a basis has been established for hypothesizing their "active ignoring," apparently on epistemological or methodological grounds. For while the idea of nationalistic chauvinism may apply somewhat to the Durkheim-Weber case (remembering that the Franco-Prussian war had occurred when they were both impressionable boys), here it would make no sense since Pareto spent his youth in France, read and wrote fluently in French, and apparently kept up with French intellectualism rather closely. Durkheim's attitude toward Italian academic developments is not as easily surmised.[8]

Yet the Durkheim-Pareto connection is less intrinsically interesting, it seems to me, than one, should it be discovered, between Weber and Pareto. As pointed out by Parsons, Hughes, and others, they shared many features: they were of similar socio-economic backgrounds, and each inherited substantial fortunes (at almost the same time, incidentally) which allowed them unencumbered time for scholarship; both began their political lives at roughly the same position, one which we would now call liberal-conservative, with great confidence in the utility of a strong state; both were fascinated with the process of "nation building" taking place as they matured; both were famous for monumental erudition and intemperate outbursts against those whom they believed ill-informed; and both were first trained as professionals, not as academics, Pareto the engineer, Weber the attorney. How intriguing, one argument goes, that their dissections of modern life, both versions dependent upon the dichotomy of "rational-irrational" (or "non-logical") culminated in such divergent theoretical statements. The question poses itself: did each know of the other's examination of their common problem—the rationalization of culture—or is it mere historical accident that each created his magnum opus during almost the same time (between about 1907 and 1916)?

Let us review what is known. In most general terms, Weber spent a tremendous amount of (therapeutic) time in Italy. He made over a dozen trips there between 1900 and 1914, many of them months in duration, when he actually became a resident, not a tourist.[9] From his letters we know that he read Italian newspapers and followed "local" events carefully. Since biographical information on Pareto is much less accessible than for Weber, and much less up to date,[10] it is difficult to make the case that they met or were in physical proximity during one of Weber's sojourns in Italy. But given Pareto's fame, plus Weber's notoriety as an important German "economist," it certainly falls within the realm of possibility.

Between 1900 and 1914 Pareto published 179 items (Pareto, 1975b: 87-94), many of them in Italian newspapers and political journals, which it is possible Weber saw. And if Weber did not come across Pareto's work while in Italy, he could have seen it in Germany since, as noted above, Pareto published three dozen reviews in Wolf's *Zeitschrift* (though it is true that during this very period, Weber was physically at his worst and complained to his wife of an inability to read technical material). All of this supports the contention that Weber *could* have known of Pareto's existence, either through his popular political analyses, his book reviews published in German, or from other sources. When it is remembered that Pareto published over seven hundred items in English, French, Italian, and German, it becomes difficult to believe that the encyclopedically learned Weber remained unaware of him.

Very few scholars have studied these matters and made informed statements based on archival data. The most thoroughly researched work is by Gottfried Eisermann, a German sociologist who has published extensively on Pareto, including one entire book (1961). In this source the following passage appears:

> Wenn man deshalb, wohl mit Recht, seine beiden Hauptwerk verdienste um die soziologische Theorie in seinen bedeutenden Beitragen zu einer grundlegenden Theorie des sozialen Handelns sowie in seiner Theorie des gesellschaftlichen Gleichgewichts als methodischen Instruments jeder konkreten Analyse erblickt, so muss einem sofort die Analogie gewisser grundlegender Konzeptionen Paretos mit den uns vertrauten Max Webers auffallen. (1961: 55)

Paraphrased, Eisermann is observing that Pareto's "theory of societal equilibrium," which represents his "most meaningful contribution to a basic theory of social action," immediately calls for a comparison with certain conceptions of Max Weber. He continues:

> Diese Analogie, die von der Betonung des sozialen Handelns als konstitutiven und fundamentalen Elements aller wirtschafts-und sozialwissenschaftlichen Forschung über die Konvergenz gewissen und das Sichüberschneiden anderer Handelnskategorien bieder und die Verwandtschaft der sozialwissenschaftlichen Gesetzenkonzeption bis zur principiellen Haltund der "Wert-freiheit" einschleisslich der "vermittelnden" Stellung zwischen historischer und formaler Soziologie und weit darüber hinaus reicht, lasst sich in der Tat, schwerlich übersehen. Man hat es deshalb als ein "univerständliches" bezeichnet, dass Max Weber "einen Mann wie Vilfredo Pareto nur dem Namen nach" kannte. "Und ein ebenso unverständliches: Vilfredo Pareto kannte Max Weber nur vom Hörensagen. So dachten, redeten, schreiben, lahrten und entdeckten die . . . grossen zwei Dioskuren der modernen Soziologie, die such soviel gegenseitig zu sagen gehabt hatten, aneinander vorbei" (1961: 55-56).

The last three sentences may be rendered thus: "It has therefore been described as 'incomprehensible' that Max Weber 'knew a man like

Vilfredo Pareto only by name'." [Here Eisermann is taking,,issue with a remark Robert Michels made in his book *Bedeutende Männer* (1927: 113, 114).] "And it is equally inconceivable that Pare-to knew Weber only from hearsay." He continued by musing that the two foremost representatives of modern sociology, with so much in common, could scarcely have been unaware of one another. As evidence, he introduces another remark by Michels, who quoted Weber as having voiced a high opinion of Gaetano Mosca, which in turn documents Weber's excellent Italian. Also, lest Pareto's Gcrman be sus-pect, Eisermann in a later sentence points to section 1580 of the *Trattato*, where Pareto translated material from the *Berliner Tageblatt*. And yet, after presenting much "circumstantial" evi-dence, Eisermann admits in a footnote that neither man referred to the other in their *Hauptwerke*, so nothing definitive can be claimed about the Pareto-Weber connection. (This was Eisermann's opinion as late as 1975 when he published an article in the "official" forum for such work, the *Cahiers Vilfredo Pareto*, concerning Pareto's influence in Germany.) And so far as I can tell, this is where scholarly opinion remained during the twenty years after Eisermann's book appeared, given that very few writers any longer even considered the issue problematic.

The Italian scholar, Sandro Segre (whose doctorate is from New York University), published an interesting article in 1982 which took issue with Eisermann's conclusions, as well as my own. He believes that Pareto did not know German at all well, that he relied on friends and family for help with translation, and that he therefore could not have read Weber's dissertation in its original form (Segre, 1982: 250, 255, esp. 258-259 and notes). I will return to his objections.

Although perhaps hard to believe, apparently no one in English-language scholarship, has made a concrete connection between Pareto and Weber, yet it can be done. (Segre mentions continental references by P. Tommissen [1972], Julien Freund [1976], and G. Guarnieri [1981]; Segre, 1982: 248n7.) A publisher in Milan, *Societa Editrice Librarie*, inaugurated a huge series in 1903 entitled *Biblioteca di Storia Economica* (The Library of Economic History), the first "volume" of which contained 1,730 pages. Five other volumes appeared in staggered years until 1929, when the series seems to have ended. Each volume, even the last, which appeared six years after his death, bears this inscription on the title page under the series title: "*Diretta dal Prof. Vilfredo Pareto*," meaning, of course, "directed" or "edited by" Pareto. Pareto's only published contribution to the bulky series[11] appears in the first volume, a simple ten-page "*Proemio*" (Preface). The series was designed to make available to Italian scholars important works in translation, from French and German, in addition to some native works. I have never seen the series cited,[12] and it seems to have slid into obscurity, even though the first item by Pareto published in the *Cahiers Vilfredo Pareto* when it began in 1963 was the *"Proemio"* mentioned above (bereft of editorial explanation or illumination). Among the authors represented in the *Biblioteca* are Eduard Meyer, Wilhelm Roscher, Theodor Mommsen, and others who figured strongly in Weber's academic world, who *were* in large part German social science toward the end of the nineteenth century.

As might have been supposed by this point, between pages 509 and 705 of Volume 2, Part 2 (just after a selection by J.K. Rodbertus and before one by Theodor Mommsen), appears *La Storia Agraria Romana in rapporto al diritto pubblico e privato*, obviously a translation (unattributed) of Weber's habilitation of 1891, *Die römische Agrargeschichte in ihrer Bedeutung für das Staats- und Privatrecht*. Since this work—acclaimed at the time of its publication by Mommsen himself—has never joined Weber's other work in the *Gesammelte Aufsätze*, it has been a scarce item bibliographically speaking, and is therefore not well known in the U.S. except by name. But its unorthodox and fruitful historiographic method, which begat unprecedented insights into the effects of Roman law upon agrarian practices,[13] virtually ensured Weber's scholarly reputation. It was obviously known beyond the limits of German academe, for why else would Pareto have chosen it for translation and inclusion in his new series, surveying illustrations and all?[14]

What can we surmise from this "discovery"? Given that Weber held the *Nachdruck* (copyright) to the habilitation (for it is so marked in the original edition), someone had to notify him or his publisher, Ferdinand Enke of Stuttgart, of their wish to reprint it. There may even have been some royalties in question. It seems in any case inconceivable that a publisher would reprint a work of 195 pages without notifying its author, even if international copyright laws at the time were such that no royalties had to be paid. The social science community of those days was certainly small enough that this courtesy would have been extended. It is *almost* certain then, that Weber knew his work was selected, presumably by the general editor, Pareto, and printed in Milan in 1907 as part of an ambitious series. It would even be reasonable to suppose that Weber was supplied with a copy of the volume in which his work appeared; or further, that he was consulted about the translation, particularly appropriate given his fluent Italian. The volume appeared precisely when Weber was spending a great deal of concentrated time in Italy, and he may have even been contacted while there.

Unfortunately, Pareto did not write an introductory essay, as would probably be called for today, so we cannot be *absolutely* sure of his familiarity with Weber's contribution. But it is, at minimum, reasonable to argue that Pareto very likely knew of Weber as an important enough German social scientist to be ranked in his series with the likes of Roscher and Mommsen. The slightly more adventurous extension can also be made, that through this publication in 1907, Weber knew something of Pareto. It seems Eisermann's skepticism (noted above) about their knowing each other "only by name" and through "hearsay" is well founded. However, virtually nothing has been said about the *quality or intensity* of that knowledge.[15] But before proceeding, we must consider one last related matter.

It is impossible to end our query without bringing up Ettore Ciccotti (1863-1939), "Professore ordinario di storia antica nell' Universita Messana" (in 1905), whose works occupy a considerable share of the *Biblioteca* from its inception till its final volume. It is important, if one wishes to establish that Pareto selected Weber's work for inclusion, to determine to what extent Pareto exercised jurisdiction over the *Biblioteca's* editorship. Since Pareto's signature, or initials, do not appear in any of the subsequent volumes (except for the imprint on the title page) following his short "Preface" to Volume I, Part 1, one suspects that someone else was aiding the distinguished professor in the tremendous labor that must have gone into the series. Pareto adds to this suspicion, in characteristically forthright style, in his opening sentence of the *Proemio*, "La presente raccolta e opera di due autori; ma del comune lavoro disequali sono le parti: grande quella del prof. Ciccotti, ristretta la mia." This tells us that "the present collection is the work of two authors; however, of the joint effort, the parts are unequal: the greater is that of Prof. Ciccotti, while mine was limited [or restricted, narrow]." Who was Ciccotti, and what was his relationship to the publisher, *Societa Editrice Libraria* of Milan, or to Pareto?

Nowhere in the standard biographical information on Pareto is there reference to the *Biblioteca*, nor to Ciccotti. The logical alternative source of information (aside from the twenty-one volumes of the *Oeuvres completes*, which yielded nothing), is his letters, which have been masterfully gathered in two principal collections: *Lettere a Maffeo Pantaleoni, 1890-1923* (1960), 1,500 pages in three lavish volumes, and, from the complete works, the *Correspondance, 1890-1923* (1975), 1,290 pages in two volumes. In his letters to Pantaleoni, there are seventeen mentions of Ciccotti, but given the immensity of this correspondence, this does not make Ciccotti ipso facto an important member of Pareto's intellectual circle (see Segre, 1982: 258n76). In the *Correspondance*, the name index cites him three times, which, in comparison with many other persons, would suggest once again that he was not on particularly close terms with Pareto. This supposition is given firm basis in Pareto's letter of July 28, 1897 (six years prior to the *Biblioteca's* first volume) to Filippo Turati (1975a: 351). He is apparently responding to an earlier question from Turati and comments that "The issue of Ciccoti is indeed exaggerated."

The "issue" according to the editor's footnote, had to do with Ciccotti's political difficulties while a professor in Milan due to his socialist beliefs. Pareto maintains almost Olympian calm in considering Ciccotti's troubles. In fact he rounds out his commentary with an allegory about cats and bacon. This relates also to the only reference to Ciccotti in the *Trattato* (Section 1713, note 3), where Pareto caustically notes, "Being a Socialist, Ciccotti ascribes to the capitalist class a trait that is characteristic of everybody [avarice and self-interest]."

Sandro Segre believes that Pareto held Ciccotti in considerable respect as a scholar of antiquity, recommending him for a chair at the University of Padua in July, 1897, some years before the *Biblioteca* project began. He also wrote a favorable review of one of Ciccotti's books. But from this Segre hypothesizes that this respect for his co-editor exempted Pareto from any serious duties vis-à-vis the *Biblioteca*, which is perhaps more guessing than the data will reasonably support (Segre, 1982: 258n76). When he writes that "Pareto failed to notice Weber's *Römische Agrargeschichte*" (p. 259), he has sidestepped the more important question, of to what extent Pareto's awareness of Weber's more mature work prior to 1920 could have influenced his way of going about theorizing the "non-logical," as he called it. While it is almost surely the case that Pareto did not help translate Weber's dissertation into Italian, this leaves a great deal unexplained as to the possibility of mutual influences.

Another two references to Ciccotti are more to the point. In the first (Nov. 27, 1905, to G. Beloch) Pareto (1975a: 556) responds to a complaint from Beloch concerning the translation of an article which failed to be printed in the first volume of the *Biblioteca*. Pareto boldly states that everything having to do with the technical aspects of translations is handled by Ciccotti, and that he has no power over such matters. The second letter, many years later (Aug. 9, 1912 to Felice Vinci) repeats that the Library is "principally" under the direction of Ciccotti and "much less by me" (1975a: 782).

From this we may hypothesize thus: Ciccotti was perhaps something of an academic entrepreneur, holding regular university appointments only with difficulty due to his politics. He engaged a Milanese publisher to print the *Biblioteca*, and somehow gained Pareto's permission to display his name as editor, perhaps because of the latter's positive review of his historiography in 1897. This may have been for political reasons, Ciccotti being a socialist and needing a more orthodox academic sponsor for such a large project. Yet it would be too much to conjecture, I believe, that Pareto did nothing but rubber-stamp Ciccotti's selections. He himself wrote that "The present collection is the work of two authors." And it is improbable in the extreme that willful, obstinate Pareto would allow his name to be attached to a gargantuan publishing venture unless he approved of its contents, for he was in no need of money. Thus, having considered the elusive figure of Ciccotti, we may return to our previous concern: what can be said about the quality or intensity of Weber and Pareto's mutual knowledge, having established the possibility of same?

Unfortunately, their writings provide practically nothing to guide us. On page 238 of the *English* translation of *Roscher und Knies*, one finds the work "residue," in a note: "On p. 266 [of an article by Meinecke in the *Historische Zeitschrift* LXXVII (1896)] he describes this 'unknown quantity'—the irrational 'residue' [*dem irrationalen 'Rest'; GazW*: 46] of the personality." While the use of the word obviously resembles Pareto's own designation, this is more a function of the translator's choice than anything else. This is because "residue" is not the necessary translation of *Rest*, and also Pareto's term *"residu"* does not appear in the German translations of Pareto as *Rest*. Also, of course, Weber's usage of *Rest* in 1905 preceeds Pareto'a *residu* by a decade. Other than this superficial commonality, their texts indicate no explicit conceptual reference to one another.

Back to our original question: could it be that, contrary to Parsons's opinion, Weber and Pareto not only knew of each other's work, but wrote in conscious opposition to one another on the problem of rationality and rationalization? Although it has been shown, I believe, that the putative mutual unawareness, not only of Pareto and Weber, but of Weber and Durkheim, and Durkheim and Pareto as well, is an illusion, the case for "conscious opposition" is made with difficulty. It is almost certainly true that had Pareto come across Weber's methodological essays of 1904-07 (especially those grouped as *Roscher and Knies* in English), he would have taken violent exception to some of Weber's opinions. And since Pareto oversaw the publication in the *Biblioteca* of Weber's work in 1907, is it unthinkable that he would have been attracted during his omnivorous reading (abetted by chronic insomnia) to some of Weber's later work? And even if he could not manage the difficult German texts himself, could he not have asked their mutual friend, Roberto Michels, or some other colleague for a meaningful precis of what Weber was trying to accomplish? Yet, on the other hand, Pareto did not suffer from intellectual diffidence. Had he objected to Weber's formulations concerning "non-logical" action, it seems reasonable that he would have attacked him in the *Trattato*. But one must ask, knowing as we now do (unlike Parsons in 1937) that Pareto reviewed Durkheim's *Suicide*, why did he fail to bring any mention whatever of the Frenchman's work into his magnum opus, either in support of his own hypotheses, or for critical dissection? This is most strange. And it accentuates the urgency and continuing perplexity of Tiryakian's unanswered question, about "the criteria used to determine what external stimuli... are cognized by a writer as being relevant to [his] own creative development" (1966: 336). How can it be, we are compelled to ask, that Weber, Pareto, and Durkheim believed each other's work to be absolutely "irrelevant" to their own peculiar theoretical tasks? How can it be, since they were all to converge in the Parsonian imagination within only a few years of their deaths, and in a way which seemed then "natural" and logically correct—at least to Parsons and his many followers. Precisely what they had so vigorously resisted in life—accord on certain basic theoretical principles—they were forced to agree upon in death. But to continue believing that they were in fact blind to one another's ideas is to attribute to the supposed convergence less violence than it may in fact have done to historical actuality.

Notes

1. Sociology in the U.S. has not yet come to terms with non- theological hermeneutics, classical and contemporary. Few sociologists writing in English have addressed this seminal body of thought (concerning method, interpretive technique, and theorizing in general), and have tried to use rather than comment upon it, e.g., Anthony Giddens, in *New Rules of Sociological Method* (1976), especially pp. 54-70, 144-162. Giddens' brief treatment does not do justice either to Hans-Georg Gadamer or Habermas, upon whom he builds his own theoretical contribution to "the hermeneutic explication and mediation of divergent forms of life..." (1976: 162); exegesis was not his primary aim, however. Janet Wolff's *Hermeneutic Philosophy and the Sociology of Art* (1975), by virtue of its brevity, deals superficially with Gadamer, Emilio Betti (Gadamer's principal rival), and other writers with hermeneutical goals. Wolff does not go very far towards employing hermeneutics in a theoretically innovative way.

   Genuine advances in the interpretation of theoretical texts (or substantive studies, for that matter) will not occur, I believe, until works such as Gadamer's *Truth and Method* (1975), Betti's *Allgemeine Auslegungslehre als Methodik der Geisteswissenschaften* (1967), and Radnitzsky's *Contemporary Schools of Metascience* (1973) are included in the sociologist's inventory of tools for "unpacking" texts, the sort that have saturated European thought for several decades. (One need only mention the advanced hermeneutical studies of Foucault, Althusser, Derrida, Barthes, Lacan, Ricoeur, Todorov, Apel, Bachelard, *inter alia*, to suggest the gulf between foreign and American scholarship along these lines.) Some emulation of our colleagues abroad, at least along the lines of interpretative precision, might be conducive to the transmission of the sociological heritage free of ritual distortion. For a brief summary of some hermeneutic theory, see Seebohm (1977). For longer exposition, see Hoy (1978) and Bauman (1978), also Shapiro and Sica (1988).

2. In a playful interchange between "Emile Durkheim" (Tiryakian) and Steven Lukes (1974), the latter charges that the former was wrong, that in fact Durkheim did refer to Weber in print (see Lukes 1972: 397, n. 19). But

Tiryakian establishes the accuracy of his earlier assertion, and Lukes concedes his mistake. The point was developed by Steven Seidman (1977). He claimed that Weber referred to Durkheim's work in his *Wirtschaftsgeschichte* (1923: 8, n. 2; n. 1). But as Gerd Schroeter suggested to me in correspondence, the editors of the posthumous Weber volume, Hellmann and Palyi, explain in their introduction (p. vi) that they took special liberties in adding bibliographical materials to the book; and since the *General Economic History* was assembled from students' lecture notes, it is probably wise to follow Frank Knight's decision and ignore such references, as he did in the English version (1927).

3.   I examined some two dozen texts in search of reference to the Pareto-Weber connection. Although text writers often juxtapose Weber and Pareto chapters—to highlight their opposing views of rationality and irrationality—only rarely does an author comment at all upon their *historical* as opposed to theoretical relationship.

4.   Another contribution to this debate, on the theoretical and interpretive merits of Parsons's early work, is that of Steven Warner (1978). Warner's bibliography lists all the relevant works, especially those of Pope, Hazelrigg, Cohen, and Jones (most of which have been published in the 1970s). Another pertinent and even more recent addition, which begins in a defence of Parsons's writings on Durkheim, but ends in a blanket attack upon "pedantic, myopic antiquarianism" of the recent hermeneutic variety, is the comment and rejoinder by Johnson (1978) and Jones (1978). Though these articles cover too much ground to permit much simplification, they revolve around comparing classical texts in hopes either of understanding or criticizing Parsons's use of same. A somewhat more ambitious essay by Alexander (1978) is sympathetic to Parsons and carries analysis in a relatively new direction. But my point is that none of these authors confronts the possibility of Parsons's "convergence" theory being incorrect on historical grounds alone. My aim is not to highlight flaws in Parsons's portrayal of Weber or Pareto (which is another task entirely), but to show that his belief in their ignorance of one another is incorrect. Had he himself not made such an issue of their mutual irrelevance, and had he not passed this tale onto so many of his readers, it would probably not merit as much attention as I have given it here.

5.   Mauss also told Aron before the Second World War that Weber "had borrowed many ideas" from Durkheim (Tiryakian 1966: 32), an improbable assertion judging from the textual evidence, not to mention their contrary ways of conceptualizing social action and social organization.

6.   Riesterer, who has written at length about Alfred Weber, supplied this information during a conversation in 1976. The "nationalistic prejudice" hypothesis is not hers, but comes from consideration of Franco-Prussian relations, political and cultural, between 1870 and 1900.

7.   The existence of the Pareto review was brought to my attention through the superb, probably definitive bibliography of Pareto's writings published in 1975 by Librairie Droz (Geneva) as No. 102 in their longterm series, *Travaux de droit, d'economie de sociologie et de sciences politiques,* and as Volume 20 in their series-within-a-series, *Oeuvres completes de Vilfredo Pareto.* The volume is entitled *Jubile du Professeur V. Pareto (avec une bibliographie des ecrits de at sur Vilfredo Pareto par Piet Tommissen et Giovanni*

Busino). The list of Pareto's writings, compiled by Busino, occupies pp. 71-110; works on Pareto are listed between pp. 111 and 249. The review in question is cited on p. 85.

Weber scholars have been equally well served by what remains the best German bibliolography: Constans Seyfarth and Gert Schmidt, compilers, *Max Weber Bibliographie: Eine Dokumentation der Sekundärliteratur* (1977), which lists 2,348 items. And for Weber's works, the definitive bibliography is Dirk Käsler's "Max-Weber-Bibliographie," published in 1975 and updated in his *Max Weber: An Introduction to His Life and Work* (Cambridge: Polity Press, 1988): 235-75, which adds more than 150 items to Marianne Weber's original list in her bibliography of her husband (not reproduced in the 1975 English translation).

8. Note should be made, however, that Durkheim did use Italian works throughout *Suicide,* but works of a special social-psychological genre. See for example pp. 53, 86, 89, 95, 100, 104, etc., in the English translation (1951).

Additionally, we should remind ourselves of Durkheim's attack upon Simmel which he published in the *Revista italiana di sociologia* ("*La sociologia ed il suo domino scientifico,*" Vol. 4 [1900]: 127-148). For details, see Heinz Maus, "Simmel in German Sociology," in Kurt H. Wolff, ed., *Georg Simmel, 1858-1918*: 188-89, and Steven Lukes, *Emile Durkheim*: 404-05. By consulting Lukes's "complete" bibliography of Durkheim's work, it is clear that he reviewed a much higher proportion of books written in French, German, and even English, and in Italian. His interest in "monitoring" German social science, for instance, appears to have been much stronger than in following Italian developments.

9. They were as follows: 1900 (Corsica), 1901 (Rome and southern Italy), 1901 (Rome again), 1902 (Florence, having spent at least six months in Rome), 1902 December (Italian Riveria), 1903 (Rome), 1906 (Sicily), 1907 (Lake Como), 1908 (Florence), 1910 (Italy), 1911 spring (Italy), 1913 spring and fall (Italy), 1914 spring (Italy). See for documentation Marianne Weber (1975: 705-706) or Eduard Baumgarten (1964: 696-704). Marianne related in the *Lebensbild* how strongly attached to Italy Weber became between 1900 and 1903 when he was at his worst emotionally: "He parted from the south as from a second homeland, and when a long winter weighed upon the land beyond the Alps, he was often gripped by an irrepressible longing for it" (p. 55, English edition); and regarding Rome: "I could live the rest of my life there" (p. 257); again, "Weber escaped to the south" (p. 261).

As for Weber's fluency in Italian, his good friend Roberto Michels (also Pareto's companion) tells the story of Weber attending a dinner in Turin during which he sat wordlessly for a while, then took the floor and entertained everyone with his "*brilliant-issimo* witticisms." See Michels, "Max Weber," *Nuova Antologia: Rivista di lettere, scienze ed arti,* Vol. 209, Issue 1170 (Dec. 6, 1920): 355-61.

10. The standard biography is that of Bousquet (1928), very brief and dated. His most recent works (1960 and 1961) do not begin to approach the detail of Marianne Weber's biography or Eduard Baumgarten's compilation and commentary for Weber. Therefore it is difficult to locate Pareto when Weber was in Italy. All that is easily determined is his hermetic existence at Celigny after 1907, though he was not as immobile as some have argued.

11. The volumes are as follows: v.1, n.l (1903): 1167 pp; v.1, n.2 (1905): 563 pp.; v.2., n.l. (1905): 731 pp.; v.2, n.2 (1907): 752 pp.; 3 (1915): 690 pp.; 4 (1909): 614 pp.; 5 (1921): 1,043 pp.; 6 (1929): 1,238 pp.
12. As mentioned above (and as Gerd Schroeter pointed out to me), the Pareto scholar, Piet Tommissen, did note the series in passing (without complete notation), in his contribution to a German handbook on "Classics of Sociological Thought": "Vilfredo Pareto," pp. 201-231, in Dirk Käsler, ed., *Klassiker des Soziologischen Denkens, Erster Band, Von Comte bis Durkheim* (München: C.H. Beck, 1976); the observation is made in a footnote: 476, n. 4. In the text Tommissen writes that the "relation" between Pareto and Weber remains "unclear" or "unsettled" (*ungeklärt*). The reason that Tommissen was aware of the connection at all is probably due to his not long before having helped edit and compile the definitive Pareto bibliography (Pareto, 1975b). His knowledge of Pareto's writings and affiliations, then, is extraordinary compared to that of most scholars.
13. Bendix (1960: 2) makes only fleeting reference to the work. Honigsheim (1949: 195-199; reprinted in Honigsheim, 2000) deals with it somewhat more satisfactorily, as do Q.J. Munters (1972: 134-135), and Guenther Roth (1968: xxxvi-vl), but an adequate study in English is lacking.
14. In further deflating claims about Pareto's unwillingness to deal with German contributions to social science during Weber's period, we should point out that within the brief compass of the *"Proemio"* to the *Biblioteca,* Pareto makes reference to [Gustav] Schmoller, Werner Sombart, G. Schmidt, and Marx (plus Croce, Labriola, Adam Smith, and the *"filosofo cinese,"* Meng-Tsue).
15. A possible reason for the fact that Pareto's use of the Weber work in his series has not been noted before may be that bibliographies, even massive, nearly comprehensive ones like the Käsler for Weber or the Busino for Pareto, do not mention the *Biblioteca,* and their respective affiliations with it. This omission I cannot explain. (The *"Proemio"* is listed by Busino [Pareto 1975b: 89], but not in such a way that would lead the usual reader to fathom its meaning, nor of course its connection with Weber.)

References

Alexander, Jeffrey C. 1978: "Formal and Substantive Voluntarism in the Work of Talcott Parsons: A Theoretical and Ideological Re-interpretation." *American Sociological Review,* 43:2 (April), 177-98.
Bauman, Zygmunt 1978: *Hermeneutics and Social Science.* New York: Columbia University Press.
Baumgarten, Eduard 1964: *Max Weber: Werk und Person.* Tübingen: Mohr.
Bendix, Reinhard 1960: Max Weber: *An Intellectual Portrait.* New York: Double-day. Later editions: Anchor Books, 1962; University of California Press, 1977, with an introduction by Guenther Roth.
Betto, Emilio 1967: *Allgemeine Auslegungslehre als Methodik der Geisteswissenschaften.* Tübingen: Mohr.
Bousquet, G.R. 1928a: *Vilfredo Pareto: sa vie et son ouevre.* Paris: Payot.
_____ 1928b: *The Work of Vilfredo Pareto.* Hanover, NH: The Sociological Press.
_____ 1960: *Pareto, le savant et l'homme.* Lausanne: Payot.

_____ 1961: "Vilfredo Pareto (1848-1923): "Biographical notes on the occasion of the publication of his letters to Pantaleoni." *Banca Nazionale del Lavoro Quarterly Review*, 58 (September): 317-360.

Collins, Randall 1998: *The Sociology of Philosophies*. Cambridge, MA: Harvard University Press.

Coser, Lewis 1977: *Masters of Sociological Thought*. 2nd edition. New York: Harcourt, Brace, Jovanovich.

Croce, Benedetto and Vilfredo Pareto 1953: "On the Economic Principle: A Correspondence between B. Croce and V. Pareto." Trans. C.M. Meredith. *International Economic Papers* 3: 172-207. London: Macmillan.

Durkheim, Emile [1897] 1951 *Suicide*. New York: The Free Press.

_____ 1900: "La sociologia ed il suo domino scientifico." *Revista italiana di sociologia*. Vol. 4: 127-48.

_____ 1978 [1906-09]: Review of Marianne Weber's *Ehefrau und Mutter in der Rechtsentwickelung* [sic]. Reprinted and translated for the first time in Mark Traugott, ed. and tr., *Emile Durkheim on Institutional Analysis*. Chicago: University of Chicago Press.

Eisermann, Gottfried 1956: "Vilfredo Pareto in Deutschland." *Kolner Zeit- schrift für Soziologie und Sozialpsychologie*. Vol. 8, No. 4: 647-52.

_____ 1961: *Vilfredo Pareto als Nationalökonom und Soziologe. Recht und Staat*. Heft 236/237. Tübingen: Mohr.

_____ 1975: "L'Influence de Vilfredo Pareto en Allemagne." *Cahiers Vilfredo Pareto*, 13:34, 155-73.

Gadamer, Hans-Georg 1975: *Truth & Method*. New York: Seabury. (retranslated under the same title and publisher, 1989).

Giddens, Anthony 1976: *New Rules of Sociological Method*. New York: Basic Books.

Hodges, H.A. 1952: *The Philosophy of Wilhelm Dilthey*. London: Routledge & Kegan Paul.

Honigsheim, Paul 1949: "Max Weber as Historian of Agriculture and Rural Life." *Agricultural History* 23: 179-213. [Reissued as part of Paul Honigsheim, *The Unknown Max Weber*, ed. and intro. by Alan Sica. New Brunswick, NJ: Transaction Publishers, 2000).

Hoy, David Couzens 1978: *The Critical Circle: Literature, History, and Philosophical Hermeneutics*. Berkeley: University of Cali-fornia Press.

Hughes, H. Stuart 1958: *Consciousness and Society: The Reorientation of European Social Thought 1890-1930*. New York: Alfred A. Knopf.

_____ 1990: *Gentleman Rebel: The Memoirs of H. Stuart Hughes*. New York: Ticknor and Fields.

Joas, Hans 1985: *G. H. Mead*. Cambridge, MA: MIT Press.

Johnson, Harry M. 1978: "Comment on Jones' 'On Understanding a Sociological Classic.'" *MS* 84:1 (July): 175-81.

Käsler, Dirk 1975: "Max-Weber-Bibliographie." *Kölner Zeitschrift für Soziologie und Sozialpsychologie*, 27:3 (December), 703-30.

LaCapra, Dominick 1972: *Emile Durkheim: Sociologist and Philosopher*. Ithaca, NY: Cornell University Press. (Reissued Aurora, Colorado: The Davies Group, 2001.)

Lukes, Steven 1972: *Emile Durkheim: His Life and Work*. New York: Harper and Row.

Makkreel, Rudolph A. 1975: *Dilthey: Philosopher of the Human Studies*. Princeton, NJ: Princeton University Press.

Michels, Roberto 1927: *Bedeutende Männer*. Leipzig: Quelle & Meyer.

———— 1920: "Max Weber." *Nuova Antologia*. Vol. 209, Issue 1170(December 16): 355-61.

Miller, David L. 1973: *George Herbert Mead: Self, Language, and the World*. Austin: University of Texas Press.

Munters, Q.J. 1972: "Max Weber as Rural Sociologist." *Sociology ruralis*, 12:2, 129-46.

Pareto, Vilfredo 1903-1929: Editor, *Biblioteca di storia economica*. Milan: Societa Editrice Libraria.

———— 1916: *The Mind and Society: A Treatise on General Sociology* [1963] Trans. Andrew Bongiorno and Arthur Livingston. New York: Dover Publications.

———— 1960: *Lettere a Maffeo Pantaleoni 1890-1923*. 3 vols. Rome: Banca Nazionale del Lavoro.

———— 1975a: *Correspondance 1890-1923*. Ed. by Giovanni Busino. *Oeuvres com-pletes*, Tome XIX. 2 vols. Geneva: Librairie Droz.

———— 1975b: *Jubile du Professeur V. Pareto 1917*. *Oeuvres com-pletes*, Tome XX. Geneva: Librairie Droz.

Parsons, Talcott 1937: *The Structure of Social Action*. New York: The Free Press.

Peel, J.D.Y. 1971: *Herbert Spencer: The Evolution of a Sociologist*. New York: Basic Books.

Pickering, Mary 1993: *Auguste Comte: An Intellectual Biography*, Vol. 1. Cambridge: Cambridge University Press.

Radnitzsky, Gerard 1973: *Contemporary Schools of Metascience*. Chicago: Henry Regnery.

Remmling, Gunter 1975: *The Sociology of Karl Mannheim*. London: Routledge & Kegen Paul.

Roth, Guenther 1968: "Introduction" to *Economy & Society*. New York: Bedminster Press.

Seebohm, Thomas M. 1977: "The Problem of Hermeneutics in Recent Anglo-American Literature, Part I," *Philosophy and Rhetoric*, 10:3 (Summer): 180-98; "Part II," 10:4 (Fall): 263-75.

Segre, Sandro 1982: "Pareto and Weber: A Tentative Reconstruction of Their Intellectual Relationship with an Excursus on Pareto and the German Language.' *Revue européenne des sciences sociales (Cahiers Vilfredo Pareto)*, vol. 20, no.62, 247-271.

———— 1986: "On Max Weber's Awareness of Emile Durkheim." *History of Sociology*, 6:2/7:1/2 (Spring), 151-167.

Seidman, Steven 1977: "The Durkheim-Weber 'Unawareness Problem.'" *European Journal of Sociology* 18: 356.

Seyfarth, Constans and Gert Schmidt 1977: *Max Weber Bibliographie: Eine Dokumentation der Sekundarliteratur*. Stuttgart: Ferdinand Enke.

Shapiro, Gary and Alan Sica (eds.) 1988: *Hermeneutics: Question and Prospects* (revised pb edition). Amherst: University of Massachusetts Press.

Tiryakian, Edward 1966: "A Problem for the Sociology of Knowledge: The Mutual Unawareness of Emile Durkheim and Max Weber." *Archives Européenes de Sociologie*, 7:2: 330-336.

Tiryakian Edward and Steven Lukes 1974: "Durkheim Confirme Tiryakian: Un Exchange de Correspondance." *Archives Européenes de Sociologie*, 14: 354-55.

Tommissen, Piet 1976: "Vilfredo Pareto." Pp. 201-31 in Dirk Käsler, ed. *Klassiker Des Soziologiechen Denkens*. Vol. 1. Munich: Beck.

Warner, R. Stephen 1978: "Toward a Redefinition of Action Theory: Paying the Cognitive Element Its Due." *American Journal of Sociology*, 83:6 (May): 1317-1349.

Weber, Marianne 1975 [1926]: *Max Weber: A Biography*. Trans. Harry Zohn. New York: John Wiley.

Weber, Max 1891: *Die römische Agrargeschichte und ihrer Bedeutung fur das Staats- und Privatrecht*. Stuttgart: Ferdi-nand Enke.

_____ [1903-1906] 1975: *Roscher and Knies: The Logical Problems of Historical Economics*. Trans. with an Introduction by Guy Oakes. New York: Free Press.

_____ 1923: *Wirtschaftsgeschichte*. Ed. by S. Hellmann & M. Palyi. Munich: Duncker and Humblot.

Wolff, Janet 1975: *Hermeneutic Philosophy and the Sociology of Art*. London: Routledge & Kegan Paul.

Wolff, Kurt (ed.) 1968: *Georg Simmel, 1858-1918*. Columbus: Ohio State University Press.

_____ 1974: "Vilfredo Pareto." Pp. 5-16 in *Trying Sociology*. New York: John Wiley.

7

Weber and Modern Philosophy: A Note

One could reasonably make the following argument, if social theory and philosophy are allowed to share the same dance floor: "With Marx temporarily set aside via historical transformations of the sort he would have enjoyed dissecting, and Freud now ritually denigrated by a growing phalanx of detractors, both learned and ignorant, only Weber survives as the principal social theorist of the twentieth century whose ideas can lead us with analytic confidence into the upcoming era, both politically and philosophically speaking." Let me explain in the few pages I have at my disposal why I hold this truth to be virtually self-evident, and admitting a priori that a thorough treatment of Weber, viewed philosophically, would fill a monograph, and perhaps someday will (as hinted at by Guy Oakes in *Weber and Rickert*).

Weber as Philosopher

It is worth remembering that Weber's dates are 1864 to 1920, paralleling almost perfectly the lives of Simmel, Durkheim, Pareto, and Freud: a rich period for social theory, but also one extremely fertile for philosophy. He died suddenly and surprisingly, a victim of the worldwide influenza pandemic, with an immediately perceived impact on the social thought of his time, not unlike the shock of Jim Henson's similar demise vis-à-vis advanced puppetry. He was commemorated by almost instantaneous festschrifts, memorial speeches, and memoirs. In fact, there were those in the 1930s, after Hitler's ascendancy, who seriously wondered if Weber's political presence could have materially helped in resisting fascism's advance. In 1986, Leo Lowenthal, at the time the last well-known living member of the original Frankfurt School, told me that he had been in Heidelberg in 1920 on that day in June when Weber's death was announced. He reflected on the interesting fact that the only other time in his long life when he could recall hearing a city come to a silent standstill in homage to the newly dead was when New York learned of Roosevelt's passing. The philosophers, literary artists, social scientists, historians, and other notables who shared enduring personal relationships with Weber (and often with his famous feminist wife, Marianne Weber) included Georg Simmel, Stefan George, Ernst Bloch, György Lukács, Emil Lederer, Ernst Troeltsch, Karl Jaspers, Paul Honigsheim, Ernst Toller, and dozens of others. Weber's omnivorous curiosity even led him to a raft of Russian emigré intellectuals who had moved to Heidelberg during their 1905 revolution, and were dragooned into tutoring Weber in their language so, after six weeks of study, he could follow political events in their homeland by means of domestic newspapers. It was Jaspers, the psychiatrist and philosopher, who coined a phrase which has been widely repeated by those with intimate knowledge of particulars, when he called Weber "the greatest German of our age." Quite poignantly, Jaspers elaborated this ultimate encomium: "When he died in 1920, I felt as if the German world had lost its heart, and as if it were no longer possible to continue living as before" (Jaspers 1995: 327). In short, this was an estimable person whose relentlessly analytic mind—one should properly call it "philosophic"—struggled most uncomfortably to interpret a store of socio-cultural, historical, literary, and economic knowledge that crowded his consciousness, the scope of which was rivaled in nearby generations only by Marx—himself dubbed "the most learned man in Europe" at his death by those who knew his work well.

In 1922, during the flurry of scholarly tributes paid to Weber (which included multi-volume *Festschriften*, and a Jaspers pamphlet that sold in the many thousands), the Freiburg legal philosopher and sociologist of law, Hermann Kantorowicz, published a short article in *Logos* called "*Weber als Philosoph*," which begins with reference to "*den Schmerz um Max Webers allzufrühen Tod*" [the pain of Weber's premature death]. It is not much known to the toilers of the Weber Industry, and is notable mainly for its title, almost unique among the many thousands of scholarly compositions Weber has inspired in one way or another. (In English alone, there now exist over 4,600 such items.) However, in a long review-essay published in a 1993 issue of *Philosophische Rundschau*, Werner Gephart of Bonn assays eleven recent additions to Weberiana under the title "*Max Weber als Philosoph?*" It is the meaning of the question mark, of course, that I want to reflect on here. This is not so much because Gephart knew of Kantorowicz's much earlier statement (which he does in fact cite), but because the interrogative, implicitly skeptical mode of expression that Gephart chose—a technique scholars may have borrowed from quasi-yellow journalism, as in "Lawyers Want Justice?"—suggests that Weber's credentials as a philosopher are worth questioning, despite contrary claims made by others, most notably Habermas and Charles Taylor (Taylor 1989). I am not the only interpreter of Weber who has wondered about his role as philosopher, whether of methodology, axiology, or culture at large: "Weber never portrayed himself as a Fichte scholar or even as a very serious student of philosophy at all, with the special exception of the antiphilosopher Nietzsche" (Sica 1990: 123).

Certainly the most profound, informed, and in many ways illuminating foray into the question of Weber's status as a philosopher was made by his junior colleague and analyst, Jaspers (whose written record of Weber's clinical analysis was destroyed by Marianne Weber for fear the Nazis would use it to defame his reputation in the 1930s). Jaspers's summary in 1932 of how we ought to view Weber's philosophical role has set the standard for all subsequent estimates, even when they strongly disagreed with his:

> Max Weber developed no philosophical system. It would be impossible to expound his philosophy as a doctrine. He declined to be called a p h i - losopher. But to us he is the true philosopher of the time in which he lived. Because philosophy is not a gradually progressing science, which recognizes a timeless truth, each philosophy must achieve its real - ity as a historical existence rooted in the absolute and oriented toward transcendence. Max Weber taught no philosophy; he was a philosophy. (Jaspers 1964: 251)

Though today it may seem a left-handed compliment or even comical to say that a person embodies a philosophy rather than presenting one in argumentative form, for Jaspers and many of his generation, who knew Weber personally, there was hardly any other plausible way of expressing their reaction to him. (Memoirs about Wittgenstein might be taken as evidence for a not dissimilar reaction many of his students and readers have had to him, particularly given the details of his life now available through Ray Monk's biography.)

Writing much later and with less emotion, Jaspers put the case even more sharply vis-à-vis Weber's standing in the world of serious thought, when Jaspers reflected that his central concern in his monumental history of philosophy was with:

> . . . philosophy of the present time in its existential gravity; not the "hob- bies" of tedious and diligent conceptual games, but the thinking that en- gages our possibilities, as individuals and in the world, in our nations and in mankind. . . . To me, Max Weber appeared as the true philosopher of the age, the philosopher who did not express his philosophy directly, but whose life and thought were based on it. (Jaspers 1995: 327)

Jaspers's deep affinity with Weber's way of viewing the social world, and the younger man's adoption of Weber's "ethic of responsibility," is documented by other sources as well.

For example, Young-Bruehl's biography of Hannah Arendt (student and lifelong friend of Jaspers) clearly illustrates how Jaspers tried, through sheer daring and courage, to emulate his hero from youth when, during World War II, he seemed to become Weber's stand-in during the ruinous "German catastrophe" (to borrow from Meinecke): "The serene confidence of Jaspers's had been like a beacon to those who needed some sign of hope for the future" (Young-Bruehl, 1982: 213). As Arendt said in her *laudatio* for Jaspers in 1958: "There is something fascinating about a man's being inviolable, untemptable, unswayable" (ibid.), which could as much have been a description of Weber at the end of his life as of Jaspers during and after the Third Reich. In fact, there is hardly a better introduction to the notion of Weber's philosophical importance than to read the letters between Arendt and Jaspers from 1926 through 1969, in which debates, arguments, and embattled positioning vis-à-vis Weber take up dozens of pages (Arendt/Jaspers, 1992: 15-17, 87-88, 148-50, 203, 208-09, 541, 546-556, 636-37, 659-663, passim). Arendt's celebratory remarks about Jaspers also stands as a fascinating, if unspoken, comparison between Jaspers and Heidegger—Arendt's lover and teacher, an arrangement Jaspers found deeply objectionable—and one in which the former comes out to far more advantage than the latter, of course. Jaspers, at sixty-two, and his Jewish wife, Gertrud, were saved from Nazi deportation by two weeks when Americans rolled into Heidelberg on April 1, 1945. One of their fellow townspersons, who was starving as were so many, was Marianne Weber, Max's widow. The "philosophy of life" about which Jaspers wrote at such great length obviously owed much to Weber's own *Existenzphilosophie*, even if the older man never announced it as such.

Weber, in partial spiritual accord with Nietzsche, even while side-stepping the latter's histrionic posturing and hyperventilated prose, found industrialized, imperialistic modernity generally repulsive, particularly in the apparent inevitability of spiritual decay, mostly attributable to headlong rationalization of structures, interaction, and even intrapsychic regimens. It is perfectly true that he supported some machinations of the German state when the only apparent alternatives were even worse, and that he thought that a reflective patriotism was not *necessarily* a degenerate state of being, particularly for intellectuals. Nevertheless, and as is perfectly clear from the more passionate passages, for instance, in *The Protestant Ethic* or "Politics as a Vocation," Weber's general response to urbanized rationalization fit very well with those of Mann, Broch, Doderer, Kafka, Musil, Canetti, and so many others who later worked the literary side of social criticism in the Teutonic realm of sensibility.

But it is not nowadays through a careful reading of highbrow literature that most educated Americans, including its philosophers, know
something about Weber. Instead, *mirabile dictu*, it is by means of Allan
Bloom's philippic, *The Closing of the American Mind* (as noted above, in
chapter 3), published to astonishing popular acclaim in 1987, that Weber qua Nietzschean devil was foisted both upon a naive laity, and also
the enormous international community of Weberian scholarship. (Even
the *Kansas City Star*, aiming to please its conservative suburbanite audience, reprinted in serial format entire sections of Bloom's book, which
must be the first time that the name Max Weber has graced the U.S. mass
market for "culture." When I saw Bloom one morning in the Agora
Restaurant (*sic*) near the University of Chicago campus, I reported this
development in suburban moral uplift, and he beamed, saying, "I love to
get good market reports!"). His studied, perverse reading of Weber (one
could not call it "ignorant") has been carried into an even wider orbit by
his student, Francis Fukuyama, in several books, including *The End of
History and the Last Man*, and *Trust*. In the latter volume, Weber is given a
more moderate appraisal. While Fukuyama is a journalist and political
analyst recently turned professor, Bloom was a bona fide philosopher
from the start, given his well-regarded translations of Plato and Rousseau,
and his life-long affiliation with the Leo Strauss operation at the University of Chicago.

In fact, one way of approaching the conundrum of why Bloom chose
to cast Nietzsche, Weber, and Heidegger as the heavies in his middlebrow melodrama is to recall Bloom's own estimate of his beloved mentor, Strauss. Quoting from the opening of Bloom's eulogy in 1973, one
hears a telling familiarity of tone:

> It is particularly difficult to speak of him, for I know I cannot do him
> justice. Moreover, those of us who knew him saw in him such a power
> of mind, such a unity of purpose and of life, such a rare mixture of the
> human elements resulting in a harmonious expression of the virtues,
> moral and intellectual, that our account of him is likely to evoke disbelief
> or ridicule from those who have never experienced a man of his quality.
> (Bloom 1990: 235)

These are virtually identical sentiments to those voiced by Jaspers
fifty years earlier vis-à-vis Weber. And as such, whether somewhat formulaic or not, they are difficult to square with less elevated stories told
by other close friends of Strauss regarding his addiction to *Gunsmoke*
and such televised drivel of the early 1960s—much the same way
Wittgenstein allegedly preferred comic books to "serious" reading.

But a more telling paragraph occurs somewhat later in Bloom's eulogy, when he writes (as I quoted earlier in the book): "Strauss recog-

nized the seriousness and nobility of Max Weber's mind, but he showed that he was a derivative thinker, standing somewhere between modern science and Nietzsche, unable to resolve their tension" (Bloom 1990: 238). So Bloom's mentor demeaned Jaspers's mentor as a "derivative"— that is, "second-rate"—thinker and "showed," presumably within a forty-two-page section of *Natural Right and History*, that the concept of "value" attributed to Weber (in "Science as a Vocation"), removed as it was from the sphere of absolutistic intentions which Strauss comfortably inhabited, eventually and inevitably became a dangerous weapon in the minds of an Hitlerian mob. And, by extension, this despicable philosophy, according to Bloom, inspired an updated nemesis which he witnessed himself: the armed black students at Cornell in 1969 and their white supporters, who, he wrote, were "nothing better than a rabble" (Bloom 1987: 313). It is fascinating to observe that Weber himself, addressing a similarly raucous crowd in Germany just after World War I, refused to bend to their desire to hear the strains of nationalist, apologetic propaganda they hoped he would voice, and which, had he expressed them, would have made him instantly a hero to young people in the same way that Bloom became a hero to elders on the nostalgic Right.

Strauss was given to writing "What Weber really meant..." (Strauss 1953: 70) and similarly dismissive phrases, thus showing his students and admirers that he had gained a philosophic high ground to which Weber had only stumblingly aspired. After all, Weber was unable to "resolve the tension between science and Nietzsche," whatever that might mean, precisely taken. Who, one asks, has successfully overcome this terrible tension? (Is it accidental that *Spannung*—"tension," "strain," or "stress"—is one of Weber's key pieces of analytic rhetoric?) The fact that Strauss knew a few things well—mostly concerning aspects of Plato, Hobbes, Machiavelli, Maimonides, and Aristophanes—and that Weber knew infinitely more about virtually everything else that mattered to the way we comprehend societal life, did not stop Strauss from allowing himself the extraordinary, one might well say "psychopathological," delusion that he was a superior thinker. If by thinker one means merely— to crib from Jaspers—a "hobbyist of tedious and diligent conceptual games," permanently and quite intentionally removed from the hustle that prompts what Habermas might call "pragmatic decisionism," then it is conceivable that Strauss and Weber were on similar planes of ability and accomplishment. But if one reads, for instance, Weber's treatises on the sociology of law, the sociology of religion, methodology in the *Geisteswissenschaften*, Roman legal practices, medieval political-economy, the sociology of music, or his massive empirical studies of Polish agricultural laborers in Prussia, it becomes clear that in addition to an exquisite education in what Strauss approvingly regarded as "the classics,"

Weber actually knew something about the way the world worked, both historically and in his day. This kind of knowledge was not given to Strauss, and he was not temperamentally suited—one could guess that he was simply not strong enough—to absorb and then conceptualize it in some global manner. But, then, who is? Weber, of course, cracked up severely in his mid-thirties, and hardly experienced a carefree moment for the rest of his short life. How would Strauss have mended his corrupt daguerreotype of Weber, I wonder, had he known that young Max, bored with class in junior high school, took with him to school the forty-volume Cotta edition of Goethe, one at a time presumably, and secretly read them as the teachers blathered on about materials of less than Weberian import (Marianne Weber 1975: 47-48)?

Let us part company with Strauss and his adoring disciple, Bloom, with one final set of observations. Their joint expectation, nay, demand, for apodictic political and cultural judgment or knowledge gave them precisely the character of those "big babies in university chairs" whom Weber chastised in "Science as a Vocation," and with calculated reference to which Bloom opens the chapter called "Values" in his bestseller (Bloom 1987: 194). According to Bloom, "The transfusion of this religious mythmaking or value-positing interpretation of social and political experience into the American bloodstream was in large measure effected by Max Weber's language. . . the Weberian language and the interpretation of the world it brings with it have caught on like wildfire," despite the fact that Weber "denies the rationality of 'values'" (ibid.: 208-209). Whether or not it is empirically the case that Weber and his wildfiery language are culpable for everything currently wrong with American society—could it be that the world looked strangely lighted during the 1980s from the heights of the University of Chicago's pseudo-gothic architecture?—Bloom's acid observations are nevertheless interesting. For this is exactly where Weber's philosophy, as it were, remains essential for contemporary social analysts, and also those philosophers who evaluate social life. It may well be possible to "do" philosophy of the most arid analytic type without reference to socio-cultural reality, but such a realm of speculation was never remotely interesting to Weber—nor to Strauss. It now seems, for better or for worse, that philosophers of European genesis or inspiration *all* have shifted into the social philosophy business, and as such, must all come to terms with Weber's particular "language," as Bloom quite correctly notes, even if for the wrong reasons. Value-freedom, rationalization, the methodology of the ideal-type and *Verstehen*, the historical force of genuine charisma, the bureaucratic force of manufactured charisma, the direction of Western music, the decline of religion as previously known and the substitution of concocted pseudo-spirituality within organizational formats, the ever-pressing Orwellization/bureaucratization of advanced societies—all of these notions and more are Weber's gifts to contemporary thought. And all of them, it may come as a disheartening shock for the novice to learn, were not only created by Weber (in close dialogue with a large salon of gifted colleagues and friends), but elaborated to an extent which to date have rarely been profitably embellished or enlarged. Or so one could argue were there enough pages and time.

References

Arendt, Hannah and Karl Jaspers 1992: *Hannah Arendt Karl Jaspers: Correspondence, 1926-1969*. Ed. Lotte Kohler and Hans Saner, tr. Robert and Rita Kimber. New York: Harcourt, Brace, Jovanovich.

Bloom, Allan 1987: *The Closing of the American Mind: How Higher Education Has Failed Democracy and Impoverished the Souls of Today's Students*. New York: Simon and Schuster.

—— 1990: *Giants and Dwarfs: Essays 1960-1990*. New York: Simon and Schuster.

Fukuyama, Francis 1992: *The End of History and the Last Man*. New York: The Free Press.

_____ 1995: *Trust: Social Virtues and the Creation of Prosperity*. New York: The Free Press.

Gephart, Werner 1993: :Max Weber als Philosoph?" *Philosophische Rundschau*, 40:1/2, 34-56.

Jaspers, Karl 1964: *Three Essays: Leonardo, Descartes, Max Weber*, tr. by Ralph Manheim. New York: Harcourt, Brace, and World.

_____ 1995: *The Great Philosophers: The Disturbers*, Vol. 4. Tr. by Edith Ehrlich and Leonard Ehrlich. New York: Harcourt, Brace & Co.

Kantorowicz, Hermann 1922: "Max Weber als Philosoph." *Logos*, 11, 256-259.

Oakes, Guy 1988: *Weber and Rickert: Concept Formation in the Social Sciences*. Cambridge, MA: MIT Press.

Sica, Alan 1990: *Weber, Irrationality, and Social Order* (rev. pb. ed.). Berkeley: University of California Press.

Taylor, Charles 1989: *Sources of the Self: The Making of the Modern Identity*. Cambridge, MA: Harvard University Press.

Young-Bruehl, Elizabeth 1982: *Hannah Arendt: For Love of the World*. New Haven, CT: Yale University Press.

Weber, Marianne 1975: *Max Weber: A Biography*, tr. by Harry Zohn. New York: John Wiley and Sons.

8

Weber and Mann

Some years ago I was asked to review at length Harvey Goldman's *Max Weber and Thomas Mann: Calling and the Shaping of the Self* (California, 1988), and I was pleased to do so because my interest in the work of Weber was only slightly more passionate than my long-term fascination with Mann's fiction and essays (literary and political). I had for some time taught my students to think of them as two sides of the same coin, and at one point tried to have them read *Doctor Faustus* in tandem with *The Protestant Ethic* so that the "iron cage" metaphor could be expanded into the twentieth century following Weber's death. Not long after reviewing Goldman, I was also asked to write an introduction to the paperback reissue of Mann's early novel, *Royal Highness* (California, 1992), and there I put to use standard Weberian thinking in order to illustrate a link that Goldman had so thoroughly forged in his two books on the topic. Because Mann and Weber are so seldom considered together, an oddity in the literature that I have not been able to disentangle, I wanted to restate my observations about Goldman's excellent work these dozen years later, mainly because his books seem to have remained isolated from the regular literature on Weber, and they do not deserve that fate.

"This book has its beginnings with a copy of Thomas Mann's *Doctor Faustus*, bought when I was a student in France and read in Heidelberg, Paris, and Lyon. I love this novel like no other," is how Goldman opens his book. Naturally, this reading event occurred during the sixties, which brings me to a similar recollection. During lunch break at the factory one day, I was reading through *Ramparts* or *Avant Garde* or some other time-bound journal frozen within that era and came upon an interview with the already superannuated Peter, Paul, and Mary, a folk-singing trio culturally and politically important between about 1961 and 1965 when the musical genre then known as "folk-rock" was concocted by their friend, Robert Zimmerman, quickly leading to their demise. In this long piece, Mary Travers was asked which were her favorite books. According to my memory, she answered: Hermann Broch's *Sleep-walkers*, Hermann Hesse's *Magister Ludi*, and Mann's *Magic Mountain*. She even disquisitioned upon Hesse for a while; so after work I shot to the library, dusted off these undisturbed volumes, and began reading. Somehow being eighteen or nineteen and led to such books by a popular singer says as much to me now about what has happened to mass versus high culture in the ensuing twenty years as any single datum: "Britney Spears, what is your favorite novel and could you describe it for us, its meaning to socio-cultural life and the future of mind in America?"

Thus in many ways Goldman and I are on the same wavelength, with one small difference. In 1968 when I sent in my check for $2.45 to Random House to get *The Magic Mountain* in paperback, it changed my ideas about the limits of fiction writing and also the nature of long-term physical and cultural decay, whereas only ten years later did I finally read *Doctor Faustus*—a text (*sic*) which I teach regularly in order to liven up my own discipline's conception of "culture." Had I come to Leverkühn first, instead of Castorp, I may have taken a different route, for the awful hilarity of the former's life—his insane but finally understandable desire to "take back the Ninth Symphony" and substitute something completely unlistenable — all of this is a far cry from the good-natured naivete of Castorp as he hangs out high in the mountains with a crew of Lukácsian dementeds.

It also happens that, while speeding through the 727 pages of *The Magic Mountain*, I was reading for the first of many times Weber's *Protestant Ethic* and related items. Yet the obvious connection between Mann's first novel, *Buddenbrooks*, and Weber's ideas about asceticism and work, seemed both unavoidable and invisible: the former, because of German intellectual currents around 1900 that affected all learned people; the latter, because Mann and Weber were so very different in their conception of duty to the craft and to their gender-role. In Mann's *Diaries* he speaks warmly of studying a young male gardener's gluteus maximus, and carefully holding in check his homophilia, whereas Weber's hyper-macho dueling scar and quick temper in questions of (masculine) honor left no room whatever for that sort of impulse. Yet both men suffered a range of severe psychosomatic troubles—Weber may well have been impotent for a while after his breakdown, or even before, though only Marianne Weber and maybe Else von Richthofen knew, and they did not tell.

One could go on in this way. It all illustrates that Goldman has probably opened a connection that now, freshly cast into the light, will seem terribly obvious to everyone who has cherished these two writers, who has had to make room in our postmodern consciousnesses for their strictly modernist, literate, politically engaged intellectualism of the most serious, maniacal kind. Their enormous writings seem to represent what some of us may have aspired to had it not been for Howdie Doodie and the Beatles. Imagine Russell Jacoby introducing Derek Jacoby on American Bandstand and asking him to read from "Tonio Kröger" or "Death in Venice," accompanied to the rear by Bon Jovi and a rank of mostly naked young men and women doing aerobic dance, and at this moment Mann's and Weber's ghosts appear in the wings and are asked to interpret this cultural condition. "Mechanized Brecht" they might say, or *Lulu* without pathos.

It is into this vortex (*sic*) of cultural matter and anti-matter that Goldman finds himself, though he does not worry about bringing his subjects up to date. Instead, he takes apart their earlier works (another volume handles the later ones) as they reveal their innermost selves vis-à-vis a "calling" and what it meant then to have a "personality." It is fascinating that a "television personality" means precisely the opposite of what Weber intended by the word, just as television is precisely the opposite of literate intelligence. But Goldman does not cross the postmodern barrier into twilight land, which is partly what gives his book its comforting anachronistic flavor and also its Linus-blanket quality, of truth before the end of truth-telling through stories and tracts begun, probably about 30 years ago when, as one of my German professors remarked, "Why bother with those dark writers anyway? Isn't the news around us bleak enough without them?" It is odd but comforting that Goldman does not invoke our own troubles when considering those of Weber and Mann, since they had plenty of their own, and also because theirs seem susceptible to rational action, bravery, ontological control, and the rest of bourgeois melodrama that is no longer in our world. Goldman is not the hip French scholar using Derrida to take apart Montaigne, hunting for codes and lapses into the unspoken/unexpressed traps. He takes his subjects' words at face value, and writes about them in ways they would have understood and appreciated.

Precisely what Goldman does is simply stated. The book comes in two parts: one, on the calling, and the other on what the word "personality" meant to Weber/Mann explicitly and otherwise. In the first part he carefully examines Weber's *Protestant Ethic*, then turns more carefully to several of Mann's earliest works, including "The Joker," *Buddenbrooks*, and "Tonio Kröger." He summarizes his findings and moves to an interesting sketch of *Bildung* and the personality type that cared about rigorous self-cultivation—from its inception with Kant and Humboldt, into its hyper-refinement with Goethe. Back to Weber, we learn about his approach to the notion of personality as a "center" for rational, ethically directed action, with reference to some of his colleagues (e.g.,

Troeltsch), and then in the early essays after his partial psychological "recovery." The most interesting part of this dissection concerns Weber's comparative religion, in which each type of religious virtuoso is evaluated in terms of how well or poorly he (sic) embodied an ethic of ultimate ends—what Mann called the *Leistungsethiker*, "the ethical man of work and accomplishment." Goldman recounts Weber's claims about the Calvinist being more suited for this-worldly achievement than other religiously dedicated social actors, but he objects only slightly to Weber's argument. Perhaps he is saving more substantial critique for his second volume. Finally, the book concludes with another chapter on Mann's "prisonhouse of personality" as revealed in letters, *Royal Highness*, "A Difficult Hour" (or "A Weary Hour" in the standard translation) on Schiller's compositional problems at three in the morning, and "Death in Venice," more elaborately and creatively treated than most of the other works. Goldman ends with reflections on redemption and the hope for meaning in the modern era. The writing is clear and imaginative, the references all to the original sources, the notes full and useful; in general, the book looks like and is a serious one of the sort we can now expect from scholars who pursue these topics vigorously.

In order to air my few objections, I return again to that hallowed period which gave both Goldman and me our intellectual peculiarities. An anachronistic but well-meaning German relative sent me for high school graduation *The Critique of Practical Reason*, for which I was gratefully uncomprehending. Shortly thereafter, during the manifold Troubles of the late 1960s, this same well-meaning, intensely moralistic and quasi--Weberian person found me reading Mann and objected strenuously, saying that *Buddenbrooks* was a degenerate novel of that typically disheartening Jewish frame of mind. Delighted I had struck a chord of righteous indignation without even trying, I allowed my elder to elaborate the critique of Mann's celebration of the uncertain, the unnerved, and the hopeless. Since I was enjoying the novel, though indeed struck by the fateful sorrow little Hanno would experience, I was truly surprised at this powerful Lutheran attack on the novel's entire theme. Not until Goldman's book appeared did it occur to me one might well put the two writers in the same box rather than in different-colored ones. This is to Goldman's credit, and now that he has pointed out this obvious congruence, it will become a normal feature of our landscape. Judith Marcus's *Georg Lukács and Thomas Mann* has done something similar, though, of course, Marcus's case was more easily built since Lukács revered Mann and wrote about his adoration at length. Such was not the case with Weber and Mann, who, according to Goldman's sources, met twice, neither time privately, and only seven months before Weber's premature death. And neither wrote about the other in any significant way. Mann did pride himself in having anticipated Weber's and Sombart's work on the Protestant ethic in his first novel, *Buddenbrooks.* That is where the overlap ends, and where my objection begins.

Goldman's chapters on Weber are skillful but not very fresh for a Weber expert—of which by now there must be quite a few worldwide—because they recount what we know well about the relation between the Puritan type and the activity that leads to great success in accumulating capital. But it certainly has its uses. For instance, Goldman's first chapter, "Weber and the Puritan Calling," and the accompanying notes is an able antidote to Luciano Pellicani's "Weber and the Myth of Calvinism" (*Telos*, #75; also in his *The Genesis of Capitalism and the Origins of Modernity*, 1994). Pellicani does what he sets out to do brilliantly—to show that not only Calvinists could behave capitalistically. Unfortunately, though, this entirely misses the point that Weber (and Goldman) make. Weber did not care in the end about who started capitalism, and he said so repeatedly. His ideal-typical Calvinist is not a sufficient cause for restructuring Europe's political economy. What he noticed and then did his best to document, given the available data, was that a type of personality came onto the political-economic scene that was extremely weird when judged by normal human historical standards, as he said repeatedly. The oddity of this new type of person involved his desire to make lots of money, then to pretend it was not there for purposes of consumption, to act bravely in the face of a truly terrifying God, and in the end to behave entirely "irrationally" by any modern conception of the term. Weber, thinking of his own extended family, was fascinated, even obsessed (as Goldman puts it) by this (and saw it lived out in somewhat diluted form in his mother, but without the desire for gain), then tried to explain it. The fact that he was assigning all three volumes of *Capital* to his students in the late 1890s before his collapse probably showed he was still hanging on to his credentials as a political-economist and historian, but by the time *Roscher and Knies* was ready for the printer (1903-06) he had loosened that identity and begun his trek into the social psychology of world religions. He was making himself over into the German William James—with history added. Henry Carey no longer interested him.

Yet for all its concentrated good sense and up-to-the-minute scholarship, Goldman's book will not shock or dismay those who have already made their way through *The Protestant Ethic* and related materials. It is only when he gets to Mann that he seems to breathe easier, feel less sat upon by his subject, and begins to carry on a livelier dialogue with the texts and their author. (Surely a Germanist with publications on Mann might feel precisely the contrary, and prize the Weber treatment more, but so it goes when one is daring enough to mix literature with social "science.") This seems readily understandable when one considers the thorny density and conceptual unknowns in Weber versus the graceful ambiguity and powerful emotional texture of Mann's prose. After all, Mann was a professional entertainer, and knew his audience well enough to win a huge following at the age of twenty-five. Weber's prose "style" is an embarrassment except in its compact strength, its ability to haul the patient reader through more ideas and information per page than is available in almost any other theorist. There are stretches of Mannheim, or Lukács, some Marcuse too, where density is as high, but not even in their work can one find the historical and cross-cultural undergirding that has always set Weber's work off from "mere" social philosophy. In a sense it is forgivable that Goldman reads better when he's dealing with Mann, since the subject presents so many choice items for quotation and parsing.

Yet a disturbing feature of Goldman's enterprise is his willingness to take Weber literally and rather unproblematically. Surely there are Mann scholars who find in his fiction (and the important scholarly essays as well) endless ironically inspired confusions that need their attention. But this is different from Weber's unintentional, even unknowing, conceptual tangles. Perhaps out of concern for space, Goldman seems to have minimized legitimate difficulties so that Weber's ideas of "the calling" and the ascetic self come across as much cleaner than they actually are. For instance, Goldman takes care of Weber's tortured excursion into "personality" theory in the *Roscher and Knies* essays with only a couple of pages. A close look at these incredible labors (which seem to me both exercises in self-administered therapy as well as solid intellectual statements) shows how amazingly at sea Weber was about what "personality" meant—not just the ideal-typical Puritan self of renunciation and control, but *any* credible self in the Wilhelmine period of overfed aestheticism and political irresponsibility. It is admirable up to a point to clarify the opaque for readers probably less accustomed to certain arguments than is the exegete, but it can be a short distance from this kind of cleansing to oversimplification.

A related and more important theoretical cloud hovers near the edge of Goldman's sunny vista. It is entirely clear that this hermeneuticist of Mann and Weber sympathizes with their overall projects and also their most precious personal values and struggles. This is no work of deconstruction or demystification, but instead an appreciative elucidation of a common theme that did not seem perhaps as closely linked in previous scholarship as it now will. In one of few summary statements, Goldman writes:

The generation of personality in any context can only be conceived on the basis of four fundamental conditions. First, there must be the creation or existence of a transcendental-like ultimate goal or value that gives leverage over the world through the tension it creates between the believer and the world. Second, there must be a 'witness' to action that is not social, seeing the 'outer' person but transcendent, regarding the 'inner.' Third, there must be the possibility of salvation or redemption from death or from the meaninglessness of the world and the attainment of a sense of certainty about it. And fourth, there must be no ritual, magical, or external means for relieving one's burden, guilt, or despair. Together these four conditions anchor the sense of meaning and may later provide possibilities that life in an age without religion has otherwise lost." (P.165)

This is technically correct, but one waits in vain for the other shoe to drop. (Perhaps it does in the second volume of the project.) Since Goldman is a political theorist and not a literary critic of the traditional kind, he has a responsibility, however modest, to tie his work to contemporary conditions of life, or so I would argue. If the reader uninterested in the Wilhelminian context and unimpressed by "dead Germans," as the *ignoranti* often call them, came upon the above quoted paragraph and tried to connect it somehow to our situation, it would seem all the recent fuss over Weber, Mann, fin de siècle Vienna, Lukács, Bloch, and the rest is a fool's paradise of nostalgia. Goldman might say he set out only to do exploration in the history of ideas, that is its own reward, and having done a bit of that myself, I understand its importance and appeal. But if ever a time for redefining "self" existed, it is now, when what "selves" there are come in mass marketed packages of predigested, misfitting fragments. The dread distance between the "self" of Mann's protagonists or Weber's ideal-typical virtuosi and what passes for same today would seem to demand some kind of theoretical response in a scholar up to his ears in the material Goldman studied. Yet he leaves it mostly to inference and polite suggestion, and I cannot imagine why. He laid the table for a hearty meal, then forgot to bring in the beast. Still, it is a good book, and one worth having on the shelves. Perhaps the concluding volume will bring us out of that ancient time of coherent, self-destructive selves and into our own.

Name Index

Subject Index